The Renaissance, the Reformation, and the Rise of Nations
Part I

Professor Andrew C. Fix

THE TEACHING COMPANY ®

PUBLISHED BY:

THE TEACHING COMPANY
4151 Lafayette Center Drive, Suite 100
Chantilly, Virginia 20151-1232
1-800-TEACH-12
Fax—703-378-3819
www.teach12.com

ISBN 1-59803-041-8

Andrew C. Fix, Ph.D.

Charles A. Dana Professor of History, Lafayette College

Andrew Fix was graduated from Wake Forest University in 1977 with a B.A. in history and philosophy. He pursued graduate study at Indiana University—Bloomington from 1977–1984, during which time he was a Fulbright Fellow in The Netherlands (1982–1983) and a Woodrow Wilson Fellow (1983–1984). He received an M.A. in history in 1979 and a Ph.D. in history in 1984. Dr. Fix taught for one year as an assistant professor of history at Spring Hill College in Mobile, Alabama (1984–1985), before taking a similar position at Lafayette College in Easton, Pennsylvania, in 1985. He published his first book, *Prophecy and Reason: The Dutch Collegiants in the Early Enlightenment*, with Princeton University Press in 1991. The next year, he published a co-edited volume of essays on 16th-century Germany, *Germania Illustrata: Essays on Sixteenth-Century Germany*, with Susan C. Karant Nunn. In 1999, Dr. Fix published his third book, *Fallen Angels: Balthasar Bekker, Spirit Belief, and Confessionalism in the Seventeenth-Century Dutch Republic*, with Kluwer Publishers. He received tenure at Lafayette College in 1992, was promoted to professor in 1998, and named Charles A. Dana Professor of History in 2000. Professor Fix lives in Coopersburg, Pennsylvania, with his wife, Carol, and son, Adam.

Table of Contents

The Renaissance, the Reformation, and the Rise of Nations
Part I

The Renaissance, the Reformation, and the Rise of Nations

Scope:

This course examines the great transformations in European society that took place between 1348 and 1715. Beginning with a look at the crisis of the 14th century that formed the immediate background for the changes that followed, the course then explores in-depth the origins and nature of the Italian Renaissance, Humanism, and art. Europe's overseas expansion during the Age of Discovery is examined, with special reference to the economic and political changes these developments brought to Europe. With the coming of the 16th century, the Protestant Reformation becomes the main focus of interest, beginning with the problems in the Catholic Church and continuing with an analysis of Martin Luther and the Reformation in Germany. The social, political, and economic contexts of the German Reformation are studied with a look at the political structure of the Holy Roman Empire, Hapsburg conflict with France and the Ottoman Empire, the Knights' Revolt of 1523, and the Peasant War of 1525. Other branches of the Reformation are also examined, including the Swiss Reformation of Zwingli and Calvin, the Radical Reformation, the English Reformation, and the Catholic Reformation. The disastrous age of religious wars in Germany, France, and The Netherlands moves the course into the 17th century, where the main focus falls on the rise of the modern state and intellectual change. Different patterns of state development are followed, such as the rise of absolutism in France and Germany, the development of constitutional monarchy in England, and the birth of the Dutch Republic. The course comes to a close with a look at the epic intellectual change brought by the Scientific Revolution and the Early Enlightenment, which usher in the 18th century. Overall, the course will focus on the elements of historical change in political, social, cultural, and economic life in the years 1348–1715 that gave birth to the modern world.

Lecture One
Crisis of the 14th Century

Scope:

In this first lecture, we begin our look at the 14th century crisis: a period of unparalleled disaster in almost every aspect of European life that had the effect of causing medieval civilization to crumble and setting the stage for the Renaissance. Demographic disaster struck in the beginning of the century with a series of famines and was greatly magnified by the arrival in 1348 of the bubonic plague. The plague in its several forms killed up to one-half of the European population and had widespread effects in every area of life. A major economic depression followed because of falling demand for food and soaring wage rates. This depression led to social unrest, such as peasant revolts and civil wars among noble factions, that set the stage for a major political crisis in the 14th century.

Outline

I.   We begin by looking at the prosperity of the High Middle Ages, contrasting what is to come in the 14th century with the previous trends of the 12th and 13th centuries.

   A. Population—population growth had been continuous since about the year 1000.

   B. Economy—the European economy had been expanding for about the same period of time, bringing prosperity to the upper and middle classes.

   C. Politics—stable monarchies in most countries provided a degree of stability.

   D. The church—its stability and continuity was a bulwark of European life.

II. Even before the plague arrived, Europe was already entering a period of population decline because the continent had become overpopulated during the previous centuries.

    A. Bad weather and starvation—in the years 1315–1320, a series of years of bad weather caused the failure of crops planted on marginal lands—lands of poor soil—by peasants without enough good land.

    B. Starving peasants ate all their grain reserves, then their seed reserves.

    C. Europe had reached its population ceiling—the land could not support the population.

    D. For example, the province of Provence, France, went from 400,000 to 200,000 people.

III. Arrival of the bubonic plague in 1346–1347—a disease unknown in Europe since the 5th century arrived in Italy by way of trading links.

    A. A merchant ship from Crimea in central Asia docked in Messina, Sicily.

        1. Rats on the ship carried fleas that had bacteria for plague in their stomachs.

        2. The fleas abandoned the rats, bit people, and transferred the plague.

        3. The population had no biological resistance.

    B. Bubonic plague caused huge dark swellings on the skin, at first near glands, then elsewhere. It spread rapidly over its victims.

        1. The bubonic plague was accompanied by a less noticeable but more deadly version of the plague: pneumonic plague. In this version, the bacteria attacked the victim's lungs, causing slow asphyxiation. It was spread by sneezing and coughing and, thus, spread even faster from person to person than bubonic plague.

        2. These two types of plague spread rapidly through Italy in 1348 and reached as far north as Denmark by 1349–1350.

IV. Certain characteristics of the plague worked to prevent population recovery, speeding population decline.

A. It was endemic—it would lie dormant in a population for a time before returning without warning.

   1. Barcelona was hit by the plague six times in the first 100 years of the epidemic.

   2. Widespread malnutrition made death rates higher.

B. The plague struck predominantly the population of individuals in their child-bearing years—preventing reproduction to revive the population.

V. This huge demographic collapse caused great social and economic dislocation, including a serious economic depression.

A. Demand for food collapsed, causing a collapse of agricultural prices and profits.

B. Fewer peasant workers demanded higher wages from employers.

C. In industry, escalating wages pushed prices of manufactured goods too high and destroyed sales.

   1. Owners and employers sought relief from governments in the form of artificial wage freezes, and many governments complied.

   2. This set off a political crisis, as both peasants and urban workers rose in revolt against wage freezes.

VI. The English Peasant Revolt began in 1381 in southern England, bringing great destruction to the countryside.

A. It was led by John Ball, a renegade priest.

   1. The peasants, incited by such leaders as Ball, made radical demands, including calling for the abolition of serfdom, church tithes, and state taxes.

   2. The peasants marched on London, burning noble estates along the way.

B. In London, the peasant army met with King Edward, who promised to redress the grievances.

C. After the peasants withdrew from London, the king mobilized the royal army.

D. The peasant force was defeated in battle by the royal army, and no peasant demands were met.

VII. Similar revolts also took place in cities across Europe.

    A. In Florence, the wool workers known as the *Ciompi* led the revolt.

        1. The Ciompi were the poorest of the many guilds of workers in the city's large wool industry.

        2. One-third of all Florentine workers worked in the wool industry.

        3. As the poorest guild, the Ciompi resented the government-imposed wage freeze intensely. They led an uprising by the lower guilds.

    B. The Ciompi and their allies were successful in seizing control of the government of Florence and ruling the city from 1378–1381.

        1. During this period of lower-guild rule, concessions were made to the workers.

        2. In 1381, the upper classes of Florence returned to power when a lockout by the owners of the wool industry brought down the lower-guild regime.

VIII. At the same time, the nobility of Europe was also involved in political turmoil brought on by economic depression.

    A. With income from their great agricultural estates falling, nobles had to seek out other sources of income to maintain their lifestyle and family honor.

        1. A lucrative source of such income was government office, but unfortunately, there were many more nobles than offices.

        2. As a result, noble factions began fighting each other in bloody civil wars to gain access to these offices and incomes.

    B. These noble civil wars brought much destruction to the countryside, decimated noble ranks, and actually accelerated the economic decline of the nobility.

        1. Some of the noble civil wars, such as the Wars of the Roses in England, stretched far into the 15th century.

2. The Wars of the Roses had far more at stake than mere government jobs. Here, the goal was the crown itself.

C. Royal financial problems, linked closely to warfare, started to break down the ability of kings to effectively govern.

    1. The cost of warfare dramatically increased in the 14th century.

        a. New weapons, such as the crossbow, longbow, and firearms, made the feudal knight obsolete as a military weapon, necessitating the hiring and paying of mercenaries.

        b. The new weapons themselves were expensive.

        c. The king's revenues from his estates and taxes had been reduced by the depression.

    2. Kings were forced to ask their nobles to contribute more funds for war than ever before.

        a. Nobles, also in a financial bind, refused additional requests.

        b. The ancient partnership between kings and nobles on which medieval monarchy was based began to crumble in an atmosphere of frustration, anger, and distrust.

        c. Without the help of nobles, and often with their open opposition, kings were unable to rule effectively.

Essential Reading:

Donald Wilcox, *In Search of God and Self*, chapters 1–3.

Questions to Consider:

1. Would the 14th century have been a century of crisis without the bubonic plague?

2. Could the political crisis that followed the economic depression have been avoided?

Lecture One—Transcript
Crisis of the 14ᵗʰ Century

Welcome to this course on *The Renaissance, the Reformation and the Rise of Nations*. I'm Andrew Fix from Lafayette College in Easton, Pennsylvania, and I'll be presenting this course to you. The course basically covers what we call the early modern period of European history, which starts around 1348 with the Bubonic Plague and runs to about 1715. This is a particularly interesting period of European history because it's a major transitional period, in which the Middle Ages pretty much comes to an end and we see the beginnings (the early beginnings) of what's going to become the modern European social, political, and economic structure.

Today we're going to be starting with the 14ᵗʰ century, and what I call the "crisis of the 14ᵗʰ century," because this really is the place where you see the whole early modern period starting. The 14ᵗʰ century is a period of tremendous upheaval and tremendous crisis in European history. In this period, you see almost all the major trends of the Middle Ages, especially the High Middle Ages, being reversed, and 100 years of disaster occurs, which will set up the Renaissance (the "rebirth") period, and will move us on into the Reformation and the 17ᵗʰ century.

So we'll start out by taking a look at the 14ᵗʰ-century crisis, and what I want to do to begin with is to sum up some ways in which the 14ᵗʰ century was really dramatically different from the High Middle Ages, meaning the 12ᵗʰ and 13ᵗʰ centuries, the end of the Middle Ages. For one thing, the population situation is much different. The High Middle Ages was a period of population growth, population expansion. In fact, in many ways Europe was overpopulated in the 13ᵗʰ century. The 14ᵗʰ century becomes a period of population decline—for reasons that you will see in a few minutes—disastrous, catastrophic population decline, which has a major effect on almost every other aspect of European life. Secondly, the High Middle Ages had been a period of economic expansion and economic prosperity for the most part, and the 14ᵗʰ century, because of the demographic disaster, becomes a period of economic depression, economic decline, economic downturn, in a major way. Thirdly, politically speaking, the High Middle Ages had been a period of relative political stability, with fairly strong feudal monarchies in England, France, and other countries, and a fairly stable social/political situation. That all completely melts down in the 14th century into a period of war, chaos, turmoil, revolt—just a disastrous political situation and social situation. Finally, the 13th century, the High Middle Ages, had been a period of a very powerful Catholic Church, which really controlled religious life, and in the 14th century the Church also begins to crumble, as a result of the Great Schism, the Babylonian Captivity, various corruptions in the church.

So in this particular lecture we're going to be looking at the first parts of these trend reversals. We'll be looking first at the demographic disaster—the demographic collapse, the population collapse, and we're going to be looking at the political turmoil and chaos.

But we'll start out with the change which really is at the root of all these other changes, and that is the population decline, or what we really should call a demographic disaster of unparalleled proportions. Most people probably realize this is a result of the Bubonic Plague, but actually, it started before the plague. The population decline did, in fact, start as early as 1315.

This has to do with the fact that in the 13th century, Europe had become so populated that they had to begin planting every scrap of land they had in food crops, just to have enough food to feed the population. That's okay as long as you can plant basically good, fertile land, but the population had reached the level where they also had to plant what we call "marginal land," which is land which is not really very good for raising crops—rocky, sandy soils; sometimes swampy and too damp—and the problem with this is that in a very good year, with good weather, this land might produce some food, but when the weather turns bad—even slightly bad—the marginal lands are going to fail. The crops won't come in, and the population depending on those crops will die. That's exactly what happens starting in 1315, and in a whole succession of years after that: 1316, 1317, again in 1339, 1340. Bad weather—for example, too much rain in the springtime, too much rain in the summer, early frosts—all these things combined to cause the marginal lands to collapse. People who were dependent on that started to starve.

So that really is the beginning of the population decline, the demographic decline: this situation with the starvation of the people depending on the marginal lands. As the marginal lands failed, people who were starving first of all ate their grain reserves. Most towns in the Middle Ages had small grain reserves for such emergencies, but they were easily and quickly eaten up, and then people started eating the seeds they were going to use to plant the next year, which, of course, just establishes a vicious cycle, where now they won't have anything to plant the next year. So the population decline actually starts a good time before the plague itself strikes.

But of course, the huge impact is the Bubonic Plague or the Black Death, which arrives in Europe in 1347-1348, and that's going to be the majority of our focus in this lecture. Plague arrives in Europe on a merchant ship traveling from Crimea in Central Asia, which docks at Messina in Sicily, in 1347. Most of the crew of this merchant ship is already sick, and the people of Messina don't really want to let the ship come in and dock, but they do let it come in and dock, and they take off the sick sailors. They don't really know what's wrong with them. They don't know what the disease is. After the sailors are off the ship, the other crew on ships of that time also comes off—and those are the rats.

The rats disembark from the ship and spread out through the town of Messina. These rats carry fleas, which is not unusual, because all rats carry fleas, but these particular fleas have in their stomachs the bacterium for Bubonic Plague, and that's how the plague begins to strike. As the rats fan out through the town, the fleas jump off of the rats, jump on to people and bite people. One fleabite is enough to transmit the Bubonic Plague to a person. So Bubonic Plague starts to spread really, really fast throughout Messina and throughout all Sicily in 1347-48. There is no biological resistance in the population, because there hadn't been plague in Europe since the 5th century. So the plague becomes quickly an epidemic—but really a pandemic, meaning it attacks everywhere, almost without exception. It spreads north into Europe. It attacks almost every place, with few exceptions that we really don't understand, but it goes almost everywhere.

As well as being epidemic, it's also endemic, which means it gets into the population and attacks. It will appear to be gone for a while, but then it will come back, and it comes back repeatedly. For example, the city of Barcelona, in Spain, was hit by the first plague in 1347, hit again in 1351, again in 1362, again in 1363, again in 1371, again in 1397—and that's just the 14th century. It goes on for several centuries after that.

Now, there actually wasn't just one kind of plague. There were two kinds of plague. The famous kind, the Bubonic Plague, is called that because people who get it get these big black swellings, called "buboes" on their bodies, which are filled with pus, and just look really terrible, and eventually it kind of just eats the person apart. However, oddly enough, it wasn't that version of the plague which spread as fast. The other version was known as "Pneumonic" Plague, as related to pneumonia, because it gets down into your lungs. It causes these same swellings, but not on the outside of your body. It causes them in your lungs, and gradually eats your lungs away and you are asphyxiated. The thing about Pneumonic Plague is that when you just look at somebody, you can't tell they've got it. It is spread by sneezing and coughing—the aerosol that comes out. This is what caused the plague to spread the fastest. It spread like wildfire throughout all of Europe.

Another thing about the plague that really hurt the population and the population's ability to recover is that the plague did not hit all age groups the same. You would normally expect a disease like this to hit maybe the very young, the very old, the more vulnerable populations, but that's not where the plague hit. The plague hit people in mid-life, say, 20 to 45, meaning the childbearing population, and by killing off the childbearing population, the plague prevented the population from recovering, and this was just a second blow to the population level in Europe. Once the plague reduced it initially, the population didn't have the chance to recover.

Of course, malnutrition caused by the failure of marginal lands made people weaker and more susceptible to get plague, so that also was a factor in this plague's spread.

This was a demographic collapse of spectacular proportion. No one knows exactly how many people died of the plague, but it's estimated that between one-third and one-half of the total European population perishes in the first onslaught of the plague. It's a catastrophic population collapse, and it's one that is bound to have ripple effects throughout the whole social, economic, political organization of society. That's exactly what you see here. The plague is the thing that sets off a much, much wider catastrophe, in social, economic, and political areas.

Just to give you some idea of the magnitude of this population collapse, let me give you a few estimated examples of population declines from different areas in the first hundred years of the plague. The nation of England, in the first hundred years of the plague, went from 3.7 million people to 2.2 million. The province of Provence, in France, went from 400,000 people to about 200,000 people. The city of Pistoia went from 43,000 to 14,000. In Germany, 40,000 towns and villages completely disappeared, meaning everybody died, and the town just vanished from the face of the Earth. So it's a huge, huge population collapse.

This population collapse has the effect immediately of setting off economic trouble. As a matter of fact, it leads to a huge economic depression, and this depression covers all of Europe, and it lasts about 100 years. Why? Why the economic depression?

Many reasons. The population collapse disrupts agricultural production. There aren't enough peasants left to do the agricultural labor to raise the food, and even those peasants who aren't killed in the plague, many of them stop showing up for work because they just feel like there's no point in working because they might die the next day. So that was one factor. Production was disrupted.

An even more major factor was that demand collapsed. With the population collapsing, of course, demand for food collapses. When demand collapses, prices collapse. When prices collapse, agricultural profits collapse. That means that the people who own and run the big plantations or estates that grow the food go bankrupt. Here we're talking about noble owners of plantations, who just can't make a living because they don't have the prices and profits anymore from their major economic activity, which is agricultural produce. So agriculture is hit really hard.

There is a kind of vise that develops. The labor shortage leads to higher wages because the peasants that are left can ask for higher wages. On the other hand, the population loss, collapse of demand, means that prices and profits go down. So agricultural owners are just in an impossible situation, where their wage levels are going up but their profit levels are going down, and many, many just go bankrupt. Bankruptcy is very common among noble estate owners in the 14th and 15th centuries.

Industry and trade is also caught in a similarly bad situation. The extremely high wages brought on by the population collapse push the prices of manufactured goods so high that most people can't afford to buy them, and that destroys sales. Of course, again, the high wages were due to the labor shortage.

In the face of this situation, a lot of businessmen and estate owners went to their governments and asked the governments to freeze wages at an artificially low, pre-plague level, thinking that stabilizing wages like that would at least help the producers to get back on their feet if they didn't have to pay really high wages, and governments agree to do this. Does it help the economic situation? Not very much. What it actually does is lead to political chaos.

It leads to revolts among workers and peasants in almost every country: a huge peasant revolt in England, we'll see, in 1381; another one in France in 1382; in Florence, the Ciompi revolt of urban workers in 1378. This is common all across Europe. Lower classes rise up in rebellion against these wage freezes and other things.

Now we're into the third stage of this crisis, the political stage: political meltdown; turmoil or chaos; war; revolt; everything you can imagine. When you talk about the political crisis, there are really about three different aspects to it that we need to look at. Number one: the popular revolts—peasant, worker revolts—and we'll take closer look at some of those. Secondly, civil wars among nobles, and we'll see why that was going on, in a couple of minutes. Then thirdly: long, costly international wars, which drained countries' treasuries and deprived kings of the ability to govern, basically.

So we'll start out by taking a look, first of all, at the peasant revolts. These are kicked off by government efforts to freeze wages, because it just enrages the peasants and workers. For the first time in history, the common person had the possibility, economically speaking, of making a better wage, and now governments are saying, "No, you can't do it." So this is a major reason that lower classes rise up in rebellion all across Europe, but there are other reasons.

Noble landlords, who are going bankrupt, have to figure out ways to squeeze more money out of the peasant workers they've got left. One of the things about the way noble estates were run is that nobles weren't supposed to just arbitrarily raise the dues and fees, the rents, the peasants had to pay. You couldn't just go out and say, "Today you pay more." But what nobles did instead was they started looking back through their estate books or account books, looking back to the earlier days of the estate, and they found out that in the earlier days, back in the Middle Ages and in the Early Middle Ages, that peasants had, in fact, paid higher dues and higher fees and higher rents. That had just fallen by the wayside in the prosperous years since then. Now, noble landlords go to their peasants and start to say, "You've got to pay these high fees and dues and rents again. It's no change. You always had to pay them. It's not any kind of arbitrary increase. We're just getting back to the way things used to be and still should be." That's a second reason the peasants are enraged.

A third reason is that kings and governments begin to raise taxes, and of course the taxes fall on the lower classes. Kings need the money because it costs them more money to govern in this situation, and peasants now have to pay even higher royal taxes.

So, all this sets off a huge series of peasant rebellions. We'll just talk about one in detail: The English peasant revolt of 1381. Led by a rebellious priest by the name of John Ball, a huge peasant crowd—army, actually—armed with farm implements and other things, marched back and forth across southern England, tearing up the countryside, burning, looting, causing all sorts of destruction. Finally the peasant army marches on London, and goes to the royal palace and demands to talk to the king about their grievances. The king comes out on the balcony to speak to the crowd, and the crowd has confidence that the king is on their side and will try to help them. They make their demands, and their demands were extreme. Their demands are for the abolition of serfdom, for example; the abolition of feudal dues; the abolition of state taxes. I mean, we're talking about the whole feudal system coming to an end if these demands are met.

The king, who happens to be a 16-year-old boy at this stage, assures the peasants that he'll do what he can; that he will take care of these demands and that they will be satisfied. So, at that point, the peasant army retires, and instead of the king trying to meet the demands, what the king does is that he musters the royal army and slaughters the peasants. So, who knows how many tens of thousands, if not more, peasants die, but this doesn't stop the trouble from happening.

An example of urban worker revolts occurs in Florence. This is the famous Ciompi revolt in 1378. As you will learn a lot more about this later in the course, Florence was a wool-producing town, and the wool industry was organized into a whole complex series of guilds, from top to bottom, depending on production roles and things. About one-third of the total population of Florence worked in the woolen-cloth industry—many different guilds, doing many different jobs. At the very bottom of this scale was the guild of people known as the Ciompi. Their entire job was to take the raw wool when it came into Florence and comb out the tangles in it with a wire brush, and then pass it on to somebody else for the next step in the process. So they obviously didn't make very much money doing this. They were terribly impoverished, and they were at the very bottom of the whole industrial hierarchy. These are the people who rise up in rebellion to begin with, against the wage freezes in Florence, but they are soon joined by a lot of the other Lesser Guilds in Florence—a lot of the relatively poorer people working in the woolen-cloth industry.

This revolt actually succeeds. The poor people, the lower guilds, take over the government and actually rule Florence for a couple of years, and during that time pass a lot of measures attempting to improve the conditions of the lower classes. I should mention that this itself is not unusual, because we see revolts of lower classes in most towns in Europe during this period, but Florence is a little bit unusual in that the revolt succeeds so dramatically and that the lower classes take charge of the government and in fact run the government until 1381, when, finally, the owners of the woolen-cloth industry decide to stage a lock-out. They lock all the workers out of their jobs, and the workers are on the verge of starvation. This causes them to give in and the wealthy people (the higher guilds) come back into power and things go back to the way they were before, but you can see, when a major city like Florence can be affected by lower-class rebellions in this way, that there's a lot of unrest going on in Europe.

So that's lower-class rebellions. Two other kinds of political turmoil that we need to mention: civil wars among nobles and then long, costly, international wars. Civil wars among nobles. What's that all about?

Well, we know that the nobles have lost a lot of money in the economic depression. They own the estates. They are the ones going bankrupt, and so they need money. Where are they going to get the extra money? There aren't that many different options for where you can get the extra money. One place you can get it is from government office. If you can get appointed to be some minister or chancellor or government official by the king, then you can draw in a pretty good income from that. Now, when I say income, you shouldn't think that these offices carry salaries, because most of them don't carry salaries, but the office holder has other ways of making money from these offices. For example, he can take gifts, he can accept tax privileges, he can get land from it; kickbacks, bribes, whatever you want to mention. It's a good source of income if you can get a government job. So, that's what nobles had their eyes on. Unfortunately there are not nearly enough government offices to go around for all the nobles that need them during this period, and for that reason we see nobles' factions breaking up, and nobles fighting each other over access to government office.

Another major cause for noble civil wars was that, in the 14th century, for some reason that we are not entirely sure of, kings had the somewhat unusual habit of dying without leaving direct male heirs. It happens in France with the Hundred Years War, as you will hear in the next lecture, but it happens in many other places, too, and when a king dies without direct male heirs, how do you decide who is going to be the next king? Well, you go down the king's family tree and you look to see who is the next nearest male relative—in most countries, it's got to be a male relative—and if you go far enough down these family trees, there are going to be several next-nearest male relatives equally closely related. That's where civil war erupts again.

Nobles choose sides; they divide up. They start to fight each other over which candidate should become the king, because if they win and their candidate becomes king, then they have access to all of these government jobs and some of their economic woes might be solved. An example of this, of course, is the War of the Roses in England, which is fought actually in the 15th century, but it is an extension of the 14th-century crisis. The civil war between the Armagnacs and the Burgundians in France is another example, but there are many others throughout Europe that occurred like this.

So, we have the lower classes rising up in rebellions in the countryside and cities. We have noble factions fighting over access to jobs, even over access to the throne (who is going to be the next king). So the political turmoil is pretty extensive.

To add to that, the 14th century becomes a period of a number of long, drawn-out, and costly international wars, the most famous of which, of course, is the Hundred Years War, which we will talk about in the next lecture. Why does this happen? Well, for one thing, royal governments are getting weaker and weaker. Kings also lose money in the economic depression, because most medieval European kings depended on personal income from their own personal lands for a substantial amount of their expenses in government, and that's not flowing in anymore. So, when they start to fight these wars and the wars drag out and become more and more costly, the kings really begin to suffer.

Why were wars in the 14th century more costly than your typical medieval war? A couple of reasons. One reason is that the mounted knight, who fought in a majority of wars in the Middle Ages, has become obsolete as a fighting tool. This is because he comes into battle on horseback, wearing chain-mail armor with his shield and sword and all, and he's met now with infantry wielding crossbows and sometimes English longbows, as we'll see in the next lecture. These crossbows and longbows—the arrows or shafts from them can penetrate chain-mail armor, which means that the noble cavalry is just mowed down as it charges. Whereas for knights you've got to have a nobleman, and he's got to buy his horse—he's got to be wealthy, he's got to be trained—for peasants wielding crossbows, it doesn't cost that much to prepare them, so you can have a whole lot more infantry with these weapons that can destroy knights. So knights become obsolete. That causes a major change in the way kings fight wars, because in the Middle Ages, when a king had to fight a war, he would simply notify his nobles and he would say, "Well, we have a war against France now. You need to come and help me fight." They would all come. They would supply their own weapons, horses, equipment at their own expense, and the king would fight the war for a certain period, and when it was over they would go home.

Now, when you can't use knights, you've got to hire mercenaries, mainly mercenary infantrymen, but also mercenary cavalry, and mercenaries you have to pay. Not only do you have to pay them to fight, you've got to equip them. If they need horses, you've got to buy the horses. You've got to buy all their fighting implements, and in the 14th century, now you have to buy firearms. This is also a dramatic increase in the cost of warfare. Firearms start to be widely used by the mid- to late 14th century. Here we're talking about not just field artillery (although that's the main thing), but also there were tiny, hand-held firearms and later on larger musket-type things called arquebuses, which are extremely expensive. So kings have to pay for all that.

How does the king get the money? He goes to his nobles. He says, "We've got to fight a war. I know you guys can't fight anymore because knights are obsolete, but you've got to give me some money so I can hire my mercenaries." The first couple of times the king asks, the nobles say, "Okay. We're not fighting, but we know that we should help out. So we'll give you some money and you can hire your soldiers and fight. The trouble is that these wars drag on so long and they are so expensive that the king has to keep going back and back and back to his nobles, asking for more and more and more money. Eventually they just say, "Sorry. No more. We're not going to pay any more. We've paid enough. You should be able to fight with this." This causes animosity between the kings and nobles, and drives a wedge between the two partners in government.

Lecture Two
The Hundred Years War and the Church in Crisis

Scope:

The lecture concludes our examination of the 14th-century crisis by showing how the crisis penetrated into the uppermost levels of both church and state. Long and costly international conflicts destroyed the ability of major monarchies to effectively govern their subjects. The increasing cost of warfare was caused by the increasing reliance on mercenary troops, rather than the old feudal levy. Mounted knights were becoming obsolete as fighting forces because of the introduction of the longbow, crossbow, and especially firearms, all of which could penetrate chain-mail armor. These new weapons were increasingly expensive, and the extended length of such conflicts as the Hundred Years War raised costs even further. Kings, who had always relied on contributions from their nobles to fight wars, now found the nobles angry about increasing costs and reluctant to pay them. Thus, the king and nobles, traditional partners in rule in medieval monarchy, became hostile toward one another, and the old ruling partnership broke down, severely limiting the power the king could exercise over his realm.

Meanwhile, the Catholic Church also was in crisis. Because of pressure from the king of France, the pope was compelled to move the church's seat from Rome to Avignon in France. There, cut off from his traditional sources of revenue, the pope resorted to new money-gathering techniques, many of which fell on ordinary churchgoers and made the pope and church unpopular among the population. At the same time, many rulers viewed the pope as a puppet of French interests. This period, called the Babylonian Captivity, ended in 1378, when the pope returned the church to Rome. Shortly thereafter, however, as a result of disagreements among the cardinals and a disputed papal election, the papacy was split in two, with rival popes vying for the allegiance of the church and populace. The Great Schism lasted for the rest of the 14th century and was resolved only in 1415 by the Council of Constance. The church's credibility had been seriously damaged.

Outline

I. The Hundred Years War (1337–1453) greatly weakened the monarchies of England and France.

    A. We start by examining the beginnings of this war over succession to the throne of France.

        1. In 1328, Charles IV, the last of the Capetians, died without a male heir.

        2. There were two claimants to the throne: Philip of Valois, a French noble and distant relative of the Capetians, and King Edward III of England.

        3. Philip's claim ran through a male bloodline, while Edward's ran through a female: He was the son of the old king's sister.

        4. The French nobles picked Philip as the new king, and at first, Edward accepted the judgment.

    B. Events in Flanders changed the situation.

        1. Flanders was part of the French kingdom, ruled by a count who was a vassal to the king of France.

        2. Both the count and French rule were unpopular in the big and prosperous cloth-producing towns of Flanders, and on several occasions, the count had been chased out by rebellious townsmen.

        3. The Flemish towns bought most of their wool from England, and they came to see the dispute over the French crown as a way to permanently escape French rule.

        4. The towns made it known to Edward that they wanted him to press his claim, and if he did not, they might stop buying English wool. Edward was still not convinced.

    C. Philip of Valois committed a blunder.

        1. The English still controlled some landed possessions in France inherited from their Norman dynasty. Over the years, the English and French had fought many conflicts over these lands.

    2. Philip chose this time an as opportune moment to renew that conflict and invade English lands in France. This move finally convinced Edward to go to war for the crown of France.

D. The war dragged on for many years, with many reversals of fortune and a few truces.

    1. Edward III prosecuted the first half of the war for England, while Henry V took over in the 15th century.

    2. The English used the longbow to decimate French mounted knights and won most major battles in the war: Crecy, 1346; Poitiers, 1356; and Agincourt, 1415.

    3. When things were darkest for the French, with only a small portion of the country in French hands, a peasant girl named Joan of Arc appeared to lead the French armies to victory, recapturing nearly the whole country.

E. There were no real winners in the war.

    1. Both countries' treasuries were left empty from fighting.

    2. The countryside of France was decimated.

    3. Neither king could effectively rule his realm.

II. As a result of events in the late Middle Ages, the king of France had gained great influence over the papacy. That influence would prove disastrous for the church.

A. The Babylonian Captivity (1305–1378) was the first disaster for the church.

    1. In 1305, the king pressured the pope to move the church headquarters to Avignon in southern France. The pope said that the move was because of a breakdown of law and order in Rome.

    2. In Avignon, the papal court fell deeper under French influence and found itself cut off from the traditional source of revenues the pope had used to operate the church: taxes from the Papal States. With the pope gone, these states declared independence.

3. To finance the church, the pope turned to papal fiscalism: charging fees and dues for services provided to ordinary churchgoers; exploiting church appointments, indulgences, and dispensations for revenue; and setting up an elaborate new bureaucracy to collect taxes.

4. The people came to see the papacy as greedy and materialistic. A wave of anti-clericalism arose. Rulers resented the flow of tax money out of their kingdoms to the papacy, as well as the French influence over the pope.

B. The Great Schism (1378–1415) was the second disaster for the church. In 1378, Pope Gregory XI finally decided that the church must move back to Rome or risk total loss of public confidence. He successfully moved the church back but died shortly thereafter.

1. The cardinals, many of whom were French, went into session and elected a new pope, the Italian Urban VI.

2. Urban turned out to have ideas about church reform that the cardinals were not aware of at the time of his election; thus, the French cardinals returned to session, declared Urban deposed, and elected a new French pope.

3. When Urban refused to recognize his deposition, the French pope and cardinals moved back to Avignon, leaving Urban and the Italian cardinals in Rome. Each pope claimed to be the true pope, and each group, the true church. The Great Schism had begun.

4. All of Europe, from kings to university scholars to ordinary people, was forced to choose sides in this dispute and declare loyalty to one pope or the other. Church bureaucracy and taxes were duplicated. All Christendom was split and the church was humiliated, its public image sinking even further.

C. Out of this disaster arose the Conciliar Movement: A group of prominent cardinals decided that only a council of all the church's bishops deliberating together could decide which pope was the true pope. There were also suggestions that, after such a decision, the council would take over as the highest authority in the church, with the pope as a kind of secondary administrator. The council would then be able to achieve true church reform, which the papacy had proven incapable of. Papal leadership in the church had hit rock bottom.

1. A first attempt at such a church council was held in Pisa in 1409. The bishops elected a new pope and declared the previous two quarreling popes deposed. However, the Rome and Avignon popes refused to recognize this deposition; now there were three popes—in Pisa, Rome, and Avignon. The conciliar solution seemed to have failed.

2. Under pressure from the Holy Roman Empire, the conciliar solution was tried again in 1415. This time, the council was held in Constance, Switzerland. It lasted from 1415–1418 and dealt with numerous matters, such as the Hussite heresy in Bohemia. But no matter was as pressing as ending the schism. Again, a new pope was elected—Martin V—and the others were declared deposed. This time, however, the results were different: under intense pressure, the other popes were eliminated, leaving Martin as the one true pope. Martin, however, was forced by the council to agree to its conditions that the council would rule the church and the pope would submit himself to conciliar decrees. Constance was a mixed blessing for papal power in the church.

3. After Constance, a struggle for power in the church developed between pope and council. Neither Martin nor subsequent popes were satisfied as subordinates of the council in church government, and several popes negotiated agreements with secular rulers to win their backing against the council. The battle came to a climax at the Council of Basel (1431–1443), where after an acrimonious struggle, the pope was able to reestablish himself as head of the church.

Essential Reading:

Donald Wilcox, *In Search of God and Self*, chapters 1–2.

Supplementary Reading:

Edouard Perroy, *The Hundred Years War*.

Questions to Consider:

1. Could the Hundred Years War have been prevented?
2. What were other options to heal the Great Schism?

Lecture Two—Transcript
The Hundred Years War and the Church in Crisis

In our last lecture we were talking about the crisis of the 14th century, which really provides a transition between the Middle Ages, which pretty much comes to an end in the 14th century, and the coming of the Renaissance, a period of rebirth. In the last lecture we talked about the terrible demographic disaster of the plague, and we talked about social and economic crisis, and we had just gotten into talking about political turmoil, and I told you a lot about peasant revolts and noble civil wars. The last aspect that we need to cover with respect to that is the long and complicated, costly international wars that were fought during the period—primarily the Hundred Years War, which was fought between 1337 to 1453.

I mentioned at the end of the last lecture that one of the most important reasons that these long and costly wars had such an impact on Europe during the 14th century was the fact that they essentially drove a wedge between the king and nobles. This was important, because throughout the entire Middle Ages, the king and his biggest nobles had been essentially partners in rule, in governing the country, because many of these nobles were almost as big and rich and powerful as the king himself, and the king really couldn't rule the country without their cooperation and goodwill. Unfortunately, during the 14th century, the cost of warfare, with the use of mercenaries and firearms and things that we talked about last time, produced financial demands by the king imposed on the nobles, which really turned these two former partners into adversaries. You start to see nobles opposing the king a whole lot more in the 14th century. The whole structure of medieval monarchy just starts to break down, because kings really can't govern their countries without the help of these powerful men. In fact, wars like the Hundred Years War make both England and France (the two principal combatants) almost ungovernable. The king just really can't effectively rule his country anymore, without the help of the nobles.

So it's important to take a look at what the Hundred Years War was all about. I'm not going to go through and fight the whole war battle for battle, but we'll take a look, first of all at the causes of the war and a few of the highlights of the war, and then the consequences of the war and its effect on the 14th century.

The Hundred Years War really was the worst of all these long and complex international wars. It was fought over succession to the French throne. Last time I mentioned that in many cases in the 14th century kings would die without a direct male heir. That is exactly what happened in the case of France in 1328, when the king, Charles IV, died in Paris without any direct male heir. That was the end of the Capetian dynasty, which had ruled France since 987, and since 987, each one had had a son, a direct male heir, so there never had been a problem, but now there was a problem. Charles was dead and there was no direct male heir. So the French nobles start to look down the family tree to find out who would be the next in line to be king. They come to a disturbing conclusion, which is that there are two people who are essentially equally closely related to the old king. There are other complicating factors as well.

One of the people is Philip of Valois, who is a relatively unknown French noble, but has a legitimate stake to the throne. That was fine. The other candidate, though, was more troubling, because he was King Edward III of England—the king of England. Automatically it's going to be a problem for the French nobles if the king of England becomes their king, but he does have a legitimate stake, or at least so it appeared.

Complicating this situation was the fact that while Philip's relationship was obviously very clear and direct, Edward's relationship to the old king was through a female. Edward was the son of Charles's (the dead king's) sister. That is complicating because the laws in the two countries hold different things with regard to female inheritance. English law recognizes female inheritance, and therefore you can come to the throne of England if your claim goes through a female. That's not really a problem, because females can inherit in England, and England, of course, later on had queens.

Under French law, however, there was no recognition of female inheritance, and so the issue about whether Edward was really legally related through this female was controversial to the French nobles. Eventually the French nobles called together a big meeting, and they decided that they really thought that Edward's claim was not as strong. Besides that, they didn't want the king of England as their king; therefore, they recognized Philip as the next king of France.

At first, that wasn't a problem with Edward. He said, "Okay. They've made their decision. I can accept that," but there were other complicating factors that pushed the situation along, one of which came from the area known as Flanders. Flanders is what is present-day Belgium. In the late Middle Ages, Flanders was an extremely urbanized area. It had a lot of big cities, industrial cities: Antwerp, Bruges, Brussels, Tournai, and Ypres. Most of these cities were deeply involved in the woolen-cloth industry, and they bought their raw wool to make the woolen cloth from English wool merchants, because England was a big producer of raw wool. Flanders had been for many centuries ruled by France, because the Count of Flanders was a vassal of the king of France.

Unfortunately, most people in Flanders didn't like being ruled by France, because they weren't French. They were Flemish. They didn't speak French. They spoke a version of what is today Dutch. Especially in the big industrial towns, they didn't take at all happily to being ruled by France, and on several occasions in the past they had actually thrown the Count out and declared their independence, and the French had to come in and re-conquer them. So this area had a long history of turmoil and resistance to French rule.

When the issue of the French throne came up (French succession came up), woolen merchants in the Flemish towns essentially told the English, "We want the king of England to press his claim on the throne, because we'd rather be ruled by the king of England than the king of France, than Philip, a more traditional French ruler."

This made Edward stop and think, because the Flemish woolen merchants further said, "If you don't press your claim on the throne, we just might not buy your raw wool anymore." If the Flemish towns don't buy English raw wool, that's just going to worsen the economic depression in England. As we've seen, the 14th century was a period of tremendous economic depression all over, so Edward was kind of pushed on the way to claiming the throne and pushing his case by what was said in the Flemish towns.

The whole thing was capped off by a tremendous blunder by Philip, who by now has been crowned as the new French king. In 1337, he took this opportunity to invade English lands in France. There had been substantial English landholdings in France ever since the Norman invasion of 1066, and throughout most of the High Middle Ages, kings of England had spent a great deal of time in France, defending English lands such as Aquitaine against French invasions and French threats. So this was nothing particularly new, but it was a very bad point in time for Philip to do this, because his invasion of English lands in France tipped the balance, and Edward decides that he will press his claim. He sends a message. He demands the throne. This is what starts off the Hundred Years War.

The French, of course, have already crowned the king, so the English have to invade France, which they do in 1337. The war lasts 100 years, although it's not 100 years of continuous fighting. There are several peace treaties or truces in the meantime, and lulls, but it drags on and on, through a couple of different kings on England's side and several different kings on the French side. There are a number of important battles in it, of which we don't really have time to go through all, but I'll talk about a couple of them, and also a number of important technological innovations that come up in the war.

Probably the first important battle was the Battle of Sluis, which was a naval battle fought off the coast just at the very beginning of the war, in which the English fleet essentially destroyed the French fleet. The reason this was important is because it assured that the war was going to be fought in France; that for the Hundred Years War the battleground would be France, and France would be the country directly torn up by all the fighting. So that was important.

There were other important battles, too: Crecy in 1346, Poitiers in 1356, and in the next century Agincourt in 1415. The interesting thing about these battles is that the English win almost all these battles, and they do it because they have what you might call a secret weapon. That secret weapon is the English longbow. Now, we know that bows and arrows had been used in combat since ancient days, so there's nothing new about the bow and arrow, but the English longbow is an exceptionally long bow with a very taut drawstring on it. The important thing about it was that you could get tremendous force behind an arrow with this huge bow length and taut drawstring, and the arrow from the longbow could penetrate chain-mail armor. So this is going to cause trouble for knights, and, in fact, the French army still employs knights to some extent in its first line of attack.

Even more important, though, the longbow has a big advantage over the main French infantry weapon, the crossbow. The crossbow also could penetrate chain-mail armor. It fires a short, stubby bolt, not a long arrow, but the thing about the crossbow is that it's big and heavy, hard to operate, and it takes a long time to reload it. It s a short, stubby cross, with, again, a very taut drawstring, but to reload the crossbow, you actually have to put it down on the ground and crank a crank that will bring back the wire before you can put the bolt in. What that means is that it takes a lot longer to reload a crossbow than it does to reload a longbow. So the rate of English fire from the longbow was many times faster than the rate of French fire from the crossbow. That meant in the initial charges in these battles the English had essentially much more firepower than the French had. Nevertheless, French knights continued to charge right into the face of the longbows, and the longbows cut them down every single time; at Crecy, at Poitiers, and even at Agincourt, the same thing happens over and over again, and sometimes the French cavalry would even charge in unfavorable conditions, like across marshy ground or when they weren't particularly well organized. So it was really a disaster for the French military machine.

At the battle of Crecy, it was estimated that a whole generation of French nobility was wiped out as the nobles were decimated by the longbow. So the English win almost all the important battles in this war; nevertheless, the French hold on. By the time we get to the 15th century, drawing towards the end of the war, the French are just barely holding on. As a matter of fact, the king of France is holed up in the city of Orleans, and he controls hardly any of the country outside of Orleans. He is there under siege, essentially waiting to be defeated.

At that point one of the really interesting things in history happens, and that's Joan of Arc. A French peasant girl shows up at the gates of Orleans and asks to speak to the king. Of course, she is turned down several times, but after repeated requests, she is allowed in, and she tells the French king that she has been sent on a mission from God to lead French forces, to break the siege of Orleans, to recapture France, and particularly to take the king of France to the city of Rheims, so he can be crowned officially, which he never had been; this particular French king had never officially been crowned. Joan's argument was that the king of France was God's favorite king. He wants to see the king of France win. He wants to see the king of France crowned properly. So she's there to do the job.

The king of France didn't have much option at this point, so he decided to try it. He had his assistants cut her hair. He gave her a suit of armor, and also gave her a number of military advisers who could help her out with strategy, and put her in charge of the French armies. They then broke the siege of Orleans, and drove the English back to the English Channel. In many ways, militarily it was a miracle, but the French forces were rallied by Joan of Arc and went from success to success. Was she on a mission from God? Did she have special powers? At the time, people thought probably, yes. More recent historians think it was the contributions of her military advisors who gave her good advice and helped her rally and inspire the forces, but there's no doubt that she did rally and inspire the forces and bring the French to victory.

At the end of the war, she was captured by the allies of the English, the Burgundians, and turned over to the English, and they thought she had special powers, because they burned her at the stake as a witch. As she was burning at the stake one of the English soldiers turned to another and said, "I think we've just burned a saint."

So the Hundred Years War came to an end. In some ways you could say the French won. They drove the English out and they didn't let the English claim their throne, but in other ways, nobody was a winner. Both countries' treasuries were drained. Both kings are left almost unable to govern their countries. Civil wars break out in both countries afterwards. It's really a major political disaster.

Which brings us to the last disaster of the 14th century: the disaster within the Church, which is equally upsetting to everybody in Europe. Since the late 13th century, the crown of France had had a lot of influence over the Papacy. In 1305, a new pope was elected, who was French, Clement V. Clement V decides that he will move the headquarters of the Papacy from Rome to the southern French city of Avignon, which was a papal city, but it was in France and very much, of course, influenced by the French crown. This move from Rome to Avignon is known as the Babylonian Captivity, and the pope resides in Avignon in this Babylonian Captivity from 1305 to 1378. Why did he move the Papacy? He said he moved it because law and order had broken down in Rome to the point that he couldn't run the church effectively from Rome anymore, but other historians estimate that yes, it was probably the king of France who pressured him into making this move. In any event, when he moves to Avignon, it really changes the whole complexion of the Church.

One of the biggest problems is that when the pope moved to Avignon he lost the revenues from the Papal States. The Papal States are a little strip of territory running through the center of Italy from Rome in the south to Ravenna in the north, controlled by the pope. These are his personally controlled territories, and he took tax monies and revenues from these tiny states and used those revenues to help run the Church. In Avignon, he obviously doesn't have access to these revenues because all the Papal States, once the pope is gone, declare themselves independent, and then stop paying the taxes and stop giving the revenues to the Church and the Papacy. So that forces the pope to find money in some other way to run the Church, and he has to set up a fairly elaborate bureaucracy of offices and new taxes, just to get the money to run the Church.

Now, if you look at it from the pope's point of view, he's got to have the money to run the Church. There are only a few places he can get it. New fees and taxes are going to be one of those. For example, he starts to exploit Church appointments; in other words, charging money to appoint people to Church office. He issues more indulgences than he had issued in the past. He starts to give out dispensations for revenue, but even worse than that, the pope causes the Church to start charging fees to common churchgoers for all sorts of things they never paid fees for before. So, where in the past, people used to get services free from the Church, now the average churchgoer, who is a peasant or a poor person, has to pay for those services. This is just to get the money to actually operate the Church. Without it, the Church couldn't have continued operating.

What this does is to make the Papacy and the Church look like greedy, money-grubbing, materialistic institutions only interested in getting money out of their parishioners and the faithful. This causes a huge wave of anti-clericalism all across Europe. Common people by the masses turn against the Church, believing that the Church is only out to make a buck, and only out to make a buck off them. To some extent that was true, but you can see what the Church's problems really were. This whole apparatus of new taxes, new fees, new charges, known as papal fiscalism, really made the Church look terrible and hurt its prestige tremendously all across Europe.

By 1378, the pope (by this time Gregory XI) has decided it's got to stop; that we can't continue down this road because the Church is going to lose all its prestige. He decides that he's got to move the Papacy back to Rome, which he does in 1378. Unfortunately, after he gets back to Rome, only a couple of months after he gets back and sets the church back up in Rome, he dies, and the cardinals have to go into session and elect a new pope, which they do. They elect an Italian cardinal who becomes Pope Urban VI.

However, it turns out that Pope Urban VI wants to reform the Church. A lot of the corruptions and abuses that people had complained about during the 14th century, he wants to clean up, and especially the fees and money coming into the Church that is being used in not the best ways. He wants to clean all that up. However, the cardinals had not realized when they elected him that he was a reformer, and especially the French cardinals did not like at all the fact that he was a reformer, because they didn't want to be reformed. They liked things pretty much the way they were. So, a good portion of the cardinals, mainly French cardinals, go back into session, declare Urban's election invalid, elect a new pope, this time a French one, and then the French cardinals and the French pope get up and move back to Avignon.

So from 1378 to 1415, we enter a period known as the Great Schism, because the Italian pope and the Italian cardinals stay in Rome. So now we have two popes, one in Rome, one in Avignon. In fact, we have two entire Churches; two entire Church organizations, one in Rome, one in Avignon. People all over Europe have to decide which pope and Church they are going to follow. Ordinary people have to decide this. Kings have to decide it. Even universities have to take sides. Some choose the French pope; some choose the Italian pope. Europe is split right down the middle.

To make things worse, each one of the rival popes excommunicates the other rival pope and all his followers, meaning that everybody in Europe is excommunicated, meaning that nobody's going to go to heaven. So, you see the situation is very, very embarrassing for the Church, and the Church is split right down the middle; perhaps an even worse disaster than the Babylonian Captivity.

This gives rise to a movement which attempts to heal the Schism. That movement is known as the Conciliar Movement. It's based on the calling of a Church council, which is simply a meeting of all the major bishops in the Church to decide some big issue. The lack of papal leadership in the Church, or I guess you could say the overabundance of papal leadership, since we have two popes now, led a lot of cardinals to think that the only way we can cure this Schism and decide who is really the true pope is to call a Church council and let the council vote on it and decide who is the real pope.

Even before the Great Schism, there had been a history to conciliorism that is worth just mentioning. In the Middle Ages some theologians had dealt with the problem or had thought about the problem: What would happen if all of a sudden the pope became insane or became a heretic or otherwise incompetent to rule the Church? What would happen then? And a lot of reformers suggested that a Church council would take control of the Church and govern it in place of a pope who wasn't able to do it. Other supporters of the Conciliar Movement went even further. They said a general council of all the bishops is really a better way to rule the Church any time. It's better than a pope, because it can do more than a pope can do.

For example, it's more democratic. It represents all the people in the Church. It might even be able to reform the Church better than the pope, because the pope is just one man and he's subject to all sorts of pressures and people can prevent him from acting, whereas a council of many, many bishops would be more able to act and perhaps reform the Church and do good things for the Church. So this whole Conciliar Movement has a history, but it becomes much more influential during the period of the Great Schism.

Also, the prominence of the Church council during this period is a measure of how far the Papacy has fallen in prestige since the Middle Ages, when the pope was unquestionably the head of the Church. Now there are a lot of people questioning whether the pope should be head of the Church, can be head of the Church, and many people are answering that, "No."

The first effort by the Conciliar Movement to bring about a solution to the Great Schism occurred in 1409, when a general council of the Church was called and convened in the city of Pisa. This was supposed to decide which of the two popes would be the real pope. One of the drawbacks of the council in Pisa was that it was in Italy, which meant that it was much more attended by Italian churchmen and not so many from northern Europe could attend because it was so far away, but it still went about its business fairly efficiently, and elected a new pope, and then declared the other two popes deposed. However, the other two popes refused to resign, refused to step down, stayed in place, and so the Council of Pisa ends with now three popes: one in Pisa, one in Rome, and one in Avignon. Now there are three Church organizations; three everything, so it just makes the situation all that much more desperate.

By 1414, a lot of people were starting to give up hope, but the Holy Roman Emperor Sigismund said, "Let's have one more try at a Church council. Let's call a Church council and really make another effort to decide which pope is going to be the true pope." This council was held from 1414 to 1418 in the city of Constance, in Switzerland. This is a much more centrally located place; therefore, much better representation from all areas of Europe, not just Italian officials. It starts to do its business very efficiently. It deposes all three rival popes and elects a fourth pope as the true pope, this pope named Martin V. This time, however, the council gets lucky and the other three popes resign, step down, give it up, and we are left with just one pope.

So the Great Schism is technically over, but the Church's problems aren't over, because when Martin was elected pope, the members of the Church council forced him to agree to a situation in which the Church council would be supreme ruler in the Church, and the pope would be like an administrator who would carry out the council's desires. The council would meet, say, every three years, and in between meetings the pope would carry out its orders, but the pope wouldn't really be the head of the Church anymore. The council would be. If Martin hadn't agreed to that he wouldn't have been elected pope, so he did agree to it, and so that's how the council ended.

After the end of the council, Martin and succeeding popes are determined to slowly but surely regain their power in the Church, and the way they do this is, in fact, quite costly. They go to various kings of Europe, the powerful kings of France and Spain and other countries, and they offer these kings, essentially, deals. They say, (the pope says to the king), "We will give you control of the Church in your country. You can make Church appointments in your country. You can take a large portion of Church taxes from the Church in your country. In return, you support the pope over the council as head of the universal Church." Kings were more than willing to do this because it would give them tremendous power over Church appointments and Church revenues in their countries. So the deal was made.

The final clash occurs at the Council of Basel, which takes place in 1431-1443. There the pope and the Church council face each other down. The pope declares he is head of the Church. The council declares it is head of the Church. The council gets so frustrated with the pope that it actually deposes the pope and appoints a new pope, who has gone down in history as being called the Anti-Pope, Felix V. However, what the council has done is essentially recreate the Schism, which it was born to heal, by deposing one pope and appointing a rival pope. This obvious re-opening of all the wounds of the Schism just turned everybody in Europe against the Church council and caused the pope to be able to come back and take complete control over the Church, and his power in the Church just grows after that into the magnificent Renaissance Papacy.

Lecture Three

The Origins of the Italian Renaissance

Scope:

In this lecture, we will attempt to answer the questions: What was the Renaissance, and why did it begin in Italy in the late 14th century? The lecture explains the Renaissance against the background of European reactions to the crisis of the 14th century. A unique Italian reaction to that crisis grew into the beginnings of the Renaissance. The lecture also explores the new view of history adopted by the first Humanists, as well as the vision of the first Humanists for a recovery of the Classical past. Finally, the lecture looks at the unique Italian urban environment in which the Renaissance was born and relates the workings of the Italian communes to the growth of Humanism.

Outline

I. There were various reactions to the 14th-century crisis.

    A. The many crises of the 14th century shook people's confidence in traditional thought and society.

        1. Many felt that society was old, exhausted, and dying.

        2. Plague and famine caused pessimism about daily life.

        3. There was a preoccupation with death, as shown in the common motif of the "dance of death" in painting.

        4. There was a general loss of confidence in the church's spiritual leadership, which bred anxiety and uncertainty.

        5. The world itself seemed to be in its last days, and apocalyptic visions proliferated.

    B. In Italy among some intellectuals, especially in the urbanized north, there was a different reaction.

        1. Instead of giving way in the face of such pessimism, they determined to make a new start.

        2. They decided to build a new world to replace the dying old one, to create a new society through a search for revival, renewal, or rebirth that would come to be called the *Renaissance*.

        3. This attitude occurred first in Italy in the late 14th century and would later spread across Europe.

C. This drive for rebirth and renewal was based on a new view of history developed by Italian urban intellectuals of the time.

   1. Reflecting on the disasters of the 14th century, these men came to see the entire period they would label as the Middle Ages as a period of disaster, decay, and corruption.

   2. By contrast, they saw the era of ancient Greece and Rome as the golden age of civilization and culture: a time of joy, prosperity, and learning.

D. To improve and renew their own society, these intellectuals sought to return to the golden age of antiquity: to remake their world in the image of antiquity. This vision of their society as a discontinuation of the corrupt Middle Ages, this determination to make a clean break with the Middle Ages and bring about a rebirth of Classical antiquity, was the heart of the Renaissance vision.

II. How was the rebirth achieved?

A. What was the plan these intellectuals had for achieving a rebirth of Classical antiquity? It was a largely educational program.

B. First, they stressed the recovery and re-reading of all the great Greek and Roman Classical writings—not just the few, such as Aristotle, known during the Middle Ages.

   1. It was believed that the classics contained the wisdom to help 14th-century people solve their political, social, and moral problems and reconstruct society on Classical foundations.

   2. The challenges lay in recovery of the works and understanding of their contents in proper historical context.

C. Second, these intellectuals hoped to revive the ancient Roman educational system based on the liberal arts.

   1. Liberal arts education, while not new historically, was a radical new departure for the 14th century—it strove to provide a broad and general education based on reading the classics, as opposed to the typical medieval vocational education in law, medicine, or theology.

2. Together, liberal arts education and devotion to the classics would come to be known as *Humanism*.

III. Why did the Renaissance begin in late-14th–century Italy and not in some other time or place? The answer lies in the social and political context.

A. Italy was the first place in Europe to begin to pull out of the economic depression brought on by the plague.

B. For centuries, the Italian towns had maintained a prosperous trade with the Middle East based mainly on spices.

C. This created a concentration of commercial wealth in the cities, some of which was invested in culture, art, and learning.

D. Unlike any other place in Europe, Italy was dominated by big cities: Florence, Milan, Rome, Venice, Genoa, Pisa, Naples, and many others.

1. This meant that life for most Italians was urban life, and it was this urban life that created the conditions for the rise of the Renaissance. Classical antiquity was revived in the cities.

2. As an urban society, 14th-century Italy resembled antiquity more than it resembled the rest of medieval Europe.

3. The ancient period had been a time of urban civilization—Athens at its height was a city of more than 300,000 people; Rome, more than 1 million people.

4. Medieval Europe, by contrast, was a largely rural, agricultural society in which towns were small and played only a peripheral role.

5. Thus, in many ways, the society of 14th-century Italy had more in common with antiquity than with the Middle Ages.

6. When political and social problems arose in the Italian cities, it was natural for people to look for solutions in the ancient classics, literary products of a society much like their own, with concerns and problems much like their own. Medieval literature, which was largely religious, was less relevant to urban problems.

IV. What kinds of problems did the cities face?

   A. Up until the 12th century, most Italian towns had been nominally parts of the Holy Roman Empire. They paid taxes and contributed troops to the emperor.

   B. In the 12th century, during the conflict between the pope and the emperor, most Italian towns established their independence, either through military action or by monetary payments to the emperor.

   C. As independent city-states—or *communes*—the towns faced many political and social problems, both foreign and domestic.

   D. There was constant political and military competition among the towns.

   E. In the late 14th century, Milan, ruled by the Visconti family, used military force to attempt to control all of northern Italy.

      1. After many victories, this goal was in sight. Milanese expansion was turned back only by an alliance between Florence and Venice.

      2. After 1450, Venice adopted an expansionist foreign policy in search of control over a mainland food supply. An alliance of Florence, Milan, and Rome turned back Venetian expansion.

      3. Florence always seemed to be the key to the balance of power in northern Italy, and as such, its leaders had to learn the intricacies of international politics.

   F. Most of the Italian towns were communes, or republics, but are best understood as complex oligarchies ruled by groups of rich citizens called *patricians*, the commercial elite.

      1. The patricians occupied the higher or commercial guilds, while less wealthy citizens were in the lower or craft guilds. In the early days of the communes, the lower guilds had shared power and office with the higher guilds, but as the years went by, the patricians gradually established their hold on power.

2. Nonetheless, the lower guilds never accepted their exclusion from power. Occasionally, they expressed their resentment in revolts, such as the Ciompi Revolt in Florence in 1378, but normally, they simply stressed the communal nature of the government and pressed for power through peaceful channels.

3. This conflict between upper and lower guilds made for an active and often turbulent internal political life for the towns. There was much political debate and confrontation.

4. The towns were highly politicized societies, which made them, again, unlike most of medieval society, where kings and nobles ruled and the church encouraged an attitude in which politics was shunned as unspiritual.

5. In the Italian towns, a new attitude toward politics developed, in which politics was seen as a worthy and honorable vocation, and a broad range of citizens participated in it. It became expected that every patrician and even lower citizens would be politically active.

6. In this atmosphere, numerous difficult political and social problems arose, whose solutions could be best sought in the writings of Classical authors.

7. This political context formed an important matrix for the birth of the Renaissance, a process that can be well demonstrated by one specific case that we will examine in the next lecture.

Essential Reading:

Donald Wilcox, *In Search of God and Self*, chapter 4.

Gene Brucker, *Renaissance Florence*, chapters 1–2.

Questions to Consider:

1. Why, in contrast to the Middle Ages, did Renaissance scholars emphasize the study of all Classics, not just a select few such as Aristotle?

2. Did any one factor have the most influence on the development of the Renaissance in Italy?

Lecture Three—Transcript
The Origins of the Italian Renaissance

We're moving now into the next major part of the course, which is the Renaissance, beginning in Italy in the late 14th century and running on for the next couple of centuries in Europe. You really have to look at the Renaissance against the background of the 14th-century crisis which we've been talking about for the past couple of lectures, because I think you could really argue that without the 14th-century crisis, the Renaissance would not have taken place in any fashion like it did. The reason for that was what the 14th-century crisis had done. All these different crises in the 14th century had basically shaken people's confidence in traditional thought and society. Society seemed to be old; it seemed to be exhausted—dying, even. The plague and famine and wars and all that caused people to just have tremendous pessimism about everyday life and about the world. A good example of that was that one of the most popular motifs of painting in the period was something called the "Dance of Death," where you have a number of skeletons holding hands and doing a little jig, and underneath was the title, "You're next," meaning we're all going to die pretty soon. So there was a general loss of confidence.

This was compounded by a loss of confidence in the Church and the Church's religious leadership, with the Captivity and the Schism. The Church didn't seem to be guiding people like it needed to, and a lot of religious anxiety and uncertainty grew up among the people for this reason. Many people thought the world was really in its last days, that it was coming to an end pretty soon. There were many apocalyptic visions about the world ending and how it would end and the chaos and disaster at the end. So it was just an incredibly dark and pessimistic attitude toward the end of the 14th century.

At that point Europeans could have just given up in hopelessness, but they didn't. In fact, they reacted in a positive way to that crisis and the 14th-century outlook. This positive reaction is what becomes the Renaissance. Europeans determined to make a new start. They determined to build a whole new world to replace the dying old world. They determined to create a new society. It was an incredibly idealistic and revolutionary and courageous kind of outlook which met the challenges of the 14th-century crisis.

Europeans begin to search for a revival or a renewal or a rebirth of society. That's what the Renaissance was. A revival, a renewal, a rebirth of society, which takes place first of all in northern Italy in the late 14th century, and then spreads throughout the 15th century to the rest of Europe and even as far north as Scandinavia.

So what happened in northern Italy to create the Renaissance? In Italy during the late 14th century and the early 15th century, a new view of history developed among intellectuals, which really made them look at the past in a dramatically different way than people ever had before. This was really because of the disasters of the 14th century. Because of the 14th-century crisis and all those horrible things that happened, a lot of Italian intellectuals began to see the entire Middle Ages (a term which, by the way, they coined— "Middle Ages")—they begin to see the whole Middle Ages as a time of disaster and decay and corruption. We, of course, know that's not true. We know that a lot of the High Middle Ages was a very prosperous, expansive time, a stable time; but they are looking at the 14th century and they are pretty much painting the whole Middle Ages with that brush, as a period of disaster, corruption, decay— horrible falling apart and decline.

By contrast, these Italian intellectuals saw the era of ancient Greece and Rome as a golden age of civilization, as a great period of culture and joy and prosperity and learning; the best of all possible times— the good old days, you might say. So, working on this new historical vision, they begin to work out ways to improve their own society, and they decided, obviously based on this notion of history, that they could improve their society by returning to the golden age of antiquity. People of the late 14th, 15th century determined to return their society, their world, to the golden age of antiquity, to remake their world; and this is really what it is—it is a remaking of the world in the image of antiquity. They wanted to make a clean break with the Middle Ages. They wanted to have nothing more to do with the Middle Ages. They wanted to have a rebirth of classical antiquity in their own day as a completely different period from the Middle Ages. So, people in Italy (intellectuals really, at the beginning) in the late 14th, early 15th century, came to see their society not as a continuation of the 14th century or a continuation of the Middle Ages, but as a rebirth of antiquity.

The interesting thing about this vision is that they saw this remade world as both something ancient and something new and modern. It was going to be a rebirth of classical antiquity, for reasons you will see in a couple of minutes. So that's like going back to the past, but they also saw this new society as something quintessentially modern and different and progressive and new. How they combined these two notions of the ancient and the modern is a really interesting thing to look at when you look at the Renaissance and humanism in Italy.

So, the next question you have to ask is, if you're going to bring about a rebirth of antiquity in your own day, how are you going to do it? Obviously classical antiquity has been gone for a thousand years. How are you going to revive it? How are you going to bring it back? The intellectuals decided on a couple of things. First of all, they could bring it back by a rediscovery and a re-reading of the writings written by the ancient Greek and Roman authors, the classical works of Greece and Rome, many of which had been present in the Middle Ages, but many of which hadn't been present in the Middle Ages and which would have to be rediscovered and re-read.

Secondly, they were going to do this with a revolutionary new idea of education, a whole revolutionary new educational program, which they called humanism. Humanism was a program of education which sought to re-make the world of the late 14th, early 15th century in the image of classical antiquity. So it's a very, very ambitious educational program. Here the intellectuals (who came to be known as humanists later) realized that if you're going to build a new society, if you're going to really change the world in this dramatic fashion, you have to start with education. You've got to start with a complete revamping of the whole educational system—and we'll look at how they did that—but just briefly, what humanism was all about was a complete refocusing of education.

In the Middle Ages, education had been primarily vocational. You went to university and from the very first day you got there you would study one of three topics: either theology, law, or medicine, and you would graduate and would become a specialist in one of these three areas. That was because those were the areas that society needed, vocationally speaking. They needed theologians, physicians, and specialists like that.

Humanism, on the other hand, sought to take a much more broad and general approach to education. They decided to base their education on what had, in fact, been the ancient Roman educational system, known as the liberal arts, and I'll be explaining in a future lecture what the liberal arts were all about. A liberal arts education was going to be based on the reading of the classical Greek and Roman authors. Its goal was not to create specialists or trained doctors, lawyers, theologians. Its goal was really to produce broadly educated individuals who could live in a new world, who could be good citizens, who could fill the role of ethical individuals; who really were a lot more flexible and a lot broader than the kind of educational product of the medieval system.

So, that, very briefly, is what the impetus behind the Renaissance was, and how humanism helped to fulfill that. We'll talk about that in a lot more detail at the end of this lecture and in future lectures, but we need to answer a few other questions first. One of the big questions is, why did this Renaissance attitude to revive classical antiquity come about when it did and where it did? Why was it born in northern Italy in the late 14th century, and not, for example, in France in the 15th century, or Britain in the 16th century? Why? How do you explain the specifics of time and place? I think you really have to do that to get a better understanding of what the Renaissance was.

Here I just want to offer a brief caveat that there are many different interpretations of the Renaissance, and especially its origins and nature. What I'm going to be offering is a combination of some of the major interpretations, with a little bit of my ideas added to it. It's not the last word; it's not the definitive explanation, but I think it's a good one, and one that's worth thinking about, and I would argue that the reason the Renaissance started in north Italy in the late 14th century had a lot to do with social and political events of the time, and the sort of stage that was set at the time.

To begin with, we'll talk a little bit about economics. Northern Italy was the first place in Europe that began to emerge from that terrible economic depression of the total 14th century. Why was that? For many centuries, Italy had had commercial contacts with the Middle East and even places farther east, and these contacts had never really died away. Especially after the period of the Crusades, they began to grow stronger, and this commercial wealth coming into Italy through Mediterranean trade, especially with the East, causes, in the late 14th century, the beginning of a concentration of commercial wealth in the big Italian cities.

As it turns out, and we'll see in later lectures exactly why this happened, this commercial wealth starts to be invested in culture and in art and in learning. That's a big reason why the Renaissance developed there, because they had the economic means for it. We'll talk a whole lot more about that a little bit later on. Another very important reason that I would say the Renaissance started when it did and where it did (north Italy, late 14th century) was because the kind of place northern Italy was at that time. Northern Italy was dominated by big cities: Florence, Milan, Venice, Rome, Genoa, Pisa. You can even go farther south: Rome, Naples. Italian life was essentially an urban life. Even the area between the cities was really controlled by the cities. The area between the cities was called the *contatto*, and usually paid taxes to the cities and was linked to the various cities. So almost all the places in Italy were controlled by cities. I would argue that it's this urban nature of life in Italy that creates the most important conditions for the birth of Renaissance culture then and there.

Classical antiquity was revived in the Italian cities. Why was that? Of course the economic part is part of the explanation, but an even more important part of the explanation, I believe, is that the society of ancient Greece and Rome had been a largely urban society. It was dominated by big city-states. Athens was a city-state of 200,000 to 300,000 at its peak. Rome was near a million at its peak. Most people don't really think of antiquity in this way, but it really was a very, very urban society.

On the other hand, medieval European society, the society in Europe since the fall of Rome through the 14th century, was not an urban society. It was a rural, agricultural society, dominated by nobles with their huge rural estates and agricultural production, and so quite different from antiquity. The society of the Italian Renaissance, the society of north Italy in the late 14th century, by contrast, was highly urban, and because it was highly urban, it was really a lot closer and more similar to ancient Greece and Rome than it was to medieval Europe. The urban nature of northern Italian life in the late 14th century just made it a place that was much more like antiquity than it was like the European Middle Ages. It was urban and not rural and agricultural for the most part.

For example, in most Italian cities there weren't even nobles by the late 14th, early 15th century. The nobles had been kicked out. They had been outlawed. They had no part in government. They didn't control society. There was no king of Italy. There was no kingdom of Italy. It was a very, very different place from medieval Europe. So when the Italian cities had to deal with political and social problems which arose within the cities, they had to ask the question, "Where are we going to look for solutions, for answers to these problems? Where are we going to look for answers and solutions that we need?" They did not go back and look for the answers to their problems in medieval sources, in the saints' lives, for example, because medieval sources represented a society that was just totally different. It was rural, agricultural, and just didn't address any of the problems that were arising in the Italian cities at this time.

Where they naturally went to look for solutions to those cities' problems and even individual people's problems in the society, they naturally went to the ancient examples. They went to classical sources: the writings of the Greek and Roman classics, because these represented an urban society like theirs, which was likely to have answers to questions or answers to problems that these Italian cities had. I think that is a very practical reason why we see the Italian intellectuals going back to antiquity, going back to the classics, because they are going back to a society like theirs. They are going back to sources written by people like them, looking for solutions to their problems because people in antiquity had similar problems and were offering similar solutions.

What kinds of problems are we talking about? What kinds of questions were they asking? What kinds of things were they looking for and finding out in the classics and the ancient sources? Political and social problems lead the list. So we'll start out by taking just a brief look at the history of some of the Italian towns in this period and the problems they faced and how they sought solutions in the classics. Later in the course we'll take a much more in-depth look at the city of Florence, its politics, its society, and we'll take a look at some of the other major cities and their history through this period.

North Italy in the late Middle Ages, meaning the 14th century, technically was a part of the Holy Roman Empire, which, of course, the Holy Roman Emperor in Germany ruled. In fact, however, most of the north Italian cities had become pretty much independent by even the 13th century, and certainly by the 14th century. They became what were known as communes, city-states, self-governing cities. What a commune is, is a form of government where every citizen is supposed to take part. It's a kind of republican form of government. It's called a commune because when the government is formed, when they actually set this government up, all the citizens go down to the central square of the town and they pledge a common oath to hold office, to vote, to participate in city affairs and to seek the welfare of the city. So, certainly by the late Middle Ages, the Italian cities had reached the stage of being communes and were virtually independent. The fact that they are technically part of the Empire really doesn't play much role anymore.

By the 1300s, the Italian cities have started to fight each other. This starts out with the larger, more dominant cities, like Milan. In the late 14th century, Milan goes on the warpath. It has a very large military machine led by the Visconti dynasty, who were the dictators of Milan. They set out to try to conquer an empire all through northern Italy. In fact, they almost do this. They conquer many north Italian states. The last major holdouts to the Milanese empire, I guess you'd say, were Florence and Venice. Florence and Venice form a military alliance, and they manage to turn the Milanese back.

But we'll see that it wasn't until it was a very serious crisis in the defense of Florence that this victory was attained, and we'll see in the next lecture that this very serious crisis in the history of Florence when they were under siege by the Milanese was a key factor in the rising of Renaissance humanism in Florence.

After Milan was defeated, then Venice became a major power, and Venice tries to start conquering its own land empire in northern Italy. One of the major factors that Venice had to deal with—as you know, Venice is a city built on islands off the coast. It was founded by refugees from the barbarians during the fall of the Roman Empire. They felt safe building a city out there on the islands, and they had prospered greatly with their city on the islands. They carried on a healthy trade with the Middle East. They traded with Constantinople. They were a very wealthy trading country, city-state, commune, but their main problem was that they didn't really have much land, and because they didn't have much land, they couldn't grow food. They became convinced by the early 15th century that they needed to conquer a mainland empire in order to gain land to grow food to guarantee their own food supply in case they were ever besieged or had to go to war against hostile forces.

So between about 1450 and 1500, Venice is on the warpath, trying to conquer all these cities, and again, Florence is caught in the middle. This time Florence forms an alliance with Milan and Rome and they manage to turn Venice back, but as you can see, Florence is always in a position of holding the balance of power in these wars. Another thing you can see is that a knowledge of diplomacy, a knowledge of military strategy, a knowledge of politics is going to be very important for these cities, and especially a knowledge of city politics and city defense and city citizenship is going to be very important for the power of these cities as they struggle against each other. So those are some of the problems that the Italian cities have to deal with. Those are some of the problems that they seek answers for, solutions to, when they go back and they read the classics.

As well as having these, I guess what you'd say, foreign or foreign military and political problems, almost all of the cities had very turbulent internal, domestic, political problems and situations. We've already seen in Florence the urban workers' revolt (the Ciompi in 1378) caused the lower guilds to rise up against the wage freeze of the 14th century and take charge of the Florentine government for a couple of years. Such a revolution was really an amazing thing, because in very few places did lower classes ever actually seize the government and control the government for a number of years.

In Italian towns though, it had not always been this way. By the late 14th century, most Italian towns were ruled by the wealthy upper classes, the wealthy upper guildsmen, and the industrial commercial world known as patricians, but it had not always been that way. When the communes were first formed, back in the 12th, 13th, early 14th century, the governments were a lot more broad-based than that. The lower guilds, the lower classes, had played more of a role in government. It had really been a lot more democratic in the early years, and only over time had the upper classes, the patricians, more or less established their own power and kind of forced out the lower classes, but the lower classes never forgot that they were living in a commune and that a commune means that it's a common thing, that everybody should be able to take part. So the lower classes never gave up attempting to press their way into power—as we can see in the Ciompi regime—attempting to gain influence, attempting to gain office, attempting to become influential in the city. When they did this, they stressed the communal nature of the government. They said, "Look, this is supposed to be not an oligarchy, as it's turned out to be, but it is supposed to be a republic, a commune, and we're supposed to have a role, and all we're asking for is our legitimate role."

So this pressure and tension between the upper class and lower class created a very lively political situation in the Italian cities. Politics was a major daily occupation. There was much political debate in the Italian cities. There was much constitutional change, much constitutional discussion. In a situation like that, you need to be able to train people to take part in debate and discussion. You need to have people who are able to hold office, who are able to give service to the commune. You need to have people who can vote responsibly. That was to be one of the goals of humanistic education: to create the kind of people needed to successfully work this political situation, this political system, in the Italian cities. That becomes a very important issue for humanism.

It also means that the Italian cities were highly politicized societies. That also made the Italian cities very different from the Middle Ages. Medieval agricultural European society had not been a political society. As a matter of fact, most of medieval society had shunned politics. The Church shunned politics, at least the people's participation in politics, as being materialistic and sinful and not something that's really good. It's a necessary evil and people ought not to be involved in it, and of course kings, who were the major rulers throughout most of agricultural medieval Europe, also shunned politics because they didn't want the people to be part of it. The people were subjects. The people were not to be voters or office holders, especially. So there was this natural aversion to politics in most of medieval society. It is very different in the Italian communes in the late 14th century. It's this highly politicized society which is another important context for the arrival and arising of humanism and the Renaissance, because, as we have mentioned before, humanism as a broad liberal arts education is designed to prepare people to take part in politics. If a society is not really political, there would be no need for this. So that's another really important contextual issue to involve and to consider.

In fact, most people did, in their own way, take part in politics in the Italian cities. True, mainly the upper classes held the important offices, but the lower classes were involved in the debate and the discussion. As we've seen in the Ciompi, they did sometimes rise up and actually take control. So it's a very fluid political situation. As more people take part in politics, whether it's only a small part or a larger part like the patricians, politics as a vocation comes to be seen as honorable; not as sinful and materialistic and to be shunned, but as good and important and vital—something we should nurture and train people to take part in. That's another big difference between medieval society and Renaissance society, the way Renaissance people, and humanists especially, valued politics and saw it as an honorable activity and an important activity that people should get involved with. In an atmosphere like that, where politics is considered so important and so vital by the upper as well as by the lower classes, you're just not going to find very many solutions and answers and ideas for societies like that when you go back and look at medieval literature. You're going to find the important ideas you need and the important solutions you need in the classics, which come from a society very much like this society was.

It's no surprising thing that one of the main things that Renaissance humanists do is revive an ancient Roman idea about politics, which actually comes from the Roman republican period, and that was this idea: that everybody in the city ought to take part in politics. Why? Because politics—what is it? It's a kind of giant public dialogue. It's a public debate. There is discussion. There is talk about different points of view. You hear other people's ideas; they hear yours. You come to a conclusion or a compromise of some kind and you act on it, and what happens in a case like that is that through this public dialogue people become educated. They learn from other people. They mature. They develop. That was what Renaissance humanists wanted citizens to be: educated, political participants. That's a big part of what the Renaissance was.

Lecture Four
The Birth of Civic Humanism

Scope:

In this lecture, we will examine events in the city of Florence during the Milanese invasion of 1380–1402 to illustrate the conditions in Italy under which Humanism—in this case, Civic Humanism—was born. Then, we will take a close look at the Humanist view of politics and how it interacted with Humanist devotion to the classics, the Humanist rhetorical tradition, and Humanist liberal arts education. We close by exploring the ideals of *Studia humanitatis* and noting the Humanist search for ancient manuscripts.

Outline

I. No particular series of events better illustrates the wider set of conditions that gave birth to Humanism than the Florentine crisis of 1380–1402, which took place in a city many see as the birthplace of the Renaissance.

   A. Florence found itself under siege.

   1. During the last decades of the 14th century, the powerful city of Milan, under its dictator Gian Galeazzo Visconti, was on the verge of conquering an empire in northern Italy. One of the last powers to hold out was Florence.

   2. Milanese forces, far superior to the Florentines, had Florence under siege, and a Milanese victory seemed only a short time away. At this critical moment in history, Visconti died of bubonic plague outside the gates of Florence, Milanese forces withdrew, and Florence was saved.

   3. After this near disaster, Florentine leaders, especially chancellors Caluccio Salutati and Leonardo Bruni, began to reflect on what had brought Florence so near defeat.

4. Their conclusion was that Florence's educational system, based on typical medieval vocational ideals, was lacking in that it did not produce well-rounded and competent citizens and city leaders who could help the city withstand such crises. They determined that a new educational structure was needed to produce more capable and active citizens.

B. Florentine leaders began to design a new educational system to prepare people for their civic roles. It was to be called *Civic Humanism.*

1. The new educational system stressed the similarity between Florence and ancient Rome and was based on reading Classical authors. It was believed that the Classics could provide a model for a stronger Florentine state.

2. To stress the idea that every citizen should be prepared for his political role, an ancient Roman ideal about politics was revived. This ideal held that participation in politics and public affairs was essential to individual human development and maturity. Politics was a great public dialogue, in which people debated and learned from one another's points of view. But to participate effectively in this community dialogue, people had to be educated in moral philosophy and rhetoric.

II. Humanist education prepared the citizen to take part in society and politics.

A. Moral philosophy and rhetoric were thought to be the two broad categories into which the education of the citizen should be organized.

1. Moral philosophy formed good judgment on an ethical basis. It was believed that all decisions, especially political ones, were essentially moral.

2. Rhetoric gave the citizen the power to communicate to others his knowledge and judgment.

3. Only the ability to make judgments and the power to communicate them made for a complete citizen. In Latin, these dual abilities were called *sapientia et eloquentia*, or "knowledge and eloquence."

4. The place to learn moral philosophy and eloquence was the classics.

B. One problem was that not many classics were readily available.

1. Many had been destroyed during the barbarian invasions of the late Roman Empire, and many of the rest had been hidden away in monastic libraries and other places for safekeeping, then forgotten and lost. These lost classics would have to be recovered.

2. Fortunately, a small stock of classics was available that the Humanists could begin with. These were available because of the teaching of rhetoric in medieval universities.

3. In the early Middle Ages, the teaching of rhetoric—how to make good public speeches and write good letters— was based on the rote memorization of long passages of Latin prose expressing certain emotions or ideas, passages that could then simply be inserted into speeches or letters.

4. Later in the Middle Ages, rhetoric teaching changed. Instead of memorizing rote passages, students were taught to imitate the *style* of great Classical authors. For this, the reading of classics was necessary, and the few available ones were preserved and utilized to this end. But they were read for their style rather than their content.

5. In the hands of the Humanists, these classics were read both for their style and content in answering pressing questions of the day.

C. In its basic structure, Humanist education was a revival of the ancient Roman educational system.

1. In ancient Rome, there were two basic divisions of people: citizens and slaves. Slaves provided the manual labor in society and needed no education. Citizens, on the other hand, did need education.

2. The system thought by the Romans best suited for the education of citizens (free people) was called the *liberal arts*. The liberal arts consisted of seven subjects organized under two subheadings.

3.   The first three subjects were the *Trivium*. They included Latin grammar, rhetoric, and logic, the arts of communication. These would become the *eloquentia* of Humanist education.

4.   The second group of four subjects was the *Quadrivium* and included mathematics, geometry, astronomy, and music. These subjects were thought of as the content of knowledge to be communicated and would become the Humanist *sapientia*. To the original four, the Humanists added a few more subjects dear to their hearts: history, poetry, and literature.

5.   Teaching of the liberal arts had been done in a rudimentary way in the medieval universities but only as a brief preparatory for the study of higher vocational subjects. The liberal arts became the full body of the Humanist educational program.

D. The Humanists called their educational system the *Studia Humanitatis*, which means the "study of the humanities" or, more to the point, the study of what it means to be human. It is from this that we get the term *Humanist*.

1.   The goal of Humanist education was to enable people to reach their full human potential: to help them be the best, most well-rounded people they could be. This would also produce the best citizens.

2.   This was accomplished because the Humanists educated what they believed to be the two primary sides of the human personality: the intellect and the will.

3.   The intellect, or reasoning power, was educated by *sapientia*, or knowledge. The will, each person's desire, was formed through *eloquentia*, or the art of convincing through communication.

4.   Humanist education served both the individual and society: It produced the best individuals and the best citizens.

E. The foundation of Humanist education was the classics. Thus, early on, the Humanists began an intensive search for the lost classics in monastic libraries and other hiding places where they had lain neglected for centuries.

1. Almost all the great Humanists joined in this search, and a large part of the Classical tradition was recovered.

2. Francesco Petrarch (1304–1374), about whom we will learn much more in later lectures, searched monastic libraries, finding important works of Cicero and Livy.

3. Giovanni Boccacio (1313–1375) searched the library of the great Benedictine house of Monte Casino, south of Rome. There, he found manuscripts of the Roman historians Tacitus and Livy. His interest in the Latin classics was accompanied by an intense interest in the Greek classics, which led him to set up a school in Florence to teach Greek.

4. Poggio Bracciolini (1380–1459) recovered manuscripts of Lucretius and Quintillian, the latter being *On the Education of the Orator*, the Roman textbook of rhetoric.

5. The search for ancient manuscripts became a craze across Europe.

Essential Reading:

Donald Wilcox, *In Search of God and Self*, chapters 5–6.

Supplementary Reading:

Anthony Grafton and Lisa Jardine, *From Humanism to the Humanities*.

Hans Baron, *The Crisis of the Early Italian Renaissance*.

Garrett Mattingly, *Renaissance Diplomacy*.

Questions to Consider:

1. How did the Florentine crisis of 1380–1402 illustrate the general conditions under which Humanism was formed?

2. How was Humanist education a forerunner of modern liberal arts education?

Lecture Four—Transcript
The Birth of Civic Humanism

We are continuing with the Renaissance in this lecture. In the last lecture we looked a little bit at the origins and causes of the Renaissance and in general terms what it was and what humanism was. In this lecture what I want to do is to look at some more specific aspects of the Renaissance and humanism, both its birth and some of the aspects of its educational system that are very relevant still to today's educational programs. Then in the next couple of lectures we'll be looking at the ideas that the humanist drew from the classics—the huge new perspectives and new philosophies that they got out of them.

I want to start today by talking about something which you don't often have a chance to do when you're talking about big historical movements like the Renaissance or humanism. Usually one assumes that it would be very difficult to pin down the beginning of the Renaissance to a certain year or a certain place because it's such a big historical movement and it's such a complex phenomenon that it's almost hard to believe that you could specifically locate it at a place in time and a place in geography. There's a really interesting theory by an historian named Hans Baron from the University of Chicago, who wrote a book called *The Crisis of the Early Italian Renaissance*. He argues that you can actually trace the birth of the Renaissance to a specific place, which is the city of Florence, and a specific time, which is the years between 1380 and 1402, a period in which Florence was in a huge crisis. So I want to talk about that just a little bit, because even though it's just one view of the beginning of the Renaissance, it's an interesting attempt to kind of pin it down and make it more specific.

So what was happening in Florence between the years 1380 and 1402? These were the years in which the city of Milan was on the warpath in northern Italy and attempting to conquer a north Italian empire. As a matter of fact, it just about created a whole, what could have been a kingdom, in northern Italy. Among the last holdouts against the Milanese was the city of Florence. Between 1380 and 1402 the city of Florence was under siege by Milan, Milan being led by its dictator, a man named Gian Galeazzo Visconti. He had a very big army, a very formidable army. Florence itself didn't have that huge of a military apparatus. So as the siege wore on, it was looking dimmer and dimmer as far as whether Florence would be able to survive and hold out against Milan and Milan's attempt to create this empire. Then, at virtually the last minute, one of those strikes of fate in history occurred that often change the course of history and you really can't say why they happen. The leader of Milan, Gian Galeazzo Visconti, got Bubonic Plague and dropped dead outside the gates of Florence. The Milanese army then retreated and the siege was over. Milan [sic Florence] was saved.

The leaders of Florence, though—this is all according to what Hans Baron has told us—the leaders of Florence realized how close they had come to being conquered, and especially two chancellors (essentially prime ministers as we'll learn later on) of Florence, Caluccio Salutati and later Leonardo Bruni, realized that it really was just a stroke of luck that Florence had not been conquered, and they asked themselves, "Why? Why did we come so close to disaster? Why were we so weak in this period of crisis?" They arrived at the conclusion that it was the educational system, that Florence really needed a new way to train future city leaders as well as future citizens of the city to withstand such crises and to exercise leadership in difficult times and to be responsible citizens and to meet all the challenges of a difficult period like Florence had just been through. So, Salutati and Bruni set out to create a new educational system that would provide this kind of background for people of Florence.

Essentially they wanted to prepare or create an educational system that would get young people ready for their roles as citizens and perhaps leaders of the city. This new educational system they named "civic humanism." As you can imagine, since it was part of humanism it was based on reading the classical authors of ancient Greece and Rome, but it was a little bit more than that. Civic humanism also stressed the similarity between Florence and ancient Rome. It essentially said, "Look—Rome was this great power based on these virtues and Florence, being very close to Rome, can recapture this glory and be like Rome was. We have the right educational system. There's no reason that we can't attain to those kind of heights that Rome attained to."

So that was kind of the overall idea behind civic humanism. More specifically, civic humanism stressed seeking political answers and solutions in the classical authors and the classical writings and also pulling the city of Florence together with a kind of patriotic appeal.

"We can be a great city. We can be like Rome. If only we can recapture some of Rome's greatness and some of their virtues and be like them, then we can be powerful and maybe even be as dominating as ancient Rome was." So that was the idea behind civic humanism.

As I mentioned in an earlier lecture, the two chancellors and other civic humanists also revived an ancient Roman idea about politics, which was that everybody in a city—not just the leaders, but every single citizen—must participate in politics. The reason for this is, it's for their own human development as well as for the good of the city. Participation in politics and public affairs is essential for human development, they argued, because politics is really nothing more than a great community dialogue—public dialogue—and in this dialogue people learn from each other. They grow and mature and become fulfilled individuals. That, of course, is good for the individual person, but also provides good citizens and good leaders for the city. So we should all want to take part in politics. Politics ought to be a good, useful, encouraged thing for everybody.

But there was more to it than just that, because civic humanists realized that you need some preparation to take part in politics. You can't just go in there completely cold and do a good job. You need some preliminary education, and this preliminary education was one of the things that civic humanism was going to try to provide. Especially civic humanists stressed that everybody in a city—every citizen, at least—should be educated in two subjects (or two groups of subjects): moral philosophy and rhetoric. Let me explain a little bit what this is all about.

Moral philosophy (which I guess today we would call ethics, but it really was a broader subject at that time than ethics) would be the branch of education that would teach people the answers to problems, the solutions to problems. It would teach them how to make good judgments in difficult circumstances. It would teach them how to make difficult moral decisions. Here I want to stress that the humanists believed that every decision, whether it be political, economic, social, personal, whatever—every decision was a moral decision. So, if you have a good moral foundation and moral consciousness, this will give you the judgment and the answers and solutions that you need to be an effective citizen or leader in the city. So that's one thing.

The second part you should all be educated in is rhetoric. The reason for that is that you need to be able to communicate the knowledge you've got. Whether we're talking about leaders or citizens or anybody in between, it's just common sense, and you can see it in today's world—if somebody's very educated and knows all the answers, but can't communicate them, they are not going to be a very successful or effective leader or citizen or even teacher. If somebody's a real great communicator but doesn't really know anything, again, they are not going to be a very effective leader or citizen or person. So you need both halves of education like this. You need both moral philosophy—knowledge to make the right judgments—and rhetoric—the ability to communicate these judgments to other people. The humanists called this in Latin, *sapientia et eloquentia*, which just means "wisdom and eloquence," wisdom being moral philosophy and eloquence being rhetoric or the art of public speaking, as well as writing and communication of all kinds. Of course, the way you get this education is you go to the classics. You read classical literature, poetry, and history and you get your foundation from the ancient classics.

That brings up the question, where did the humanists get the classics to read? One of the kind of accepted notions is that in the Middle Ages they really hadn't read the classics and so, as a matter of fact, they didn't really have the classics in the Middle Ages, and therefore for the Renaissance and the humanists it was all a hugely new and totally, perfectly new thing. That's not really true. In fact, the Middle Ages did possess a number of classics, but they read them in a very different way than the humanists did. So what's new about the humanists is that they do, in fact, find a lot of other classical works that weren't present in the Middle Ages, but the real new thing is that the humanists read them differently and get different things out of them.

You might recall that at the fall of the Roman Empire, a lot of especially Roman classics had essentially disappeared. Either they had been destroyed when the barbarians attacked cities or, in effect, a lot of them had been hidden away in monastic libraries and other hiding places to save them from the barbarians, but then after that they were kind of forgotten. However, there were a number of classics available during the Middle Ages, and they were preserved in the medieval education. The classical, literary, rhetorical tradition was preserved in a certain branch of literary education. This is an idea that is given to us by a very famous Columbia University historian, Paul Oscar Kristeller. There were classics available to medieval readers, but it's the way that they read them and used them that was so different.

Where were they read and used, and where were they available? The major place that the classics were used in the medieval educational system was in the teaching of rhetoric, which is public speaking, essentially, which was a pretty important branch of even medieval education—good speaking, good writing, arts, communication. Early on in the Middle Ages, what they did in teaching rhetoric was they would essentially force students to memorize rote passages of Latin from classical authors. The passages would be ones that would express, say, sadness, happiness, thankfulness, whatever, and they would memorize these passages, and when they wrote their own letters, they would just plug them in. The problem with that, of course, is that all the letters sound alike, because they are plugging in all the same passages, and it's just not a very effective means of teaching eloquence.

So in the late Middle Ages, they changed, and instead of making people memorize rote passages, they said instead find classical authors that you think have a good style, read the works, and imitate their style—not necessarily the very words, but just imitate their style, and that will make you write better and be more eloquent. This is what they were using the classics for, for the most part, in the medieval educational system. They were using it as a way of learning good Latin style. So they were reading them for the style, not really for the ideas. That's what makes a big difference when the humanists come along and start to read these works for the ideas, although, we shall see in a couple of minutes, the humanists also uncover a lot of "new" classics—recover a lot of lost classics.

What I want to do next is to say a little bit about exactly what the foundations for humanist education were, because it really was a radically new kind of education. It wasn't the old medieval doctor-lawyer-theologian kind of vocational education. In fact, humanist education provided the foundation for the modern liberal arts education that people at Lafayette College where I teach get, and people all across the U.S. and even some in Europe get still. What this humanist education was, was essentially a revival of ancient

Roman education, the ancient Roman educational system, which was known as the "liberal arts."

Why did they call it the liberal arts, first of all? In Rome there were essentially two kinds of people: there were citizens, who were free and took part in everything: state, government; and there were slaves, who were the manpower behind the economy. Slaves don't really need to be educated to maintain, to provide manpower for the economy, but a free person does need to be educated. A free person needs to be educated in order to make good decisions, to lead the state, to pull his weight in the government. So the seven liberal arts ("liberal" meaning "free") were the seven subjects the ancient Romans thought should be taught to every free individual, and by extension they were the seven subjects that the ancient Romans thought every free citizen should know, to be prepared for life and for their role in society.

So what were these seven liberal arts or seven subjects, really? The ancient Romans broke them down into two parts. The first part was called the *Trivium*. That included three subjects: grammar (Latin grammar, of course), rhetoric (Latin rhetoric), and logic. These were the subjects of communication. In the humanist view, these were the subjects of eloquence. These taught people how to get their ideas across to other people, which was very important.

The second group of the liberal arts was called the *Quadrivium*, a group of four subjects: mathematics, geometry, astronomy, and music. These were thought of as the subjects of providing the content of knowledge, the ideas to be communicated, the way to make good judgment. So you can see how these ancient ideas paralleled later humanist ideas.

When the humanists adopted the liberal arts education, they expanded upon the liberal arts. So they really weren't any longer the seven liberal arts. The *Trivium* they kept the same: grammar, rhetoric, and logic—classical Latin grammar, rhetoric, and logic that had to be learned, and we'll see how that was learned. To the *Quadrivium*, they added subjects, because they thought that people needed to be a bit broader than what was prescribed there. They added the study of history (which humanists thought was very important), they added the study of poetry and other forms of literature, and they even added other things beyond that. So they really expand the basic system, but the idea is the same: that these are the subjects that every individual who is going to be a responsible citizen should be educated in.

The humanists called this—they didn't really call it a "liberal arts education—they called it the *Studia humanitatis*, which means—you can translate it various ways—it's usually translated "study of the humanities." But I think it's better translated as "study of the human" or "study of what it is to be human," because that's really what the humanists were all about. They were about trying to make people the best individuals they could be. They tried to help people reach their full human potential. They tried to make people the best people they could be. That was the idea behind this educational system. It was believed that, to do that, you had to educate both the intellect and the will. The humanists imagined that these were the two basic parts of the psychological make-up of people: the intellect (the reasoning part); and the will, which provides the desire and the motivation to do things.

We no longer today think that there are just these two sides of the human personality, but the humanists thought this pretty much summed it up. They thought you had to educate both these equally, and that's where they came up with moral philosophy and rhetoric—*sapientia et eloquentia*—because the intellect, the reasoning part of the mind, is educated with knowledge. We'll see in later lectures exactly how they did this and what their plan was for doing it, but knowledge would fill up the intellect and give people the ideas that they needed to create or to make good judgments and decisions and so forth.

The will, the other part, which was, for the humanists, at least as important a part, had to be educated with eloquence. What that means is that the will had to be inspired. It had to be motivated properly to do the right thing and make the right judgment and make the right decision. Here we see a basic difference between Renaissance humanist education and medieval education, which we'll talk a lot more about in the next lecture or two. Medieval thinkers tended to believe that the intellect was by far the more important part of education, and if you educated that, you'd really done most of the job. The humanists disagreed. They said without properly forming the will, without properly inspiring and motivating the will to do the right thing, it doesn't really matter what you know. You need both. You need the answers, but you need the motivation to carry out the answers, to carry out the solutions, to put in practice. So the humanists stressed the will, and that's really another reason why rhetoric was so important to the humanists, because it was through rhetoric, as you will see later, that the will was inspired and motivated and moved to make good judgments and to do the right thing that the intellect knew. We'll come back to that a little bit later on, in a later lecture.

So humanist education (*Studia humanitatis*) was designed to help develop the human faculties, both intellectual and moral, to their fullest potential. That's what it was all about. This was seen as being important both for the individual and for society. It's obviously important for the individual, because this is how you get a mature, fully rounded individual, and this is still the way liberal arts education works today in our modern educational system. We believe in broadly educating people to create the best prepared individual—prepared for life, prepared for citizenship, prepared for making good judgments—but the humanists also thought it was important for society. So it has a social role, as well, because these fully developed people are going to be good citizens and good leaders, and there you get back to Salutati and Bruni and civic humanism, which really did have a kind of social, political focus to it, but that was, as we shall see, only part of humanism. So that was the theory behind humanist liberal arts (*Studia humanitatis*)—that kind of education.

I want to end by just talking a little bit about the search for the classical writings and some of the answers and perspectives they got out of these writings. We'll continue a lot more with that next time.

Humanist education, obviously, has got to be based on classical writings. In the early years, it was largely based on Latin classics. As you're going to see, in the later years, particularly from the mid-15th century on, they put a bigger stress on the Greek classics and on learning Greek and reading Greek, but early on, it's mainly the Roman classics (Latin classics). One of the problems is that even though, as we've seen, some classics existed in the Middle Ages and were known, there were a lot that weren't, and there really weren't enough classics available to fill out this whole educational program. So the humanists had to somehow find, search for, uncover more classical writings and put them in the educational program.

There were several really difficult problems with this. Some of the classics had just been destroyed. They were lost and would never be recovered. We know them today only by their titles. Nobody's read them since antiquity. A number of the classics did survive and were public, but a huge amount of the classics were hidden away. You'd think that being hidden away, they would be preserved for later users, but there were a lot of difficulties to the way they were hidden that made them essentially lost to European intellectuals. For one thing, when the classics were copied down in antiquity and written out—they were, of course, all written out longhand; there was no printing or anything—they were bound into books for the most part, but the books just had blank covers. They didn't bother to write the title of the book, and as a matter of fact the books often didn't have titles. They didn't bother to write the author of the book on the cover. They would take these books and when they hid them away they would hide them in monastic libraries or cathedral libraries, along with other books that were in similar condition, and so what you would have when you entered one of these libraries is you'd have just rows and rows of books, but they are all blank on the outside. There is no indication of who wrote them or what their title or subject might be. So the humanists faced this daunting prospect. First of all, they weren't totally sure that there were a lot of them out there. There were rumors that there were, but they weren't totally sure. They had to figure out a way to get into these monastic libraries and find the works, which had been sitting there, in many cases, for centuries, unopened, unread, totally unknown, without any indication in the book who wrote it, even.

So the humanists had a big problem, and when they set out to search for these manuscripts, they had to employ a new science that they had developed, a new study they had developed, called the study of philology. The study of philology (or philology as a subject) is the study of the changes in language over time, in this case, the study of changes in the Latin language over time. From the classics that the humanists had, they pretty much mapped out how Latin had evolved throughout the years, from early Latin in the early Republican period to the golden Latin of Cicero, to the more ornate silver Latin of Tacitus and even later writers. They developed a sense for, when they would read a manuscript, what period it came from by the style of the Latin in it.

Some of the humanists became so good at this, they knew individual authors' styles. When they read a book, they could actually tell who the author was by the style, especially a distinctive style like Cicero or Livy, for example. They could pinpoint who wrote the book, the manuscript, the original of it, by the style. So, they simply had to go into these libraries and take the books out, one by one, read through them and try to figure it out. If the book were a medieval book, its Latin was such a different Latin; it was a very decayed form of Latin, where they had lost the endings; they hadn't adopted word order yet. It was very difficult to interpret. We'll see this more later on. They could pretty much pinpoint a medieval book and they could put that back on the shelf. They could also pretty much pinpoint a classical book, and they would take that one out and would say, "We need to know more about this." Many times they could even figure out the actual author of it.

When it came to a title, since there were no titles, and it was unknown—well, there were some titles, but a lot of the works were untitled and it really wasn't known what the authors intended for a title—the humanists would just take the first line of text, called the *incipit*, and put that on the front and say that was the title.

So they go into these libraries and they start searching, and they begin to find things. A lot of the famous humanists begin to find some really important things. For example, Francesco Petrarch, who we'll hear a whole lot more about in the next lecture, went through monastic library after monastic library, and you just have to imagine the incredible patience of a man like this to go in day after day and sit there at these tables in these cold, dark places and read through book after book after book. He went to a lot of famous libraries in Italy, and he made some amazing discoveries. He found works of Cicero, and he found works of Livy that were unknown up until then. He found a lot of really important stuff.

Another important humanist, Giovanni Boccacio, the famous author of the *Decameron*—which is a book of sexy stories often said to be typical of humanists, but it's really just a book of sexy stories—he went to the very famous monastic library of Monte Casino, which is the biggest monastery, the biggest library in all of Italy at that time. He patiently searched through and he found Tacitus, the famous historian of the imperial period; he found Livy, the historian of the Roman republican period; and a number of other important works.

It was also Boccacio who began to point out that, "Hey! Look! We need to study the Greek classics, too, not just the Roman classics," and people said, "Well, nobody reads Greek." Boccacio said, "We've got to teach them to read Greek." So he sets up a school in Florence to teach people to read Greek, and he starts looking for the Greek classics; a real pioneer in that area.

Poggio Bracciolini, who has the reputation of being the most difficult to get along with of all the humanists, also searched very diligently through monastic libraries and cathedral libraries, and he found a book by an author called Quintillian, called *On the Education of the Orator*, at the monastery of St. Gallen in Switzerland. This was the ancient Roman textbook of rhetoric. It was just like finding a gold mine.

Other humanists found other works. They begin to incorporate these works into their educational program, and you have a full panoply of classics to read. The Renaissance is really underway.

Lecture Five
Humanist Thought

Scope:

In this lecture, we will take a closer look at Humanist modes of thought and the lessons Humanists drew from their reading of the classics. We will start out by examining the educational theories of Francesco Petrarch, the founder of Literary Humanism. We will see how his theory of language led him to a new view of history. We will also take a close look at how the Humanist view of history differed from the medieval view of history. We will see how Petrarch created a cult of the classics for the Renaissance. Then, we will examine the Humanist devotion to ethics and show how Humanist teaching of ethics grew out of rhetorical concerns. We will conclude by looking at how Humanist rhetorical culture contributed to the Renaissance view of history.

Outline

I. In reading the classics, the Humanists got new ideas and new perspectives on the issues of their day. Many of these new ideas helped build the foundations of modern thought. They included ideas about education, history, and ethics, among many other topics.

    A. One of the fathers of Humanism was Francesco Petrarch (1304–1374), founder of Literary Humanism, a branch of Humanism chiefly concerned with ethics.

    B. Petrarch was born in the papal city of Avignon to an exiled Florentine family. His father was a notary.

        1. He was sent to study law at Montpellier and then at Bologna, returning to Avignon to take a job as secretary to an important churchman.

        2. Petrarch disliked his legal studies. Because they were based on Scholastic philosophy and logic, he found them too abstract and impractical. They did not teach the one thing Petrarch thought everyone needed to know: how to live a good life.

C. Petrarch advocated an education with moral and ethical meaning.

1. He believed that one could learn how to live a good life by reading history, poetry, and literature. In these works, one would find examples of people who lived good lives, and these examples could be emulated.

2. But to be effective as educational tools, history, poetry, and literature had to be written in beautiful Latin style, in order to make its lessons clear and to inspire readers to follow the examples of good lives they read about.

3. Petrarch believed that medieval literature was not up to this task. It was written in a decayed and unclear Latin that, over the years, had dropped its case endings but had not yet developed a firm word order to indicate parts of speech. Thus, it was ugly, uninspiring, and unclear.

4. For this reason, Petrarch advocated that education be based only on reading Classical Latin, such as that of Cicero or Livy, because this Latin was beautiful, clear, and inspiring and, thus, perfect for teaching moral lessons.

D. By observing the changing shape of Latin over time, Petrarch also drew lessons about history.

1. Medieval thinkers saw little change in history. They saw a unity and continuity between ancient times and their own day.

2. This was because they referred to the Bible for historical knowledge, specifically, the Book of Daniel, with its prophecy of the four empires. This prophecy was interpreted in the Middle Ages to mean that the Roman Empire would be the last worldly empire before the end of time. Thus, medieval thinkers believed themselves to still be living in the late Roman Empire, saw themselves as latter-day Romans, and saw little change between antiquity and their own day.

3. Petrarch, on the other hand, adopted a distinctly modern view of history that stressed change over time. He saw history divided into three distinct periods: antiquity, the Middle Ages, and the present.

4. Petrarch saw this change in history because he saw change in language. Antiquity had been a period of beautiful and clear Latin and was, thus, the golden age of civilization. The Middle Ages was a period of corrupt and decayed Latin and was, thus, an era of decline. Petrarch's own age was one that was reviving both Classical language and culture.

E. Petrarch idolized antiquity and helped begin the Humanist rage for Classical studies.

    1. He wrote a book of personal letters to Classical authors entitled *Letters to the Ancient Dead.*

    2. In this book, he addressed such authors as Cicero, Livy, Virgil, and Horace just as if they still lived, because for Petrarch, they were alive in their writings.

II. The Humanists cultivated rhetoric and ethics.

A. Rhetoric—the art of communication—was a central part of the Humanist educational program. It influenced how Humanists approached teaching such other key topics of concern as ethics.

B. From Petrarch on, the Humanists were especially concerned with the teaching of ethics, in part because they felt medieval education had failed to do this job effectively.

    1. The teaching of nearly all subjects in the medieval university was based on Scholastic philosophy derived from the works of Aristotle and Thomas Aquinas.

    2. The Humanists claimed that the medievals had failed in their effort to teach ethics using philosophy and logic. This was because what they taught students was an intellectual definition of the good life that was too abstract and theoretical to be practical. It did not motivate people to live the good life.

    3. This medieval approach to ethical education rested on one of the primary assumptions the university system took from Aristotle: that man is a rational creature. Therefore, if man knows the good, he will do the good. Under this definition, an intellectual idea of the good life was all that was required to impart ethics.

4. The Humanists, having lived through the 14th-century crisis and having their intellectual roots not in the tradition of ancient philosophy but in that of ancient rhetoric, thought this idea of man was too optimistic. For them, man needed more than simple knowledge of the good life in order to lead the good life. They recognized that man's will was corrupt and, thus, he was likely not to do the good even if he had the idea of what the good was.

5. Thus, for the Humanists, the key to ethical education was to change man's will: to motivate and inspire the will to lead the good life that the intellect understood. This was to be done through rhetoric—*eloquentia*—which the Humanists viewed as the great missing element of medieval education. Following Petrarch's ideas, the rhetoric studied had to be beautiful and inspiring Classical Latin rhetoric.

6. Therefore, the Humanists actually had a *less* optimistic view of human nature than medieval Scholastics. But they were true to their educational ideal of *sapientia et eloquentia*, of educating both the intellect and the will.

C. Humanist rhetorical culture also produced a critique of the medieval teaching of history that aided in the emergence of the modern view of history based on change.

1. According to the Humanists, medieval education based on Scholastic philosophy stressed the discovery of one universal and objective truth. This had been the goal of philosophy since ancient times.

2. In following this model when thinking about history, the medievals saw all of history as governed by one universal truth. That truth was believed to be Providence: God's plan for all people throughout time. History was simply the working out of this great divine plan.

3. Thus, medieval thinkers tended to see history as one long, continuous period based on one plan and not involving change and development from period to period.

D. With their intellectual roots in ancient rhetoric rather than philosophy, the Humanists were led to a different view of history.

    1. Since ancient times, rhetorical culture had been linked to the ideas of the Greek Sophists, teachers of public speaking whose job it was to train people to make convincing arguments.

    2. Because their stress was on making the convincing argument and not on finding one objective truth, the Sophists imparted to the rhetorical tradition a notion of the relativity of truth. To a certain extent, truth was relative to the convincing argument. There were many truths, not one.

    3. While the Humanists did not explicitly teach this idea of the relativity of truth, the idea influenced their view of history.

    4. They did not see history as one long, continuous period dominated by one truth. Rather, they saw history as a series of unique and different periods, each with its own set of rules and truths determining its character.

    5. Each period had to be understood on its own terms. Different periods were hard to compare. It seemed doubtful that history repeated itself. Change from period to period was the rule. Here, the Humanists approached a modern view of history.

E. Their view of history caused the Humanists to read the classics in a new way.

    1. Medieval readers did read the classics, but they read them as if they had been written by people much like themselves in times much like their own. This came from the medieval view of history as one long, continuous period.

    2. Because of their different understanding of history, Humanists read the classics as products of a historical period unlike their own. They placed the classics in a very different historical context and treated them as windows on the Classical past, as ways of learning about peoples and times unlike their own.

F. Just as the Humanists' appreciation for change over time arose in part from their devotion to rhetoric and their recognition that the Latin language had changed over time, the Humanists developed a new field of study to carefully trace the changes Latin had undergone. The new study was called *philology*.

    1. Soon, Humanists could date unknown manuscripts from the style of their Latin.

    2. Master philologist Lorenzo Valla (1407–1457) used the new science to write a textbook of Latin style, criticize the Vulgate translation of the Bible, and prove the Donation of Constantine a fraud. With Valla, the revolutionary potential of Humanism became more apparent.

Essential Reading:

Donald Wilcox, *In Search of God and Self,* chapters 7–8.

Nancy Struever, *Rhetoric and Humanism.*

Questions to Consider:

1. Was the Humanist view of education and history essentially ancient or modern?

2. How might the Humanists' view of history influence their efforts to revive antiquity?

Lecture Five—Transcript
Humanist Thought

In the last couple of lectures, we've been talking about the social and political origins of Renaissance humanism. In this lecture what I'm going to do is to take a look at some of the ideas and the answers that humanists actually found in the classics, because they got ideas and especially new perspectives from the classics, which not only helped them solve a lot of their own problems, but also created many of the fundamental ideas of modern thought.

We have already seen that civic humanism, born in Florence with Salutati and Bruni, sought to read the classics for political, social education and the good of the community; you could say, in service to the state, but this was not the only focus that humanism had. Humanism also read the classics to get new perspectives on other issues, and not just issues of politics and society, but other, deeper, more age-old—you might say eternal—human questions about the nature of man, society, God, people's relationship to each other. So what I want to do in this lecture is take a look at some of these other answers, kind of the broader answers, that humanists got from the classics.

We'll start by taking a look at a very famous Renaissance humanist, one of the fathers of humanism, Francesco Petrarch, who lived from 1304 to 1374. You could call him the co-founder of humanism, along with Salutati and Bruni, but he really founded a different branch of humanism. Whereas civic humanism was more politically and socially oriented, Petrarch was interested more in individual ethics and morality and the individual conduct of a person. So what I want to do first of all is take a little bit of a look at his life, his ideas on education, and then we'll look at some of the other perspectives he got from the classics.

Although he was from a Florentine family, his family was exiled from Florence, and he was actually born in the papal city of Avignon, the son of a notary. Like his father, he went to law school. He attended law school at Montpellier and Bologna, both, and came back to Avignon and got a good job as a secretary to a leading churchman there. When he came back to Avignon, he brought some ideas about education that he'd gotten during his legal education that made him really question medieval education and develop his own new ideas, which really were one of the foundations of humanist education.

For one thing, he found his legal studies turned him against the vocational, professional nature of medieval education, because he basically found that, even though he got a good job with it, he found the education too abstract. It was largely based on scholastic philosophy and logic, as most things were at a medieval university, and for that reason he found it rather impractical, at least for himself. He said it was impractical because it didn't really teach him (or anybody else, as far as he knew) the one thing that people should know more than anything else, and that is how to live a good life. He didn't feel like it had taught him how to live a good life, and that's what he thought education should do. So Petrarch sought to develop an education that had more of a moral, ethical focus than medieval education had, and would teach people how to learn how to live a good life. Well, how do you do that?

Petrarch said it's not really by reading scholastic philosophy or logic. It's by reading poetry, history, and literature, because they will teach you how to live a good life. The reason is that poetry, history, and literature contain examples of good lives that people have led in the past that you can read, and you can basically emulate or copy these examples and let them be your guide to living a good life; but it's more complicated than just that, because to be good, effective educational tools, Petrarch believed this poetry, history, and literature had to be written in a very clear, beautiful Latin style, the reason being that this style would make its lessons clear, and the style would also inspire and motivate and convince people to follow the examples that they read about, and actually live the good life that they were reading about.

The trouble Petrarch had was that Latin literature from the Middle Ages was just not up to this task. It was corrupt and unclear and uninspiring because it had decayed since classical times. In the Middle Ages they lost a lot of the word endings from Latin. They had not yet developed word order, so it wasn't always clear what the subject and object and verb were in sentences, and it could be very difficult to read. Petrarch just said, "This medieval Latin is uninspiring. It's ugly. You can't learn anything from it. On the other hand, classical Latin is totally different. The classical Latin of people like Cicero and Livy is beautiful. It's clear, inspiring, and so it's perfect to teach moral lessons, and ethical education can really only be based on the classics, because of the nature of the language, which makes it so much more fit for teaching the kind of moral lessons that people needed to learn." So Petrarch called for a revival—a return to the classics to learn these moral lessons and to learn how to live a good life.

In fact, language was extremely important to Petrarch in many different ways. One of the ways that it became important was not just in teaching or giving him a new idea of moral education. It also gave him a new perspective on history itself, which becomes a kind of characteristic humanist perspective on history, which is very different from the medieval perspective on history and really much closer—it's the ancestor of the modern idea of what history is. To understand this, though, we first have to look a little bit at how medieval thinkers understood history, and it was very different from how we understand history today.

In the Middle Ages, they saw very little change taking place in history. They saw a kind of unity and continuity between periods, between classical antiquity and their own day, with not much changing over time. Why did they see that? Well, because their only source for learning about history was the Bible, and in the Bible specifically it was the Book of Daniel, where there is the prophecy which had been interpreted by medieval theologians to be explaining how history took place. According to this prophecy in the Book of Daniel, there are four empires in history: the Egyptian Empire, the Persian Empire, the Greek Empire, the Roman Empire, and then the end of history. That's how the Book of Daniel was interpreted by medieval thinkers, and since the last empire was the Roman Empire, and then the world came to an end, medieval people could look around and clearly see that the world had not yet come to an end, so they must still be in the last empire, the Roman Empire, and they tend to see themselves—and you don't really think of the Middle Ages this way—but they tend to see themselves as latter-day Romans, and they saw little change taking place in history between ancient Rome and their own day. So it was a kind of a planum.

Petrarch had a very different idea. He saw three distinct and different periods in history, based on changes in the Latin language over time (the development of the Latin language). Antiquity, of course, he saw as the golden age of civilization, because it had beautiful, clear, inspiring Latin. The Middle Ages he saw as a corrupt period of civilization—a period of decline—because it had a corrupt Latin style, and then, in his own time, he saw that as an attempt to return to the clear, inspiring, golden age of antiquity. So he emphasized change in history, because he saw change in language, and that's how we look at history today, as a matter of change over time. For Petrarch, the corrupt Latin style of the Middle Ages meant that the whole civilization was corrupt, and the beautiful Latin style of antiquity meant that the whole civilization of antiquity was beautiful and a golden age. So he really pioneered the modern way of looking at history as being based on change.

He also idolized antiquity so much that he wrote a book called *Letters to the Ancient Dead,* in which he actually wrote personal letters to dead ancient writers, just as if he expected that they would write him back, because they were still alive for him and he had a kind of personal relationship with the classical writers of antiquity. When one person asked him, "Why do you admire the classics so much?" he just said, "It's because it's so much better than what has gone after that."

From Petrarch we can see that humanist culture is based heavily on language and especially on rhetoric, and this humanist concern for rhetoric, eloquence, good public speaking has an impact on how they attempted to teach ethics, which we also know is extremely important to the humanists; how to live a good life; moral philosophy; what good ethical decisions were. Here again they differed greatly from the Middle Ages.

In medieval education, according to the humanist viewpoint of this, they had failed to teach ethics properly, because they had attempted to teach ethics based on scholastic philosophy and logic—Thomas Aquinas and Aristotle, for example—and in doing that they had used logic and used reason to teach ethics, and they had succeeded to some extent because they had given their students an intellectual idea of the good life, or an intellectual definition of what the good life would be like.

But Petrarch believed, and other humanists believed, that this intellectual idea or definition of the good life was just too abstract and theoretical and not very practical and applicable for people. Well, why did medieval education do that? Why did they give just this definition of the good life and kind of stop there? That was because, oddly enough, in some ways medieval education had a more optimistic idea about human nature than the humanists did. Medieval teachers believed that people were essentially rational creatures, and that if they knew the good, if they had an idea or a definition of the good, they would automatically do the good. So an idea or a definition was really all you would need to lead a good life and to go out and make the right decisions. If you have knowledge of the good you will then automatically, basically, do the good. That was the medieval view. They thought that man's will was by nature inclined to do what his intellect knew to be the right thing.

Contrary to the other views of the Renaissance in some cases, the 14th-century crisis had given humanists a more pessimistic view of human nature than this, especially with relationship to the human will. The humanists came to believe that people really need more than just knowledge of the good, more than just a definition of the good life, in order for them to do the good and live the good life. So for the humanists, to know the good was not necessarily to do the good; whereas, for medieval thinkers, to know the good was pretty much to do the good.

Well, why was that? Because the humanists believed that people's will was corrupt, and it was inclined in many cases not to do the good, even if their reason knew what the good was. Why did they have this pessimistic view of human nature? Well, it could have come from the 14th-century crisis and the humanists' view of the Middle Ages in general. It is also a deeply Christian view that man's will is by nature corrupted by original sin and inclined not to do the good. For whatever reason, the humanists really thought that just having the definition or the idea of the good was not going to be nearly enough to get people to actually live the good life, and they would say that ethical education had failed if it didn't lead people to lead good lives, if it didn't actually inspire and motivate people to practice good lives and to make good ethical decisions. Just the knowledge was really not the end point.

So the humanists believed that a good, moral, ethical education had to change people's will. It had to inspire the will. It had to inspire the will to do the good that reason knows. So they believed you had to do both things. You have to teach the intellectual idea of the good, obviously; but then you also have to inspire and move and change the will and motivate people to go out and practice the good, do the good, live the good life, and that was going to be the difficult task for the humanists. Medieval philosophy, medieval education had supplied only half the job. They had supplied only the idea and not the inspiration, so the knowledge but not the motivation.

How did the humanists solve this problem? They solved it through one of their basic, fundamental ideas: rhetoric; eloquence. Rhetoric and eloquence could be the tool that would inspire and motivate the will to go out and do the good that the intellect had learned about, that the intellect had knowledge of. So you have to have both these halves to education for the humanists. You've got to give the intellect the idea of what the good life is. Then you have to use rhetoric, eloquence, to motivate and inspire the will to follow the idea and to live the good life and do what is right. That was where the humanists really had a very different view of ethical education than medieval thinkers had had. You need both *sapientia* and *eloquentia*, knowledge of the good and inspiration to actually do the good. That was the full picture of education for the Renaissance thinkers.

This humanist stress on rhetoric also affected their view of history and kind of fed into the idea of history that Petrarch had developed. Humanist stress on rhetoric led to a specific outlook on history, which we would probably identify more closely with the modern outlook on history than with the medieval outlook on history. It probably was the beginning or the basis for modern historical thinking. Again, here we have to look at medieval views, first of all, and then we'll take a look at how the humanist thinkers changed this and had a different view.

Medieval education had been based on scholastic philosophy and stressed the use of reason and logic to discover one universal truth, because that's what philosophy had always taught since antiquity: that people are rational, and they can use reason to discover the one objective truth that is true for all people at all times and places. This led to a particular medieval view of history, where they saw all history as governed by one universal truth, one overriding plan or truth, which you could identify with religion or philosophy. It would be God's plan for all people in all periods in all times, and history the medieval thinkers saw as more or less just a working out of this universal plan or universal truth. Because history was just the working out of this one continuous, one long plan, history was a kind of continuous period, without too much change, again, following one plot line, one blueprint, one plan throughout all times, and that doesn't really provoke a lot of change. So they, again, as we've seen earlier, saw very little change occurring in history.

That's not how the humanists saw it, and the reason for that is the humanists—their basic intellectual viewpoint—was not based on philosophy. It was based, rather, on rhetoric. There's a big difference between the two, especially in the way that they look at the nature of truth, and the way to really understand this is to look at where rhetoric comes from.

Rhetoric, like philosophy, goes back to the days of ancient Greece. Some of the earliest teachers of rhetoric were the Sophists in ancient Greece, who claimed to be teachers of wisdom, but who actually were, in fact, teachers of public speaking, and their job was to teach people how to make good arguments. The Sophists developed an idea of truth which we should call a kind of relative idea of truth. They saw truth as being relative to the good argument. The Sophists would teach you how to make a good argument, and if you're convinced of it, then that, in fact, is the truth. So the convincing argument is true, for those convinced, and there could be different truths for different people, depending on who is convinced in what ways, and it's all based on this art of speaking, art of arguing, rhetoric, and convincing people of a point of view. So rhetoric, in its very beginnings, was based on a kind of relative notion of truth. Of course, the humanists inherit this relative notion of truth, because they have such a deep concern for rhetoric in their educational program. We have already seen why they had such a deep concern for rhetoric, because of the need to motivate the will, and because of the need to communicate ideas effectively in society, and all that was extremely important.

When we say that they inherited a relative idea of truth, we have to be careful, because there's a conflict here, there's a tension here, because the humanists were also deeply religious, deeply Christian people, and of course Christianity has a rather objective view of truth. It is the truth of religion and what God has said. So there's a kind of tension between the humanist rhetorical culture on the one hand and their Christianity on the other hand, and whereas the tension does make things more complicated to explain, tensions like this also tend to make thinking and thinkers more creative, because they have to play off different ideas against each other and consider different points of view. It becomes, as we will see later on in the course, a very productive kind of thing.

A lot of textbooks on the Renaissance and humanism will claim that humanists were essentially secular thinkers, that their whole movement was a kind of secular movement, but in fact, as we have seen from Petrarch, they were deeply concerned with morals, with ethics, they are deeply concerned with religious belief, and you have to look at both sides of them; but from rhetoric they do inherit this relative view of truth, to some extent, and the rhetorical idea or perception of relative truth feeds into the way they look at history.

We have already seen that Petrarch looked at history as three distinct periods, not as one continuous planum of not much change, like the medievals did, but as three very distinctive, different periods. For Petrarch, that was because of the change he saw in the linguistic culture of the different periods—the language and how that fit into the culture of the different periods—but humanist concern for rhetoric also plays a role, because when you start off with at least a partial appreciation for a relativity of truth, then you have the possibility for looking at history as not governed by one universal truth, as not governed by one universal plan, although they certainly did believe in providence—here again we have the tension with their Christian inheritance—but the humanists' historical perspective tended to see each historical period as unique and different: antiquity, the Middle Ages, the Renaissance. Each of these periods has its own set of truths that it operates on, its own set of truths that rules and governs it. Each period has its own characteristics and conditions and circumstances, just as different truths can be relative in different arguments.

History doesn't repeat itself. That would follow from this, because each period is unique and different. Each period has its own truths and circumstances and conditions. This leads to other, more disturbing ideas that the humanists had to wrestle with. If each period of history is unique and different, then that pretty much means that it's very difficult to compare periods. If each one operates on its own set of truths, its own values, its own laws, then it's really hard to compare periods because they are just so different, but of course the humanists made their living comparing periods. They said antiquity was better than the Middle Ages; the Middle Ages, worse; our period, better. So they do compare the periods, and it's difficult when you consider each period operating on its own truths and conditions and circumstances.

Even more disturbing is the fact that if each period is unique and different, then you shouldn't be able to bring a past period back. In other words, the humanists should not be able to replicate antiquity in their own day, because it as a unique period is past and gone, and you can't really replicate it. A number of humanists realized these contradictions and what they argued was that they were not really trying to bring back antiquity exactly, not to imitate it or bring it back like a photograph and just slavishly imitate it. They were saying that they would bring antiquity back in a modified version, using its answers in modified ways to apply to problems of their own day that would make these answers practically useful. In fact, many of these humanists argued that if you just bring back antiquity completely like it was, it's not really going to perfectly match up with the problems that you've got. You need to be flexible; adapt, change some of the solutions a little bit to apply them to your own day. In that sense you can actually do it. You can bring back a version of antiquity, although it's not going to be the same thing, and the period you create, while being very, very, classically influenced, will not be classical antiquity itself. A number of humanists realized this. Some of the others really didn't discuss the problem very much, but it shows you the tensions and complexities that develop when you start to have this quintessentially modern view of history as a series of different periods with great change between the periods, and it being difficult to compare the periods and difficult to replicate past periods.

Also, for modern historical thinkers this humanist historical perspective stressed some things that are very important for the way we think about history today. For example, the humanists would argue that you can't judge periods of history based on ideas and conditions and standards taken from another period, meaning you really can't judge antiquity based on standards and conditions and criteria that you take from your own period, and vice-versa. You can't judge your own period from conditions and standards you take directly from antiquity. Again, that's going to stress the humanists' desire to bring back antiquity as much as they can, but it really feeds into the modern notion that when you are judging history, you have to judge periods on their own standards. You have to judge antiquity by the standards of its generation, and the modern period by the standards of its generation. I think that's what most modern historians do, although you can see the tensions that created for the humanists when they realized that you can't make these direct comparisons and judgments using classical ideas; for example, to judge 15th-century Florence. So there are tensions and problems and complexities there.

When you see all these ideas, the humanists' idea of ethics and their idea of history, you start to see how deep and sophisticated and, in fact, varied humanist thought really was. Even though we kind of sketched out this picture of humanist education as being a very clear, goal-oriented, driven kind of thing, which it was, most humanist thinkers were sophisticated thinkers and had to deal on many theoretical levels with a lot of these problems we've been realizing.

This humanist view of history did have practical consequences. For example, we've already noted that the humanists were not the first people to read the classics. The classics were read in the Middle Ages, but this humanist view of history caused the humanists to read the classics in a different way. Here's what I mean by that: In the Middle Ages, because of their view of history as one long, continuous planum, and the Roman Empire as still really here, and we're latter-day Romans, and all that, when they read the classics, they tended to read them as if they were written by people pretty much like them in times pretty much like theirs, where not much had changed since then. That's the way they interpreted the classics, and they got a very specific picture of the classics from that.

The humanists read classics in a different way, as being from a different period, representing a different culture, giving a window onto a different society, a different way of life in many ways, and they recognize the difference. They attempt to draw lessons from the past without assuming that the past is like the present, that nothing much has changed. They see the classical writers as writing in a different period, with different concerns in many ways, and giving ideas far on into the future that can be used, but that aren't exactly the same as ideas and concerns that people in the 15th century would have had. So it causes the humanists to read the classics in a different way.

It also leads—and this is the final point I'll make—to the humanist stress on the science or the new discipline of philology, the study of the change in the Latin language over time. Incredibly important for the humanists: They could date books from it, as we've seen. They could assign authors from it, as we've seen. They could tell you what style was from what period, from what author. They knew the language backwards and forwards.

This had also some very practical consequences. For example, the famous humanist philologian Lorenzo Valla, who essentially was probably the father of humanist philology, was the guy who discovered that the Donation of Constantine, trotted out by the pope for many centuries as proving his supreme rule over all of Europe, was a forgery. Valla just said—he worked in the papal library, he took out a copy of it, he read it—and he said, "The Latin style here is not in the style of Constantine's day. It's 8th- or 9th-century medieval Latin. So this is a forgery." That showed people that philology and the humanist concern for language could have a very practical effect—a very important practical effect—as well.

Lecture Six
Renaissance Florence

Scope:

In this lecture, we will look at the economic, political, and social structure of Florence during the Renaissance period. The woolen industry dominated the economy of Florence during this period and provided the economic backbone of the Florentine Renaissance. We will examine the structure of the woolen industry, as well as the economic cycles of both the woolen industry and the city. We will also investigate the influence of the woolen industry on the political life of Florence and take a close look at the complex governmental structure of the city. The government was designed to disperse power into many hands as a result of Florence's historical experience with dictators, which will be covered in a future lecture. We close by noting the highly political nature of Florence, a spur to the Renaissance in Florence.

Outline

I. The woolen industry was the mainstay of the economy of Florence and the economic backbone of the Florentine Renaissance.

   A. The woolen industry experienced cycles of expansion and contraction that generally followed population cycled.

      1. In the year 1330, the population of Florence had reached its medieval peak at about 100,000.

      2. Of the 100,000, about 30,000 worked in the wool industry.

      3. The output of woolen cloth was worth 1.2 million florins per year.

   B. A booming banking industry complemented the cloth industry, banks springing up as branches of cloth companies to allow the companies to do business abroad by changing currencies for them.

      1. Florence had more than 80 separate banking firms and more than 300 branch banks abroad to aid the cloth industry.

2. Florentine banks pioneered Bills of Exchange, paper instruments that facilitated currency exchange and transfer of funds by utilizing Florence's many foreign branch banks.

C. The bubonic plague of 1348 initiated a widespread economic downturn in Florence that would have some unexpected effects.

   1. Nearly 40,000 people died in Florence alone, and the Florentine population remained at a level of between 50,000 and 70,000 up to 1715.

   2. By 1350, between one-third and one-half the total European population had been destroyed by the plague. As a result, the markets for Florentine woolen cloth, both domestic and foreign, were decimated. Serious economic depression in Florence resulted and would last for more than 100 years.

   3. Even before the plague hit, weaknesses in the Florentine economy had been evident. In 1338, two giant banking firms, the Bardi and the Peruzzi, had collapsed.

   4. The Bardi and Peruzzi were arms of wool companies, and they did most of their business in London, where they provided banking functions to enable their companies to buy English raw wool and ship it to Florence for manufacture into cloth. The cloth was then often re-shipped to London for sale.

   5. Both banks had gotten into the practice of making loans to the English crown. When King Edward III became involved in the extremely expensive Hundred Years War, the status of these loans became shaky, and before long, the king defaulted. Both banks immediately collapsed.

   6. The collapse sent shock waves through the Florentine economy and raised questions about the structure of the banking industry.

D. Conventional wisdom suggests that periods of economic depression are not conducive to cultural creativity, but the case of Florence shows the reverse. In Florence, the economic depression helped to create the Renaissance.

1. We have seen in earlier lectures how the people of Italy responded in a positive way to the crises of the 14th century, and Florence was no exception to this rule. But other factors were also at work in Florence.

2. Historian Robert Lopez has argued that specifically economic factors helped give rise to the Renaissance in Florence.

3. With the depression in full swing, investments in commerce and industry yielded little and uncertain returns. Investments in art and culture, on the other hand, were much safer. Art and manuscripts slowly but surely gained in value over the years, and thus, they became attractive investments.

4. Investment in art and culture also offered the investor a source of pleasure, comfort, and enjoyment that other investments did not. Investment in culture soared and the Renaissance gained economic support.

5. Further, people in Florence had money to invest despite the depression. As the plague killed family members, the surviving members of the family inherited the victims' money. Although there were fewer people in Florence, they were richer per capita than before.

6. These people bought paintings, books, and other cultural products both as investments and as ways to gain enjoyment in times that could be grim. The uncertainty of who would be hit next by the plague also caused people to spend rather than to save.

II. The organization of the woolen industry provided the skeletal structure for all economic, political, and social organization in Florence.

   A. The industry was organized in a complex structure of guilds.

      1. Guilds were organizations of masters or trained workmen who specialized in certain tasks. The object of the guild was to control access to each trade, working conditions in the trade, the quality of the trade's product, and the price for which the product sold.

2. The ultimate goal of the guild was to ensure a good living for every member. Every economic activity, every commercial or industrial activity, had its guild. Town law prohibited practicing a business or trade without belonging to the guild.

B. The woolen industry in Florence was organized into 7 Great Guilds and 14 Lesser Guilds.

   1. The Great Guilds were merchant guilds. They controlled the industry, dominated Florentine politics, and contained the town's wealthiest citizens.

   2. Most important of the Great Guilds was the Cambio, the guild of bankers. Here was Florence's greatest wealth. The most prominent families, including the Medici, belonged to it.

   3. Another Great Guild was the Calimala. This was the guild of wool merchants. They bought raw wool, then took it to the artisan guilds for manufacture into cloth.

   4. When the cloth was finished, it was bought from the artisans by members of the Lana, another Great Guild. They took the cloth to foreign and domestic markets for sale.

   5. The 14 Lesser Guilds were guilds of artisans or craftsmen who actually manufactured the cloth from raw wool. Each guild focused on only one step in the manufacturing process—what Adam Smith would later call *division of labor*. But because the manufacturing process was so subdivided and the task of each lower guild so limited, guildsmen's wages were often low

   6. Among the lower guilds would, of course, be spinners and weavers but also included were the fullers, who beat the cloth with boards to fill in holes; softeners, who applied alum to the cloth to soften it; washers, who washed the cloth in the Arno River; dyers, who applied colored dyes to the cloth; shearers, who cut the cloth; menders, who sewed up breaks in the cloth; pressers, who pressed the cloth; and the lowly Ciompi, whose job it was to use an iron comb to comb out tangles in the raw wool.

7. Alongside the master worked one or more apprentices. These were usually the sons of well-to-do townsmen. They did much of the work in the shop and were there to learn the trade from the master. Their hope was to someday become masters themselves with their own shops. This was difficult because shops and capital were hard to come by. Some hoped they could inherit their own master's shop. Also in the shop was the journeyman, hired labor who was not learning the trade and had no future in the guild.

8. The shop was almost always in the master's home, on the ground floor. Any tools were the property of the master. The master and his family lived on the upper floors, and the apprentices boarded there, receiving room and meals in place of a salary. This system of economic organization was called the *domestic system*.

C. The first guilds to be formed in the Middle Ages, around the 11th century, were merchant guilds. As they formed, they gained legal rights to regulate their trade from town governments. Guilds of artisans, or craft guilds, were prevented from forming, by towns, until the 14th century, when artisans gained political power as a result of the plague-induced labor shortage.

D. The structure of the woolen cloth industry and the hierarchy of guilds within it provided the blueprint for nearly every other aspect of Florentine life. Politics and government were a direct reflection of the economic structure. The social structure emerged out of the economic structure of the town. All this we will see in the next lecture.

Essential Reading:

Gene Brucker, *Renaissance Florence*, chapters 3–5.

Supplementary Reading:

Gene Brucker, *Two Memoirs of Renaissance Florence*.

Robert Lopez, *The Three Ages of the Italian Renaissance*.

Questions to Consider:

1. To what extent can the Renaissance in Florence be attributed to economic factors?

2. Why would the economic structure determine the political structure of Florence?

Lecture Six—Transcript
Renaissance Florence

Now that we've taken a look at the origins and nature of the Renaissance—why it happened where it did and when it did—and what humanism was and humanist education and some of the ideas the humanists had, we're going to spend the next couple of lectures looking at one of the centers of Renaissance culture, the city of Florence. We'll take a look at the social, economic and political structure of the city, first of all. Then we'll take a look at the history of the city, its political history and military history. Then we'll also look at the histories of some of the other major Italian cities that were part of the Renaissance.

We do this because you have to ask yourself the question, exactly what kind of society was it which gave birth to the Renaissance? We have already said in earlier lectures that it was essentially an urban society, and that was very important because it was very similar to antiquity, which was also urban. We've also seen that according to Hans Baron and others that it was particularly Florence which was the place where the Renaissance was born, or certainly one of the initial centers of Renaissance culture. So it's worth taking a look at the actual city of Florence and its internal structure, its politics, and dynamics, just to see what kind of a matrix gave rise to these ideas which have changed the course of Western history.

So what we'll do first of all is start by taking a look at the population and the economic structure of Florence, which are very closely tied together. Then we'll look at the political structure a little bit later and move on from there.

When you look at the economic structure of Florence, it's actually very simple. The woolen-cloth industry was the most important industry and the most important economic activity in Florence. You could say that Florence was a one-industry town. Because of this it was the woolen-cloth industry which provided the money that was the backbone for the birth of the Renaissance. Now, we've already seen that Italy's trading links with the Middle East, especially through Venice, Genoa, Pisa, and other cities, also provided a great deal of money that provided the economic means for the Renaissance. So you can't discount that by any means, but the huge role of the woolen-cloth industry in Florence and the amount of money it produced really makes it worth taking a look at that.

The woolen-cloth industry in Florence, like in the rest of Europe—and I should point out at this point that the woolen-cloth industry was the most important sector of the very small industrial sector of the European economy in the early modern period—the woolen-cloth industry ran in cycles of expansion, contraction, boom and bust, if you want to look at it that way. This is very typical of other places in Europe all through the early modern period. These cycles of boom and bust tend to follow population cycles, and typically what you will see is, when the population expands, the economy expands; when the population contracts, the economy contracts. You might expect this to be bad news for Florence during the Renaissance, because we know the population collapsed and there actually was a serious depression in the economy, which we're going to look at. Surprisingly, in some ways, you will see that it was actually this depression which played a major role in giving birth to the Renaissance. Even economically speaking, had it not been for the depression, things might not have developed as they did in Florence. So it's really an interesting story.

We'll start out a little bit before the Renaissance, about 1330 in Florence. In 1330 the population of Florence was at its medieval peak of around 100,000. Now, to put that in perspective, compare it to the population of classical Athens, which was about 300,000. So what you see is that medieval Europe had not been very urban, and even at this period in the most urban area in Europe, cities are not terrifically big, but even at 100,000, Florence in 1330 is one of the biggest cities in Europe, and can be compared favorably to such huge places as Paris and London at this time. Of the 100,000 people in Florence, about 30,000 worked in the woolen-cloth industry, so that shows you how significant the industry was. The output of woolen cloth in 1330 was 1,200,000 florins per year—a pretty substantial output of woolen cloth. So the wool industry/cloth industry is the number one industry.

The number two industry in the city is banking, and in many ways Florence is the leading banking city in Europe during this time. There are 80 separate Florentine banking firms, of which the Bardi and Peruzzi are one. We'll talk about them in a couple of minutes. Of course, the famous Medici bank is another. There are some 300

Florentine branch banks abroad. This is very important, because not only does it expand Florentine banking internationally, it has a real key role in the woolen cloth trade, because what we'll see is that all of these banks initially grew out of woolen-cloth companies. They grew out of the woolen-cloth industry. They did so because their initial purpose was not to accept deposits and make loans; their initial purpose was to help transfer funds and change currencies and help Florentine woolen-cloth companies do business abroad, which they had to do, really, to make a profit. To do that, the Florentine banks had developed a kind of revolutionary financial instrument which is not adopted in the rest of Europe for some time, known as the "bill of exchange." The bill of exchange is a way that banks developed not only to transfer funds out of the country to another country, but to actually change currencies from one currency to another. This was made possible by the fact that Florentine banks had branches abroad.

The way it essentially would work, if you were a Florentine merchant doing business in London, for example, and you had to pay off your people in London in pounds (pounds sterling), which is what they accept in London, and you're in Florence and you're doing business in florins, you've got a problem. So you go down to the local branch of the Bardi Bank, for example, which has a branch in London. You say, "I would like to buy a bill of exchange worth 100 pounds sterling," and they would then sell you this bill of exchange worth 100 pounds sterling for however many florins it would cost (let's say 300 florins). You get this piece of paper with your name on it, which says, "Pay to the bearer upon presentation at the Bardi branch in London 100 pounds sterling." That's a terrific advantage, because now you can take this one piece of paper, which is specific to you, it's got your signature on it, and you can travel to London. You don't have to carry cash, gold coins, or anything with you. The risk of being robbed is much, much lower. It's much easier to carry this one piece of paper. You get there. You do your business. You go down to the bank. You cash it in. You get your pounds and you pay off the people you are doing business with, and bring your product back—and you could do it in reverse. The English could do it through a branch of the Bardi to go to Florence. It really made business a lot easier, a lot safer, and made the transfer of funds swifter, easier, and therefore made businesses work a whole lot better. Bills of exchange weren't only used in Florence, but they were pioneered in Italy, and, in fact, had not even made it to France by the 18th century.

1348, the onset of the Black Death, is a very important point for the economic history of Florence, because it damages Florence's economy in a very fundamental way. In 1348, the first year of the plague, about 40,000 people in Florence died, which is approximately one-half the total population. So this is a huge, huge demographic collapse, and of course it disrupts wool production, wages shoot up, all the things we've seen in past lectures as being difficult. The population of Florence stays at a level of between 50,000 and 70,000 for the rest of the early modern period, which still ranks it as one of Europe's bigger cities.

By 1350, after the first year and a half of the plague, somewhere between a third and a half of the total population of Europe has been destroyed, which is a further blow to Florence's market. Florence has basically lost over a third, maybe as much as a half of her total domestic and foreign market for woolen cloth, which is going to lead directly into an economic depression, which starts in Florence around 1350, as it starts in the rest of Europe around that same time, and will last for about a hundred years in most places in Europe, although it may not be as severe in Florence as in other places.

In fact, though, the Florentine depression in some ways had begun even before the onset of the Black Death. This had to do with two huge Florentine banks, known as the Bardi and Peruzzi banks, which both run into serious trouble in 1338, and in fact they collapse. The Bardi and Peruzzi banks were branches of the Bardi and Peruzzi woolen-cloth businesses. They were pretty typical of Florentine banks in that they were very hierarchically structured, with most instructions coming down from the Florentine headquarters and not a lot of local flexibility, but it had worked out in the past. The Bardi and Peruzzi had been effective in providing banking functions for the woolen companies to buy raw wool in England. They then took this raw wool all the way back to Florence, through a process that we will see later, manufactured it into woolen cloth, and then sold it, and in many cases took it all the way back to London to sell. So we are talking about huge distances being covered here; large transfers of funds. A lot of money is involved. In the 14th century it's quite an achievement to think you're doing business on this kind of scale.

And they were doing good business. They handled money transfers that were substantial. However, because they had money sitting around and they wanted to make it work for them, the Bardi and Peruzzi made the mistake of loaning money to the king of England, Edward III, who just happens at that time to have been involved in the Hundred Years War, which we talked about earlier on. As you know, the war was extremely expensive; it was not particularly successful for anybody. As a result of this, the king defaulted on his loans and both the banks collapsed. When the king says he's not going to pay off a loan, there's not much you can do to make him pay it off, because he can just simply kick you out of the country. So the banks just collapse, and this collapse of these two very large banks sent shock waves throughout the entire Florentine wool and banking industry. So that was kind of the onset of bad times for the Florentine economy.

Then, of course, comes the plague. Combined with the plague and the loss of markets there, you have a very serious economic depression in Florence. Interestingly, however, this economic depression actually helps create the Renaissance in Florence, and there might have been a very different situation had the depression not occurred. On the one hand, there was the general explanation we've already looked at, that when the economy was bad and things were disastrous, that your Italians (Florentines and others) chose a creative, positive, intellectual reaction—cultural reaction to the crisis—which became the Renaissance, and so, in that sense, a depression created the general conditions for a reaction, a kind of response, which became the essence of the Renaissance.

There is actually more to it than just that. There is a more specific economic explanation for why the depression helped to cause the Renaissance. This explanation was offered by historian Robert Lopez from UCLA a number of years ago in a book he wrote, in which he argued that during the depression in Florence, because commercial investment—investment in business and commerce—had become risky at best and even disastrous in many cases, that investors were tending to redirect their investment. Instead of investing in business and commerce, they begin investing in art and culture: buying paintings; buying books; building libraries; commissioning sculpture and things like that. The reason, Lopez argues, that they did this was because art and culture are safe investments. They may not give you huge returns in times of economic expansion, but they are always going to increase gradually in price and cost and return over the years. So you're not going to lose any money on it. It's the kind of investment you can kind of count on, although it's not going to bring you huge returns, but in a time of depression, you're not likely to get huge returns in commercial or industrial investments, either, so it was attractive for that reason.

Another thing that was attractive was that art offered people a kind of pleasure and a kind of comfort in these terrible, depressed times. So they were buying things that they enjoyed having in their homes or reading or handling, and this comfort that they provided for the people who invested in them also is a significant factor as to why funds tend to be invested in art and culture—books, manuscripts, paintings. We see a lot of examples of this.

Another factor here is that even though the plague is killing off a large portion of the Florentine population, the people who are left, who are not killed, inherit the family money. The survivors inherit the family wealth. This means that even though there are fewer people in Florence, the ones that are left are richer than they were before, but of course that's not going to make much difference unless they are willing to spend the money. In this case they did tend to be willing to spend the money, especially on art and culture, because they wanted to make and buy things that would make them feel better, bring them comfort. They didn't know how long they would be around, so they didn't really want to make industrial, commercial, long-term investments. They wanted to buy things that would give them a better standard of living, a kind of luxury, luxurious living. So they tended to buy books and art and commission chapels and things like that, with the money that they inherited from the family becoming smaller along the way. So for all these reasons the economic depression actually did, in fact, help kick off the Renaissance in Florence.

Next, what we'll do is take a brief look at the way the woolen-cloth industry was actually structured and how it worked. Then we'll move on to take a look a little bit at how this affected other areas of Florentine life.

The structure of the woolen-cloth industry in Florence really determines the structure of most other things there. It determines the structure of the political system, social life; a lot of other aspects of life were determined by this. As we have seen before, when we talked about the Ciompi, for example, the woolen-cloth industry, like every other industry every place in Europe in the early modern period, is controlled by guilds.

Guilds, as everyone knows, are organizations of master businessmen who organize themselves into a group which essentially controls trade in the branch of commerce or trade that they happen to be involved in. So, for example, blacksmiths had their guild, the woolen merchants had their guild; every craftsman, artisan, merchant— whatever their area of industry—they all belonged to a guild, because you can't carry on commercial activity in any area without belonging to a guild. In the woolen-cloth industry there were two basic kinds of guilds: on the top, in charge of the woolen-cloth industry, there were the seven Great Guilds. These were guilds of merchants, who did the buying and selling of the product. They are really at the top of the whole structure. These were also the people who tend to monopolize political power in Florence. Also in the woolen-cloth industry, there are 14 Lesser Guilds, guilds of people lower down, for example the Ciompi, but we'll see many others in a couple of minutes. These are guilds of artisans or craftsmen, who actually provide the industrial activity which produces the product. So you might call them industrial guilds, in a kind of early modern way, whereas the seven Great Guilds were commercial guilds.

Like I said before, political power in Florence pretty much rests with the seven Great Guilds, and you will see why this was at the end of this lecture and the beginning of the next lecture. Of course, the Medici were members of the Great Guilds.

What I'm going to do is describe just a few of these guilds to give you some idea of what they were and how they worked. We won't go through all of them. Of the seven Great Guilds, the three most important were these: on top of the social structure, number one, pretty much, is the Cambio. That's the guild of bankers, and that's the guild the Medici belong to. That tends to be the guild of the people who have the most money. The bankers were always kind of at the top of the social structure. Second down, in second place, is a guild called the Calimala guild. This was a guild of wool merchants, and what they did was, they bought the raw wool from various places. They would often go as far, as we've seen, as England, which was a major supplier of raw wool. They will buy the raw wool and bring it to Florence. They will then distribute it to domestic spinners and weavers. This is very often a commercial exchange, here. They will bring the raw wool in and actually sell it to these domestic spinners and weavers, who spin it and weave it into cloth in their homes. That's basically what the wool merchants do. These wool merchants only handle the raw wool. They don't handle woolen cloth, the finished product, so to speak.

The third guild down, called the Lana, was a guild of woolen cloth merchants. They are the ones who would go around to the domestic spinners and weavers and purchase the finished cloth, usually in very large bolts, usually unfinished, undyed. They would pay them; again, a commercial exchange. They would take the woolen cloth and distribute it to other Lesser Guilds, where it would be finished, dyed, and made into pretty much the final commercial product. There were also other Great Guilds, but those are examples that pretty much make it clear what they are doing.

Further on down, the Lesser Guilds have a very different kind of picture. I'll just mention a few of these and tell you what they did, and you will see that in many cases their activities were pretty limited, as were their incomes. There was the guild of fullers, for example. What they did was take the woolen cloth and beat it with boards, to fill in any kind of holes that might be in the cloth. That was their entire job: take this woolen cloth and beat it with a board. There was the guild of softeners. They would take the finished cloth and apply to it a substance called alum, which they would kind of rub into it, which would make it somewhat softer. Now, if you know anything about woolen cloth, you will know it's not very soft. It has all sorts of problems, like it's difficult to wash it, and so forth, but without alum, it might be unbearable. So these people were important. The guild of washers, another Lesser Guild, would take the woolen cloth down to the River Arno (the main river running through the middle of Florence) and wash it. After they washed it, they would stretch it out to make it a little bit longer.

The guild of dyers would apply dyes and make the wool different colors. You can't apply too many dyes to woolen cloth. There are no chemical dyes in this period, so it's all vegetable-based dyes like yellow dye from onions and blue dye coming from indigo—which is expensive, so you don't see a whole lot of that—red dye taken from clay, and things like that to make the cloth a little bit more attractive.

It's still in these long bolts, though. It's a little bit softer. It's now got some nice colors. The next guild, another guild of the Lesser Guilds, is the guild of shearers. They cut the cloth into various different lengths, so that it is sold, not as a huge bolt, in many cases, but in different lengths. Then the cloth is given to people called menders, who sew up any damage done through all these other processes—and it's going to be damaged at almost every step. Another guild called the guild of pressers will take a big iron and iron it out, to make it flat and get the wrinkles out. That's pretty much what they do. And, as we all know, at the very bottom of the social scale was the Ciompi, whose job was to comb out the tangles in the original raw wool.

So, all sorts of different guilds and different tasks. Each guild only does its own task, and it's illegal for anybody who is not in the guild to do that task. It's illegal for anybody in another guild to do a task of another guild. There is no crossing over. It's a very compartmentalized thing. Wage levels are strictly regulated, and of course the people on the bottom are not making very much, where the people at the top who buy and sell the product and the raw wool are doing pretty well.

As you probably know, the typical guild—and this is especially characteristic of the artisan guilds—has three different people in it. This is kind of important for the structure of the industry in general. The guy who actually belongs to the guild is the master craftsman, the master dyer or presser or mender or whatever else. He will be the guy who owns the shop and also owns whatever tools might be being used. He basically owns all the hardware being used at that step in the process, and almost—well, in every case—he will have his shop on the bottom floor of his house. His family will live on the top floors, and it will be all one building. He'll do his work on the bottom floor. In many cases, he has a big, kind of window he can open on the first floor, forming a kind of table, and he would put his wares out to let people see what he is doing. So it's all very public activity.

The other major person in the guild is the apprentice, who is learning the trade. His family has apprenticed him to this master. He doesn't really get paid a wage. He lives in the master's house. He eats at the master's table at the master's expense. He often does other things for the master, and he learns the trade as much as he can by watching the master, although, in actual fact, the way guilds worked is that very often the masters just sat back and told the apprentices what to do, and the apprentices did almost all of the work. In some cases, even, the master would contract out the work to wage workers and get other people involved, but in most cases, the master is more like the supervisor instead of a guy actually doing the work, although he does supervise.

Then finally, you will have a journeyman or journeymen, who are just wage workers. They are not learning the trade. They are not ever going to move up. They are not going to go anywhere. They just sweep the floor and empty the garbage and do the manual labor and get paid a really poor wage. They are called "journeymen" because they tend to leave one job and go to another and travel around quite a bit. It's an important aspect of the industry, but those people are really in dead-end jobs.

Even the apprentice, though, there is no guarantee he will ever move up and become a master and join the guild, because there has got to be a spot for him, and there aren't always open spots in a guild. As a matter of fact, more often than not there are not open spots. So a lot of apprentices lived in hopes that the master would die and leave the shop to the apprentice. Maybe he would marry the master's daughter and move into the family and kind of inherit the business. He could move up and become a guild member that way.

However, even becoming a member of the guild, even if, for example, the master died and basically said to the apprentice, "You can have the shop" and everything, the apprentice would have to show to the guild that he could do the quality of work that the guild required. He would have to gain admission to the guild in his own right. He would do this by producing an example of whatever work he does, for example, pressing cloth or washing it, and his example would be called a "masterpiece." He would take it to the guild, the guild warden, the guy in charge, and if the guild warden liked it, he'd be admitted to the guild—after he pays a huge fee. If you can't pay the fee, you don't get admitted, even if you do do good work.

If you do produce good material and you can pay the fee, you get in to the guild. Now you're really lucky—but now you face the fact that your industrial activity is heavily regulated. The quality of the stuff you make is determined by the guild. They inspect it. You've got to make up to a certain quality, but you can't make better than that. The price you sell it for is regulated. They inspect that, too. The whole impetus behind this is, in some ways, restraint of trade, or at least restraint of competition. Guilds are designed to make sure everybody in the guild makes a similar living. Nobody undercuts the others and makes more money. Nobody's going to lose out because he can't charge as much. It's all going to be an even playing surface for everybody.

That's not competition, and, as far as I know, that's not capitalism. It's a guild-based economy, often called a domestic economy. This was the economy in Florence and in the rest of Europe up until the 18th century. So when you read in various books that capitalism was born and flourishing in Renaissance Italy—well, maybe, but since everybody is in a guild and everybody in a guild is regulated, it doesn't seem like modern-day capitalism—to me, at least.

So that's kind of how the guild structure was organized. The guild structure directly influenced the political structure of Florence. It's almost as if one were an imprint of the other. Florence was officially a republic, a commune, as you know, but in fact it was ruled in large part by a group of wealthy men who belonged to the seven Great Guilds. We'll talk a lot more about this in the next lecture. In our modern point of view, it's a small group of wealthy people; an oligarchy. In Europe at this time, it really was a fairly broadly representative government, which could correctly be called a commune. So Florence in the Renaissance is politically based in this communal structure.

Lecture Seven
Florentine Politics and Society

Scope:

In this lecture, we will take a close look at the structure and functioning of the government of the commune of Florence. We will also examine Florentine political life and the political environment that fostered the Renaissance, as well as the different levels of Florentine society and the families who filled them. Finally, we will begin our examination of the political history of Florence to see how the town evolved its institutions.

Outline

I. The political structure of Florence was closely linked to the economic structure of the town. It decentralized power into many hands as a way of preventing one family from gaining total power. Although this goal was not always achieved, Florence did become a very politicized society, creating one of the conditions for the rise of Humanism.

    A. Officially, Florence was a republic or commune, but in reality, it was an oligarchy controlled by a fairly large group of wealthy citizens, members of the seven Great Guilds.

        1. The government had not always been so oligarchic. In the early days of the commune, the 1100s, there was broader participation in government. Over the years, the rich established their hold on power.

        2. During the Ciompi period (1378–1381), the lower guilds came to power for a time. The same thing happened in many European towns as a result of the 14th-century labor crisis created by the plague.

        3. By 1380, the Great Guilds were back in power in Florence, and the trend toward aristocratic rule continued. Soon, individual patrician families were coming to exercise dominant control over the government, as we will see later.

4. The narrowing of the ruling circle in Florence seemed to challenge Civic Humanist ideals about citizen political activity. But the façade of the republic was never dropped and the ideals of Civic Humanism were never abandoned. Historian Lauro Martinez even suggests that Civic Humanism was used by the ruling class as a way to legitimize its position.

B. The city council was called the *Signoria*. Its seat was a fortress-like building in the center of the city.

1. The Signoria consisted of many offices, elections to which took place in an indirect process known as the *Scrutiny*.

2. The first step in the Scrutiny was to draw up a list of all the members of the Great Guilds. This was the group from which officers would be elected.

3. This list was passed on to a committee that took names off the original list to create a list of eligible candidates. The names of men were taken off if they were in debt, in exile, absent from the town for other reasons, sick, or dead.

4. The new list was then passed to another committee, which struck off still more names to create the list of nominees.

5. The name of each nominee was then written on a bean. The beans were put in a sack and some were blindly drawn out. Those drawn out were elected.

6. The numbers of names on the lists varied and tended to contract as the oligarchy narrowed. In 1343, the list of eligibles contained 3,000 names, and the list of nominees, 300; in 1382, just after the Ciompi period, the eligibles numbered 5,000, and the nominees, 750. After this period, the number of names on the lists declined rapidly.

7. Control of this electoral process could be achieved by gaining control over the selection committees. This was how the Medici would later establish their control over the government.

C. The duties of the Signoria were executive and administrative. It did not make law or policy.

  1. It appointed judges, regulated commerce, and oversaw foreign affairs.

  2. The Signoria was the day-to day administrative power in the town.

D. There were many different officials making up the Signoria, each with his own responsibilities.

  1. There were 9 *Priors*, or chief executive officers. They were elected for terms of two months each and led the government. Nothing better illustrates the dispersal-of-power principle at the core of the commune.

  2. There were 12 *Buonomini* ("good men"), who supervised commerce. Each was elected for a term of three months, and each administered one section of the town.

  3. There were 16 *Gonfalonieri*, or police officials. Each was in charge of one section of the city.

  4. There were 15 *Magistrates*, or administrators. They were in charge of day-to-day business, such as tax collection and fortification repair.

  5. For extremely unpopular jobs, such as the quarantine of a part of the town when the plague hit, electoral reform, or forced loans, special committees called *Balia* were formed. They did the dirty work and were then dissolved.

E. The making of policy and law took place in two large representative bodies.

  1. The Council of the Commune and the Council of the Popolo ("people") together were composed of about 500 members, each elected for a term of six months.

  2. They debated and made policy, and the policies were then recorded by an official known as the Chancellor.

3. Originally just a secretary, the Chancellor had to be an educated man. In later years, he was almost always a Humanist. Over time, he came to represent the two assemblies before other bodies of government, and he turned this position into one of leadership of the two councils. He could be compared to a modern prime minister.

4. Leonardo Bruni and Caluccio Salutati, the founders of Civic Humanism in Florence, were both Chancellors.

F. One very unusual official was the *Podesta*. He was the police chief and commander of the army and was always chosen by the Signoria from outside the city for a term of one year. He lived in the Bargello, another fortress-like building in the center of town, and enforced law and order. The choice of a foreigner for this important job showed the Florentines' fear of turning military power over to one local family, who might try to seize power.

G. Compared with most other political structures in Europe at the time, oligarchic Florence was a very political society.

1. There was relatively broad participation in government: In any one year, about 1,165 men would serve in office.

2. There were, thus, large numbers of politically active citizens despite the oligarchs' control.

3. This situation fostered civic pride, political thinking, and debate; highlighted the importance of public speaking; and ultimately, provided a home for the growth of Civic Humanism.

4. These conditions were, in part, the creation of the Humanists themselves, but to a much greater degree, the broad nature of Florentine government evolved over the years from a fear that the city would be taken over and ruled by dictators. This fear emerged out of Florence's historical experience, which we will soon examine.

II. The social structure of Florence also was closely tied to the economic structure.

A. Unlike in most of medieval society, there were no nobles in Renaissance Florence. Conflict between the nobles and Florence's commercial classes resulted in the nobles' ejection from the town in the 13th century.

  1. Social status in Florence was, thus, not determined by noble birth but by commercial wealth.

  2. At the top of society were the patricians, members of the Great Guilds, citizens of great wealth for generations, holders of high office.

  3. This was a relatively, but not absolutely, closed oligarchy. Its members intermarried. Mobility into the class was possible but slow and difficult. Guild membership was, of course, necessary to enter the oligarchy, but so was great family wealth over several generations.

B. The greatest of the Renaissance patrician families were the Albizzi, virtual rulers of Florence from 1382–1434; the Strozzi; the Pitti; and of course, the Medici, rulers from 1434–1498.

  1. All of these families lived in magnificent palaces, many of which still stand.

  2. They all came from generations of wealth: Cosimo de' Medici, who ruled Florence from 1434–1464, as we will see, came from four generations of wealth in the Cambio, or bankers guild.

Essential Reading:

Gene Brucker, *Renaissance Florence*, chapters 3–5.

Supplementary Reading:

Lauro Martines, *Power and Imagination: City-States in Renaissance Italy*.

Questions to Consider:

1. Did the political structure of Florence help to create the Renaissance or vice versa?

2. What was the role of the lower guilds in Florentine life?

Lecture Seven—Transcript
Florentine Politics and Society

In our last lecture we were looking at Florence, the economic and social structure of Florence, as one of the contexts of the Renaissance and humanism. In this lecture we're going to continue with that theme by looking at the political structure and political life of Florence and seeing how that provided a context for the Renaissance. In fact, we'll see how the Florentine political structure actually helped create the Renaissance and civic humanism.

So we'll start out with a kind of brief overview of how the government worked, and then we'll look a little bit at how people were elected and served in the government. Officially, Florence was a republic. In Italy at this time they were known as communes, because they were formed when people took common oaths to serve the city. In fact, however, Florence was ruled by what we, with our modern eyes, would see as a relatively small group of wealthy men. Today we'd probably call it an oligarchy, although it really wasn't perceived that way at the time, so much. This oligarchy was made up of the members of the seven Great Guilds, who controlled the woolen-cloth industry. So what we'll see in Florence is that city officials are elected from within a fairly small group of eligible, wealthy people. We'll have to consider the extent to which this actually qualifies as a republic, not to mention a democracy.

Just to take a look back in time, very briefly, the government of Florence had not always been so oligarchic, had not always been so restricted to just a small group of people. In the early days of the commune, when it was first organized back in the 1100s and early 1200s, the government was, in fact, a lot more popular and a lot more democratic, but over the years what had happened was that the rich just gradually assumed more and more power, and there was a trend towards rule by the wealthy people throughout the years. This trend was, of course, reversed during the Ciompi period, from 1378 to 1381, when the Lesser Guilds actually seized power and controlled the government for a couple of years, unusual in the history of Italian towns and even European towns, but for the late 14th century not that unusual, because in the 1380s, for example, because of the plague, depression, and labor shortage, there were lower guild regimes in power in a number of cities across Europe.

None of them lasted very long, but at least Florence was not the only one to have a regime like the Ciompi regime.

After the Ciompi period is over though, by 1400, the Great Guilds are back in command, back in control, and the trend towards rule by a smaller and smaller wealthy group continues on throughout the 1400s and the 1500s, and in the Renaissance period climaxes with the Medici period. This brings up a point that has been debated, as to exactly how popular, how democratic this government was. Could it really be called participatory? The historian Lauro Martinez has suggested that Renaissance humanism—civic humanism—was developed as an ideology by this ruling class to legitimize their power and make it seem as though the government was more participatory and democratic than it actually was. So if you take this interpretation, you actually see humanism as a kind of ideological program of the upper classes. I think that's not a terribly accurate description of what's going on in Florence, however. As we'll see, even though to the modern person it seems like the group of rulers in Florence is small, for the time it actually was a fairly broad government. There was fairly broad participation of the people in government. I'll give you examples of that in just a couple of minutes.

So I don't think people at the time would have considered it to have been a narrow government. As a matter of fact, in most countries in Europe, of course, there was simply a king who ruled and subjects who followed. Most towns were ruled by various different versions of this situation. It was about as republican a government as you would find in the early modern period. So I wouldn't really say that humanism was an attempt to cover up rule by the elite.

The chief organ of government in the city was the city council. That was called the Signoria. What I want to do first is tell you how people were elected to the Signoria. You will get some sense for not only who was elected, but how many people would be elected and serve, and you will get a better sense for the nature of participation in this government.

The elections were held—and this was fairly typical of a lot of towns in Europe—by an indirect electoral system. In Florence, it was called the "scrutiny." Here's how it would work. What they would do is, first they would draw up a list of all the members of the seven Great

Guilds. That would be a fairly lengthy list. You have to be in the seven Great Guilds to even qualify to run for office. So they make a list of people in the Great Guilds. Then they hand that list down to a committee, and the committee strikes names off and makes a new list, which it calls the list of eligible candidates. It will strike names off the original list, in the cases that maybe a person would be in debt, because being in debt makes you liable to bribes and things like that, and it's not good to have those people in government. People who were in exile would be stricken off, obviously. People who were absent on business trips would be stricken off because they couldn't serve. People who were too sick to serve would be taken off, and, finally, people who were dead would be taken off. So then you have your list of eligibles. That's handed down to another committee, and that committee goes through a whole other process of striking off names. I won't go through all the reasons why they strike off names here again. This produces the final list, called the list of nominees.

At that point, the name of each nominee is written on a bean. The beans are put in a chest, and somebody who is blindfolded reaches in and draws beans out. Whoever's name is on the bean drawn out gets elected. Over the years, over the 14th century, the number of people on these various lists grew, and then at the end of the 14th century it began to contract again. For example, in 1343, the list of nominees (the final list) contained 300 names, out of a list of eligibles of 3,000. In 1361 the list of nominees contained 500 names, out of a list of eligibles of 3,000. In 1382, right at the end of the Ciompi period, the list of eligibles was 5,000, and the list of nominees was 750. So it is growing all through the 14th century. Then it begins to contract again as we move into the 15th century and into the rule of the wealthier families.

Whoever controls these various election committees, striking off names, can basically control the election, because you can control who is eligible to be elected. In the 15th century, for example, the powerful Medici banking family had all their friends on these committees, and they struck off people who weren't their friends and got all their friends elected, and that's how they basically ruled Florence from behind the scenes. It was a system that was not too difficult to manipulate if you had people in the right positions.

So that's how you get elected to the city council. Now, what does the city council do? The duties of the Signoria? They are executive and they are administrative, but they are not policy-making. There are two other bodies that I'll tell you about later that make policy. The Signoria is going to do things like appoint judges, enforce the law, regulate commerce. It has some foreign affairs responsibilities and that kind of thing. On the Signoria or city council there are number of different officials, and I will tell you about these different officials and what their duties were. First of all, the top officials were nine men called *Priors*. These were nine chief executive officers. You might think of it as nine mayors of the city—nine to spread out the responsibility, so nobody gets too much power. Each one of the *Priors* is elected for a term of two months—two months, and then another election for that spot. The *Priors* live in the Signoria building, which is a huge, fortress-like building in the center of Florence, which you can still visit today if you go there. It was really built to resist attack by people who didn't like what the city council was doing.

Another type of official on the city council were the 12 *Buonomini*, or the 12 "good men." These 12 officials basically supervised commerce. They are elected for terms of three months each, and each one of them administers commerce in one section of the city. The city is divided into different sections, and one official regulates each one.

Then you have 16 officials known as *Gonfalonieri*. These are 16 police officials. This job actually evolved from the medieval position created to police the nobles in Florence, before the nobles were kicked out in 1282. Now the *Gonfalonieri* are just general police officials. Each one controls one section of the city. He doesn't really have a police force. He's just like the lone official for that section of the city.

There are also 15 officials known as *Magistrates*. These are just basic administrators. They take care of day-to-day business: tax collecting, road repair, repairing of fortifications of the city, things like that—whatever mundane jobs need to get done.

If a really bad job came up, none of these officials would do it. They would appoint a special committee, called a *Balia*, which would undertake the very unpopular task at hand, such as, in a forced loan, where the government is forcing people to loan it money; or electoral reform, reforming the process of scrutiny; or quarantining a section of the city because of the plague. Of all these jobs, probably the most unpopular, the job that no one wanted to do, was quarantine. Whenever the plague hits, and you know it hits very often, the section of the city it hits first is quarantined; cut off. Nobody can go in. Nobody can go out. The people can't see their relatives in other neighborhoods. They can't do business. They can't go to work. It's a very, very unpopular kind of thing. These committees would do it, and then after the task was over and the situation was resolved, the committee would dissolve, and no one would have to accept responsibility for doing the unpopular thing. That's pretty much how the city council worked. Executive and administrative.

Policy making—actually making laws and making policy for the city—was carried out by two legislative bodies. One was known as the Council of the Popolo. "Popolo" in Italian just means "people." The other was called the Council of the Commune. Together these two legislative bodies had about 500 members, and each member served for a term of six months. They debate and they make policy. That's what they are all about. The policies they make, the laws they pronounce, are recorded, written down, and announced to the city by an official known as the chancellor. This official actually becomes very important in Florentine government as the years go by.

In the beginning, the chancellor simply represented these two legislative bodies. He would go in, listen to their debates, write down what they decided, and he would go out and announce it to the rest of the city. As the years went by, however, the chancellor gained more and more influence and then more and more power in these two legislative bodies. He came to manipulate the agendas. He came to control or at least influence debate, and actually came to lead and direct these two bodies and their formulation of policy and law. At that point, the chancellor had become a lot more than what he was earlier. Earlier he was just kind of a secretary. Now he's become almost something, we would say, that would be equal to a prime minister. So the chancellor becomes probably the most important single official in the entire Florentine government.

Because from the beginning the duty of the chancellor was to write down laws and policies, he always had to be highly educated. By the late 14th, early 15th century, chancellors tended to be humanist scholars, not really professional politicians so much as people who were qualified by their command of Latin and their learning to provide the functions that they had to provide. You might recall that the two founders of civic humanism in Florence, Leonardo Bruni and Caluccio Salutati, were both chancellors. Salutati was chancellor at the very end of the 14th century, Bruni at the very beginning of the 15th century. Both of these people, as you know, had tremendous influence on the evolution of humanism in the Renaissance in Florence, but their influence started in this political position that they held, which has become very, very influential as a position by the late 14th century.

One final official I want to mention just briefly is an official called the podesta. The podesta is basically the army commander, the commander of the Florentine militia or army. The nature of the Florentine army changed over the years. At some points it was a mercenary army, professional soldiers hired from all around, men called *condottiere*. Other times it was a militia. You might recall that Machiavelli in *The Prince* argues for the virtues of militia over other forms of government [sic army]. The podesta is the commander of this military force. The odd thing about him is that he's always chosen from outside the city. He is never a native Florentine. They go out to some other city, usually some city really close by, and they hire somebody from there to come in as army commander. Why do they do it this way? Why would such an important position be always restricted to non-Florentines, non-citizens of the city? It seems kind of odd at first when you think about it, but the reason was that the Florentines didn't want to let anybody—any Florentine family—have this kind of military power, because with this military power you could take over and control the town. Families were always feuding, always disputing. There were always arguments. They didn't want to put this kind of power in the hands of any family who might use it against other families, or any particular local man who might use it to increase his own power and become a dictator.

As you are going to see in the next lecture, there was a tremendous fear of dictators in Florence. One of the reasons why the Florentine government evolved with such a broad, really participatory government, from contemporary standards, was the fear of a dictator taking over. This fear was very real, because in the early, mid-14th century, as you will learn in the next lecture, there were episodes when dictators did take over and created serious problems for the city. So the government is designed to move away from that, to spread power out, especially in the case of the *Podesta*, but just think: there are nine priors—nine mayors—all these different officials. Power is really diffused, really spread out, and no one really has enough to walk in and take over.

Also, another factor which prevented people from accumulating too much power in this governmental structure is that their office terms are so short: two months, three months, maybe six months, then they are out. They are not immediately eligible to be re-elected, so they can't become ensconced and develop a power base. All these things were developed to spread out power. So, in a sense, it was a practical situation. It was a practical guard against any kind of tyrannical government.

Another result of this kind of government was that Florence developed into a very, very political society. Really, it has a relatively broad participation of the citizenry in government. For example, in any one year, about 1,165 different people would serve in some government office, and, for the time, that was a broad participation. So there were a large number of politically active citizens in Florence.

Because of this large number of politically active citizens, a number of other conditions were fostered; for example, civic pride. There was a tremendous amount of civic pride in Florence, people proud of being Florentines. This was promoted, in part, by civic humanism, which, you will recall, compared Florence to Rome and the Roman Empire, and said over and over again, "We can be great like Rome and we can attain Roman virtues and we can be just like the Romans were: powerful." This fostered real patriotism in the city, and that's one of the things that civic humanism was supposed to do.

Another condition that the government fostered was political thinking. So many people were in government and had to make governmental decisions that the average citizen was used to thinking about politics. Political thinking was considered important. It was something that people did on a regular basis, and that was very, very different from the typical subject of a king in medieval Europe, who never thought about politics, never talked about politics and wouldn't even know what politics was. There virtually was no politics in monarchies, but in a situation like this, there's a lot of political thinking.

Another thing that it fosters is a stress on rhetoric. You will recall that rhetoric is one of the bases of humanist education. The humanists believed that you had to be able to communicate your ideas effectively, both to be a good citizen and participate in politics, but also you had to be able to communicate your ideas effectively to motivate and inspire people, in particular to motivate people to make good moral decisions and lead good moral lives. So there's a tremendous stress on communication, on rhetoric, on good public speaking, and this is, in fact, dictated in part by the fact that the Florentine government is such a broad government and so many people take part in it. You really need to be able to communicate ideas back and forth in a situation like this.

Finally, the governmental situation fostered all sorts of debate and discussion of problems that you wouldn't find in many other places. You certainly wouldn't find in monarchies and medieval Europe debate about the best kinds of governments, best kinds of armies, the best kind of person to serve in government—all sorts of political problems were discussed, and the discussions often became quite heated. Sometimes there would actually be disputes and sometimes even physical confrontations over political issues among the various different people involved. They took it very seriously, and they debated political ideas in a very serious way, and that also makes Florence very different from other places in medieval Europe.

So all of these conditions that I have talked about that the government fostered—civic pride, political thinking, stress on rhetoric or communication, the frequent debate and discussion of political problems—all these created the need in Florence for an effective system of political and civic education. This is a very important point, because here you see that the governmental structure is actually giving rise to the creation of an educational system, and this, of course, this system of political and civic education, was civic humanism, developed by Salutati and Bruni, the two great humanist chancellors. It was designed to create people who could be good citizens, good leaders, good office holders, and it was, as we know, a civic education drawn from reading the Greek and Roman classics. Especially, histories like Livy and political and social thinkers like Cicero were very important in this educational process.

So the governmental structure of Florence really has a big role in giving rise to civic humanism by creating the need for an effective civic and political education. We saw this in the Florentine crisis of 1400 when the Milanese almost conquered Florence, and Salutati and Bruni sit back and say, "Why did we almost get conquered? Because we don't educate our citizens very well. We need a more effective way to educate citizens and create leaders and office holders and governors for the city." So we can see how that works.

So, in many ways, the Florentine government helps give rise to conditions that foster the Renaissance, and you might even say, create the Renaissance. So in this case you can see actual factors in Florence effective in creating a new cultural milieu, but it is important to realize that the broad nature of this government did not evolve because of civic humanism. It evolved because of the fear of dictators, the desire to spread out power, the desire to keep families apart—feuding families apart and not gaining too much power—and out of these conditions grew the need for political education and that's what really created civic humanism and helped create the Renaissance. So it's a broad government and we see exactly what all that led to.

Now, just a little bit, finally, about the social structure of Florence. Unlike most other medieval societies, or earlier medieval societies, there was no such thing as nobles in Florence. There were no nobles in Florence, for reasons you will see in just a second. Social status in Florence was not determined by whether or not you were of noble lineage. Why were there no nobles in Florence, and, in fact, no nobles in most of the Italian cities? The reason for that goes back to the Middle Ages. In the earlier Middle Ages, there had been nobles in Florence. They had estates out in the countryside, they had townhouses inside the city, and they would commute back and forth, back and forth. However, the nobles were only one group of people in the city. The other big group, of course, was the commercial middle class.

These two groups of people did not get along. The commercial middle class, the guildspeople, they had their own outlook, their own agendas. They were concerned with commerce and the accumulation of wealth. They needed a legal structure and a governmental structure to the city which would promote commerce and promote their business activities. That's what they were totally focused on.

The nobles, on the other hand, cared nothing about commerce. They cared nothing about the middle class accumulating wealth or industry and trade prospering. They had no care about that at all. Their main concern was for their own wealth and power, and they believed that they should be the ruling class in town, even though in many cases there were more middle class than there were nobles. The middle class was wealthier than the nobles; the nobles still thought they should be the ones in control. This led to tremendous tension.

Another thing that led to tremendous tension was that nobles legally had the right to feud, and, legally at least, other middle-class and lower families did not have the right to feud. This is what nobles did in the Middle Ages, in Italian towns most of the time. They feuded with each other, the different families of nobles. They would hire huge groups of retainers, basically toughs; bodyguards with the livery of the noble on front, carrying weapons. They would go back and forth through the town fighting each other. They would bull right into a city market in the middle of a business day and have a sword fight and tear things up, and really create havoc all through the city, and in their townhouses, or city houses, they built these tremendous towers, way up, so they could go up in the towers and throw stuff off at each other. You can still see some of these towers when you go to Italian towns today, especially in San Gimignano, near Pisa, you can see these towers. Of course they are up there throwing stuff over at each other, and anybody walking beneath, meaning the middle-class people—they are getting hit with all this stuff.

It all came to a head in the 1280s. In the 1280s in Florence, and around that time in other cities, the nobles were first excluded from the guilds. They could not be a member of any guild. Then they were excluded from government. They could not hold government office. Then they were kicked out. Many left voluntarily, but others had to be forcibly kicked out. After that, you got no nobles. After that, the ruling class in Florence and other Italian towns was simply the wealthy upper guildsmen. They took the name of patricians, "patrician" simply being the ancient Roman designation for "rich person." So the rich people, the patrician families, they control things. They intermarry. Mobility into their class is possible, but slow. You've got to have several generations of wealth, not just one, to move up and become a patrician. They control the Great Guilds.

They hold the government offices. They pretty much run the town. It's not easy to move up into this group at all.

Of course, the greatest of all these patrician families was the Medici. Cosimo de' Medici, the first, the patron of this whole family, rich from the wool and banking industry, ruled Florence from behind the scenes from 1430 to 1464. His family, when he took power (or sort of assumed power) had four generations of wealth, in the Cambio, the bankers' guild. So the Medici are a perfect example, but there are many other patrician families who played a role in government, as we shall see in the next lecture: the Albizzi, the Strozzi, the Pitti, and many others. You can still see their palaces in Florence today. This was a very interesting class of people who controlled Florence's culture and politics.

Lecture Eight
The History of Florence

Scope:

In this lecture, we will take a look at the political history of Florence from the Middle Ages through the Renaissance to see how the town's history helped to shape its institutions, traditions, and culture. Just as we have seen that economic conditions and Florence's political structure helped to create the conditions for the coming of the Renaissance, we will now see that Florence's political history was no less influential in this regard. We will see the rise to power of the great patrician families, their contributions to the Renaissance, and the many changes in government brought by the fall of the Medici. Ultimately, we will examine events that some consider to signify the end of the Renaissance in Florence with the rise to power of the radical monk Savonarola.

Outline

I. Medieval Florence was a city of turbulent politics and frequent social unrest.

   A. In many ways, the central political struggle of the high Middle Ages was the battle between the pope and the Holy Roman Emperor for political domination of Europe, but especially of Italy.

   1. In this struggle the supporters of the pope made up a party known as the Guelphs; the supporters of the emperor made up a party known as the Guibellines.

   2. The struggle between Guelphs and Guibellines was especially intense in Italy, which the emperor was intent on dominating and the pope intent on defending. Within towns, Guelph and Ghibelline parties struggled for control of the government, while on the wider scene, Guelph cities made war on Ghibelline towns.

   B. In the 13th century, Florence was a Guelph town, allied with the pope.

1. In 1260, however, Florence lost the Battle of Montaperti to neighboring Siena, a Ghibbiline town, which caused the Guelphs to fall from power in Florence and the Guibellines to take over.

2. Only a few years later, in 1310, the Guelphs returned to power in Florence when Emperor Henry VII launched an invasion of Italy but lost to a coalition of Guelph towns.

3. Guelph control proved very profitable for Florence as the pope awarded Florentine banks all of his banking and tax-collecting business. An economic boom followed in Florence from 1310–1338.

C. Meanwhile, the 13th century also saw the destruction of noble power in Florence.

1. The high Middle Ages had been a time of conflict in most Italian communes between the nobles and the commercial classes, who styled themselves the *Popolo* ("people").

2. Nobles carried on destructive feuds that hurt commerce, considered themselves above town laws, and had no regard for the civic good. Efforts were made to disenfranchise them.

3. In Florence, the turning point was 1282, when the Great Guilds got a law passed stipulating that only their members could hold communal office. Then, in 1293, another law was passed excluding nobles from the guilds. Soon, most nobles left the city.

D. Perhaps the most important political development of the late Middle Ages in Florence was the town's fateful experimentation with rule by dictator, which left an indelible mark on Florentine political structures.

1. During the imperial invasion of 1310–1313 by Henry VII, Guelph Florence felt that it could not defend itself against such massive forces.

2. Thus, Florence invited the powerful king of Naples to bring his army north to defend the city, during which time he would be given powers to rule Florence as a dictator. He would be paid by Florentine tax revenues for his defense of the city.

3. Fortunately for Florence, the arrangement worked relatively well and the king left when the crisis was over. But this seeming success encouraged the Florentines to depend again on such a dangerous tactic.

4. During the period 1320–1323, Florence found itself on the losing side of a war with the tiny town of Lucca. Riots broke out in Florence and law and order crumbled.

5. In this crisis, Florence invited the foreign noble Charles of Calabria to bring his army to town and use it to restore order and prosecute the war. As before, this strongman was given dictatorial powers to rule Florence until the emergency passed. Again as before, Florence had good fortune in that, when the emergency was over, the dictator left. Such good luck, however, was not to hold.

6. During the economic depression of the 1340s, law and order again collapsed in Florence. Again a dictator was called in to restore order, this time the noble Walter of Brienne. Walter got firm control of Florence, restored order, but then refused to relinquish power when the crisis was past. Only a long and bloody civil war succeeded in ejecting Walter and teaching the Florentines a lesson about one-man rule.

E. The 14th century brought other political changes to Florence. The Florentines fought a war with the pope and lost his banking business. Then the period of lower-guild rule of the Ciompi ended only in 1382 with the return of the Great Guilds to power.

II. In many ways, Renaissance Florence was the birthplace of Humanism.

A. Rule of the Albizzi.

1. When the Great Guilds returned to power in 1382, the patrician Albizzi family controlled the government. They ruled until 1434.

2. During this period, Civic Humanism was born in Florence against the background of the struggle with Milan in 1380–1402. Although Florence survived this war, it fought and lost a second war with Milan in 1425. Not long after this defeat, the Albizzis fell from power.

B. Rule of the Medici, the architects of the Renaissance in Florence: Cosimo.

1. After the defeat by Milan, law and order once again broke down in Florence. This time a local leader, the banker Cosimo de' Medici, stepped forward to restore peace with his private mercenary army, led by Francesco Sforza. After Cosimo succeeded in this task, he assumed great power in the government and began the period of Medici rule in Florence.

2. Cosimo himself held no office, but he controlled the election committees and got his supporters elected to office, ruling through them. For support, he had the muscle of Sforza's troops. But the façade of the republic was maintained.

3. Cosimo was for all intents and purposes a dictator, but he was also a great patron of artists and scholars and the main financial promoter of the Renaissance in Florence.

4. In foreign policy, he pursued a policy of peace. In 1447, he was able to install his general Sforza as ruler of Milan, afterward signing a peace treaty with Milan. In 1454, he signed the Peace of Lodi, an alliance of Florence, Venice, and Milan designed to create a balance of power in Italy with the two southern powers the Papal States and Naples. A period of peace and prosperity resulted, in which the Renaissance flourished.

C. Lorenzo the Magnificent was perhaps the greatest of the Renaissance rulers of Florence.

1. He took over the reins of government when Cosimo died in 1464 and ruled for 30 years.

2. During his rule, Humanism and art flourished.

3. He pioneered the modern diplomatic system by sending permanent resident ambassadors from Florence to all the major Italian powers. He maintained Cosimo's policy of

peace and the Renaissance continued to flourish in Florence.

4. He built a huge library.

5. When Lorenzo died in 1494, crisis struck Florence. His successor, Piero de' Medici, was not a competent ruler. Meanwhile, Italy faced an invasion by the armies of French King Charles VIII, who had a claim on the throne of Naples.

6. As the French marched south in 1498, Florence was conquered and the Medici were ejected as rulers, leaving a power vacuum.

D. The waning of the Renaissance in Florence was the inevitable result of this political crisis.

1. Into the power vacuum as the new ruler of Florence stepped the radical monk Savonarola. He blamed Florence's defeat by France on the excess luxuries brought by the Renaissance.

2. Savonarola preached against luxury, culture, learning, and Humanism. He even had books burned on the city square. Many consider him to represent the end of the Florentine Renaissance.

3. In 1502, Savonarola fell from power after attacking the pope for being a heretic—now he himself was burned on the city square.

4. A republic was installed as the new government, led by Piero Soderini and his deputy Niccolo Machiavelli. This government lasted from 1502–1512. It made concessions to the lower classes of Florence, which led to its unpopularity with the patricians and its eventual collapse.

5. In 1512, the Medici returned as rulers of Florence, this time with the title of duke. This return to power was made possible by pressure created by the Medici Pope Leo X. The creation of an aristocratic court in Florence has been further seen as evidence that the Renaissance had come to an end.

Essential Reading:

Gene Brucker, *Renaissance Florence*, chapter 6–end.

Questions to Consider:

1. Would there have been a Renaissance in Florence without the Medici?

2. What factors brought about the end of the Florentine Renaissance?

Lecture Eight—Transcript
The History of Florence

In the last couple of lectures we've been looking at how the political, social, and economic structure and conditions in Florence helped to cause and foster the Renaissance and humanism. We are going to continue with that in this lecture by taking a brief look at the actual political history of Florence. Before we get into the political history, though, just to briefly review what we've seen already, we've seen that, economically speaking, the depression which hit Florence and the rest of Europe in the mid-14th century caused a positive response, which actually produced the Renaissance and humanism. We've also seen how the economic depression caused or promoted investment in art and culture as safe investments, and this helped to bankroll Renaissance culture and Renaissance learning. We've also seen how the money from the Florentine woolen industry and banking and also foreign commerce were part of the economic backbone of the Renaissance. We've also seen how the governmental structure and political life in Florence caused a need for civic and political training, which led people back to the classics, and which also promoted the growth of humanism and the Renaissance.

What we're going to be looking at in this lecture is Florence's actual political history and relations with other Italian cities, and we'll look and see how that influenced the growth of the Renaissance and humanism in Florence, because the actual political history is quite influential in this process. To understand really how it develops, we have to go back into the Middle Ages again, and start there, as far back as the 13th century, and we'll bring Florentine political history up into the late 15th century, when the Medici basically lose power.

So we'll start with medieval Florence. We'll go back to the 13th century. In 13th-century Italy, the main political conflict—and it really was all-pervasive, throughout the whole peninsula, and it affected the rest of Europe, as well—was a struggle between two political parties called the Guelphs and the Guibellines. The struggle was about who had the right to claim or be supreme ruler over all of Europe. Would it be the pope or would it be the Holy Roman Emperor? Those who said the pope belonged to the Guelph party. Those who said the Holy Roman Emperor belonged to the Ghibelline party. In fact, both these parties had somewhat legitimate claims, or at least plausible claims, that their leader should be supreme ruler over all of Europe.

For example, the pope said, "On the one hand I'm God's representative on Earth, and you know, God is the ruler of everything, and therefore, as God's lieutenant on Earth, I should be the main political ruler over all of Europe," which was an argument that many people accepted. The pope also had a thing called the Donation of Constantine, which he very often brought out. That was a very interesting document. It supposedly was a document written by the Roman Emperor Constantine at the time that Constantine moved the capital of the Roman Empire from Rome itself over to the new city of Constantinople in Greece. This document supposedly said that when Constantine left and went to Constantinople, he gave the pope the right to be ruler over Western Europe. So the pope would always bring this out and say, "Look! Right here! It's written down. I've been legally given the right to rule all western Europe." We know that later on the Donation of Constantine is found to be a fraud by Lorenzo Valla, using the new humanist science of philology, but for many centuries it was thought to be legitimate, and was a very effective way the pope was making his claim.

The Holy Roman Emperor, of course, had his own legitimate claim to power. He was ruler over all of Germany. He claimed that his power over all of Europe came from the fact that he was the heir of the Roman Emperor who had ruled all of Europe and, like the Roman Emperor, he should rule all of Europe. Technically speaking, legally speaking, most of Italy was part of the Holy Roman Empire in the late Middle Ages, although the emperor didn't have a lot of control over most of the areas; the communes were becoming independent, the pope had tremendous influence in the south. However, the Empire did extend into Italy, technically at least.

So there was this huge argument between these two parties, and it was very heated, and became more heated in the 11th century, when the two parties (pope and emperor) became involved in what's known as the Investiture Struggle, which was a big fight over who had the right to appoint bishops in the Church, and of course whoever had the right to appoint bishops in the Church could control the Church. You might think right now, "Oh, well, this seems simple. The pope is the head of the Church, right? So he should appoint the bishops." But by tradition the emperor had appointed bishops in Germany, and he was unwilling to give this up. The pope was trying to make him give it up and take full control of the Church. In the end the pope is actually successful in stopping what was known as "lay investiture," and getting control over most bishops, but it was an ugly, long, drawn-out political struggle that really dominated the Middle Ages.

We see this political struggle in Italy almost everywhere. In Italy, some cities belonged to the Guelph party. Some cities belonged to the Ghibelline party. These cities would fight each other in battles over this issue. Inside individual cities there would be Guelph political parties and Ghibelline political parties, and they would fight each other, and not just in elections. They would go out and fight in the streets. There would be real riots over these issues, and cause a significant breakdown of law and order in many cases. So it was a very controversial thing, and it varied, depending on where you are in Italy, as to exactly what the minor issues were.

In Florence, the control of the government tended to move back and forth between the Guelph and Ghibelline parties in the late Middle Ages, depending on circumstances. For example, in the year 1260, Florence loses a military battle, known as the battle of Montaperti, to the city of Siena. Siena happens to be a Ghibelline city, so when Florence loses that battle, the Ghibelline party takes political control of the Florentine government for a period, but it doesn't last terribly long. By 1310, the Holy Roman Emperor Henry VII invades Italy with a very large army, but loses a number of battles to an alliance of Guelph towns. As a result of this Guelph victory over the emperor, the Guelphs return to power in the government of Florence. So, you see it really goes back and forth, just depending on which way the prevailing winds are blowing, basically.

The Guelphs stay in power in Florence until the 1340s. In fact, Guelph control of the Florentine government turns out to be very profitable for Florence, because during this control, the pope gave to Florentine banks the complete right to be exclusive papal banker and papal tax collector, so bank all the pope's money and collect all his taxes. This, of course, meant a lot of money; it meant an economic windfall for Florence, and there was, in fact, an economic boom in Florence between 1310, when the Guelphs take over, and 1338, when the Bardi and Peruzzi banks collapse and the depression starts to come on. So that's kind of how things were going in Florence in the late Middle Ages.

As we move into the 14th century and into the 15th century, the main trend in Florentine political history and government is a movement from a more democratic, more popular regime, to a more oligarchical regime, but it's not a steady movement. There are lots of backs and forths and other kind of reversals in this process, and I want to take a look at that now.

The first big step was actually taken in the late 13th century, when the power of nobles was destroyed in Florence. You will recall from the last lecture that there was a big conflict in most Italian cities, Florence included, between the middle class and the noble class: the noble class feuding, causing havoc and the middle class not liking it, and huge tensions developing over who should run the towns. In Florence, the nobles lose out in this struggle in the years between 1282 and 1293. In 1282, a really momentous occurrence happens in terms of the Florentine governmental structure. The Great Guilds get a law passed that says that only Great Guild members can hold government office, and this becomes, obviously, very, very important to the Florentine government from this point on.

A few years later, in 1293, there is another law passed, which says that nobles cannot belong to the guilds. Not that many nobles did belong to the guilds, but now, if you wanted to hold office, you had to be a guild member, and so this essentially meant that nobles couldn't hold office, and they couldn't participate in commerce, although they didn't much, anyway. After 1293, the nobles leave Florence—many voluntarily, some not voluntarily—but the noble presence is gone. There is no nobility in Florence after that. Patricians become the ruling class, as we've seen in the last lecture. These events were fairly typical for other Italian towns around the same time.

In the 14th century, however, the Florentine government is not particularly stable, and there are a number of different problems which develop. Included among these problems are several experiments with the use of dictators to rule the city. We've already seen in the last lecture that by the time the Renaissance arrives, the extremely broad participatory nature of the Florentine government is, in large part, the result of an effort to diffuse power and prevent any dictator from taking over. The reason that happened was because of what happened with these experiments in the 14th century, when dictators were, in fact, tried.

The first case, the first experiment with a dictator, occurred during the imperial invasion of Henry VII, from 1310 to 1313. Florence was afraid of being attacked, and Florence did not feel capable of defending itself, so it sent a message to the king of Naples in the south, and said, "Would you please bring your army up here? Defend our city against anybody who might attack it during this invasion, and while you do that you can take over the government and you can run the town." So the deal essentially was that the king would supply military protection, he would be paid off by Florentine tax revenues, and he would defend the city. Perhaps amazingly, this situation worked. He did defend the city. He never got really firm control of the government. When the crisis was over in 1313, he left. So the initial experiment with a dictator turned out to seemingly work, and the Florentines had kind of dodged a bullet.

But another crisis evolves in 1320. Between 1320 and 1323, Florence becomes involved in a war with the tiny town of Lucca. Lucca was a very small, insignificant power in Italy, but nevertheless Florence was losing the war, which is, I guess, testimony to the fact that Florence didn't have a very effective military structure at this time. Because they are losing the war and it's so embarrassing, pretty soon riots break out all through Florence. At that point the Florentine government invites a noble named Charles of Calabria to come up to the city and use his army to restore law and order. Again, the deal is he will bring his army, he'll be paid off by tax revenues, he'll restore law and order, he'll put down the riots. He'll fight the war against Lucca, and hopefully he'll win that war, and he'll run the town as a dictator while he's doing all this. Then, when the crisis is past, he'll go. Again, amazingly, this works out. By 1328 Charles has left Florence, and the deal seems to have worked again.

However, in this case, in the case of Florence, three times was not the charm. The third crisis really shows them the danger of dictators and fooling around with dictators. During the economic depression of the 1340s, which followed the collapse of the Bardi and Peruzzi banks in 1338, again law and order in Florence essentially collapsed. The government invites another noble, Walter of Brienne, this time, to come in and restore order. The deal is basically the same. "You come in and we'll pay you with tax revenues. You can run the city.

Just defeat the riots, restore law and order, and that's what we really ask you for." So Walter comes up. He does restore law and order, but he gains firm control of the Florentine government, and when the crisis is past, he refuses to leave. He wants to remain as dictator. He finds it a pretty good job. Because of that, civil war erupts in Florence between the citizens and Walter and his army. It's a very bloody situation for a number of years until Walter is forced to leave—is ejected, essentially—and the last experiment with a dictator ends.

So in two out of three cases it did turn out benignly, but in the last case it was very traumatic, and this attempt to use dictators to run the government turns into a bad experience and an important learning experience for the Florentine government, and really reinforces the government's commitment to a broader-based, semi-popular kind of government.

Now, we know already that the period of greatest democracy in Florence was the late 14th century. We've had the plague hit by then; the depression is in full swing. To make things worse, Florence fought a war with the pope and therefore lost all his banking business, which is a huge blow to the Florentine economy. Unemployment and poverty soar. This is the period, in 1378, when the Ciompi, the lower guilds, rise up, defeat the greater guilds, and seize control of the government. There is a government by the Lesser Guilds for a couple of years, which was not all that unusual for late 14th-century Europe, but in the history of Florence it's the only time you see the lower guilds with any significant political influence. However, it doesn't last long.

By 1382, the trend towards a more oligarchical, narrower government resumes. This happens when the Great Guilds stage a lockout of the workers in the woolen-cloth industry. They can't go to work, they can't earn money, they can't feed their families. As a result of that, the Ciompi regime collapses and the Great Guilds return to power. Politically speaking, you might see this as the beginning of the Renaissance period in Florence.

In 1382, as the Great Guilds come back to power, it is the patrician Albizzi family which takes control of the government. The Albizzi family controls the government from 1382 to 1434 by controlling the electoral process. This is the period, 1382 to 1434, essentially, in which the Renaissance is born in Florence. This is the period of that great crisis with Milan in 1380 to 1402. This is the period when civic humanism is born with Salutati and Bruni and the whole idea of civic education. This is the period that Salutati and Bruni whip up popular and patriotic support for the government by comparing Florence to Rome and saying, "We can be as great as Rome, and we can obtain Roman virtues and be like Rome was." Also, this is a period in which Salutati the chancellor stresses the fact that the war with Milan, the crisis with Milan, was more than just a kind of political power struggle. It represented a struggle between the Florentine republic, which was a good form of government, and the cruel and evil dictatorship of Milan, which was a bad form of government. Of course we know that in Milan—and we'll see this more in the next lecture—the Viscontis were dictators, and Florence did have a form of republic. So this is not too far from the truth.

Salutati further argued that the republic in Florence—in fact, a republic in general—was the best form of government that you could have. It was much better than a dictatorship, because political participation by the citizens allowed individual personal development and allowed the city to be governed more wisely by more different heads and more different efforts than a dictator could. So we see the political ideas of the Renaissance developing here.

We know that Florence survived this crisis with Milan in 1382 to 1400, but by 1425, Florence becomes involved in another war with Milan, and again we find that Florence does not have the military power to really be successful, and in fact they lose this war to Milan in 1425. As a result of that loss, the Albizzi family falls from power, and it is at this point that the Medici family takes over and becomes the great Renaissance ruling family of Florence. The Medici rule essentially from 1434 to 1494.

The father—"father of his country" he was called; *Pater Patriae*— the father of this family, the great patriarch, was Cosimo de' Medici, a very wealthy banker. He seized power during the loss to Milan by using his political connections to create a mob riot all through Florence. Then he stepped forward and he said, "I've got my personal mercenary army here, led by my personal general, Francesco Sforza. I'll restore law and order in Florence." In fact, he does step in, restores order, and as a result he gains control of the government, from basically solving a situation he created himself. So

Cosimo, in many ways, you could say, seizes control of the government through a plot.

Cosimo rules from behind the scenes from 1434 to 1464. He never holds any office, but has his friends sitting on all the election commissions. He strikes off all the names he doesn't like and gets all his friends elected. He's there pulling the strings behind the scenes, and if there is ever any trouble, he's got his personal mercenary army with his personal general, Francesco Sforza. They are going to be there to be the muscle if he needs it. In most cases he doesn't need that kind of muscle.

A lot of historians argue that Cosimo ruled as a dictator, but he never changed the structure of the government, and we have seen what that structure was. The republic was kept. It was never done away with. The electoral process was kept; it was manipulated, but it was kept. So whether he was actually a dictator or not is, I think, kind of open to debate. He didn't rule arbitrarily. In fact, he was a tremendous patron of artists and scholars, of books and learning and painting and so forth, and was a huge factor in promoting the growth of Renaissance culture, art, and learning. Some historians like Lauro Martinez will argue that he was this great patron of the arts to legitimize or even perhaps to cover up the fact that he was ruling as a dictator, but I still think that's going a little bit too far. I think the Medici—Cosimo and his family—had a sincere interest in Renaissance culture, and they were governing the city not as dictators, but as probably a pretty small oligarchy.

In the international realm, Cosimo pursued a policy of peace, because he knew peace would be the best thing for the Florentine economy and for Florentine art and culture. In 1447, a power vacuum developed in Milan, as we will see in the next lecture. At that point, Cosimo uses the opportunity to install his personal general, Francesco Sforza, as the new ruler of Milan. We'll see how that worked out in the next lecture. Immediately thereafter, Florence and Milan sign a peace treaty. Cosimo goes one step farther in 1454, when he engineers what is known as the Peace of Lodi. The Peace of Lodi was, in effect, a military alliance of northern Italian cities, the most important of which were Florence, Venice, and Milan. It was really put in place to offset a southern power bloc which had grown up when the pope (the Papacy) and the kingdom of Naples had come together in an alliance. So what Cosimo is trying to do is to maintain a kind of balance of power between north and south Italy. This balance of power maintains the peace of Italy, maintains the prosperity of Florence and other cities, and helps Renaissance culture—the Renaissance art and learning—grow during this period.

I should also point out at this point that the whole notion of balance of power was, at this point, a kind of new concept in diplomacy, and Cosimo should get some credit for thinking in these terms and engineering this new idea of diplomacy.

Eventually, Cosimo died, in 1464, and was followed as ruler by his son Lorenzo de' Medici, also called Lorenzo the Magnificent. It was during Lorenzo's rule that the Renaissance really reached a zenith in Florence. He was a tremendous patron of art, culture, and learning, just like Cosimo had been. Humanism flourishes. Art flourishes. There is peace and prosperity in the city. Lorenzo pretty much continues Cosimo's foreign policy of maintaining peace, a balance of power, for the prosperity of the whole Italian peninsula.

One way Lorenzo does this is by pioneering the modern diplomatic system. You can read about this in a very famous book by a historian named Garrett Mattingly, called *Renaissance Diplomacy*. What exactly happens is that for the first time, Lorenzo sends permanent ambassadors from Florence to the other Italian cities—the other Italian powers. Before this, there had been no permanent embassies or ambassadors. If you were going to send a diplomatic message, you had to send a special envoy to Milan or to Rome or whatever. He would take the message down and bring the answer back, but there was no permanent presence.

Lorenzo now develops a permanent ambassador presence in all the major powers, meaning he's in continuous contact with them, can negotiate with them, and can ensure the peace—or at least try to ensure the peace. So in many ways this is the birth of the modern diplomatic system. Other cities do the same thing. They send out their own ambassadors and the system begins to work.

Things are going very well in Florence up to 1494. In 1494, the good times end, and a series of events start to unfold which a lot of historians say brought about the end of the Renaissance in Florence. The big blow was that Lorenzo died. He was replaced by his brother, Piero de' Medici. Whereas Lorenzo was called "The Magnificent," and Cosimo was called "the father of his country," Piero was called "the gouty," because apparently his greatest achievement was having gout in his feet, which is a very painful illness. He was a terrible ruler. As bad luck would have it, that during his period in power, which was a very vulnerable period for Florence, Italy underwent a major foreign crisis.

That foreign crisis was caused by the French king, Charles VIII. The French king, Charles VIII, had a claim on the throne of the kingdom of Naples. This claim came from the fact that Naples and Sicily had been conquered in the early Middle Ages by the Normans, in 1054, and had been ruled for a number of years by an Angevin dynasty, a French dynasty. There had been since then other intervening dynasties, a couple of Spanish rulers, and others, but Charles still believed that when the king of Naples died, that he had a legitimate claim to the throne of Naples. So to enforce this claim, he invades Italy.

A huge army, a much bigger military apparatus than anybody in Italy has, marches down from the north, and conquers Florence easily. Piero runs away. The Medici family is ejected, and in place of the Medici, after Charles marches on and leaves Florence alone, a radical monk by the name of Savonarola takes over. This radical monk Savonarola believes that Florence has lost the war and been conquered because of Renaissance culture, because the Florentines had been sinful. They've had too much luxury, too much culture, too much learning, too much humanism. They have gotten soft, and now we've got to get back to obeying God and being strict and religious and all that. So, among his first acts, Savonarola takes huge numbers of Renaissance books out to the city square and burns them, just to demonstrate that this was wrong and we've got to go back to the straight and narrow path. A lot of historians think that Savonarola's reign was the end of the Renaissance in Florence, and this book burning could kind of symbolize that, but it's controversial to maintain that the Renaissance ends at this point.

Savonarola does in fact end. He doesn't last very long. In 1502 he makes the mistake of claiming that the pope is a heretic. The pope then sends forces to the north which eject Savonarola from power. He is taken down to the city square and burned at the stake as a heretic. So that was the end of Savonarola.

At that point, a republic is restored in Florence, with the chancellor being a man named Piero Soderini, and his right-hand man being a man I am sure you have heard of: Niccolo Machiavelli. This republic is a broader government than even the Medici regime was. It makes a number of concessions to the lower classes but is very unpopular with the patricians. Later it falls from power and the patricians bring back the Medici as dukes of Florence in the 16th century.

Lecture Nine
The Italian State System

Scope:

In this lecture, we will take a brief look at the other major political powers of Italy during the Renaissance period. Their governmental structures, foreign policies, and interactions will be examined, as well as their roles in Renaissance culture. We will also look at Milan and Venice, the two north Italian rivals of Florence, in some detail, while we make a briefer examination of the southern powers, the Papal States and the Kingdom of Naples. The dynamic interactions of all these states made up an important element of the Renaissance.

Outline

I. Milan was an industrial city of the far north in Italy and Florence's most dangerous rival.

    A. Milan was an industrial town that was smaller than Florence but still of significant size. It was linked to Florence in many ways, not the least of which was its main industry: the production of tools used in the woolen cloth industry.

        1. More important was Milan's location right at the foot of the Alps. The Alps divided Italy from the rest of Europe and saw tremendous traffic in trade and travelers passing between the two areas. Milan controlled nearly all trade routes north through the Alps and grew wealthy from the hefty tolls charged for passage.

        2. The Visconti family ruled Milan as dictators in the early Renaissance period. Their seat of power was a huge fortress that dominated one entire side of the city walls. They had emerged as rulers during the late Middle Ages and made no pretense, as did Florentine rulers, of maintaining republican government.

3. In the late 14th century, Gian Galeazzo Visconti began his campaign to create a Milanese empire in Italy. With a powerful military, he succeeded in subduing nearly all of northern Italy. During this period, Milan was the most powerful force in Italy, and the campaign was halted only when Gian Galeazzo died of plague and the siege of Florence was broken in 1402. These were the events that led to the birth of Civic Humanism in Florence.

4. Gian Galeazzo's successor, Filippo Maria Visconti, ruled Milan from 1402–1447. He was a less competent ruler and military leader than Gian Galeazzo, and although he managed to defeat Florence in a war in 1425, he eventually lost most of Milan's conquests in north Italy in conflicts with Florence and Venice. Even worse, when he died, he left no heir.

B. When a power vacuum developed in Milan, the Medici in Florence were determined to use it to their advantage to neutralize the rival state.

1. Cosimo de' Medici sent his private general, Francesco Sforza, and his army to conquer Milan and take power there in 1447. Sforza became the new dictator of Milan and Milan aligned itself as an ally of Florence.

2. Perhaps surprisingly, Sforza proved to be a good ruler for Milan. He built up the Milanese economy by introducing the cultivation of rice and silkworms in the Po valley. Like his patron Cosimo, he was a great champion of Renaissance art and learning. Under his rule, Milan became a center for Renaissance culture with such figures as Leonardo da Vinci working there.

3. Sforza's heir was Ludovico Sforza, known as il Moro ("the Moor") for his dark complexion. During his rule (1476–1500), Milan continued as a center of Renaissance culture. Sforza rule and the Renaissance in Milan came to an end with the French invasion of Italy, when this foreign power took control of Milan.

II. Venice was a state and power in northern Italy like no other.

    A. Built on a series of islands off the Adriatic coast by Roman citizens fleeing the barbarian invasions, the city had built-in defenses and soon became a major maritime commercial and naval power.

    B. In the Middle Ages, Venice joined with Genoa and Pisa to exploit the spice trade with the Middle East opened up by the Crusades. To protect this extremely profitable trade, Venetian naval forces fought frequent conflicts with Arab pirates and naval forces of the Byzantine Empire, a rival for the eastern trade. The major item the Venetians traded for spices in the Middle East was Florentine woolen cloth.

    C. Venetian society and government was unlike that of other Italian towns.

        1. Like other Italian towns, Venetian society was controlled by rich commercial families. But unlike in other towns, such as Florence, where nobles were banned, these Venetian families declared themselves nobles.

        2. Government office and even significant areas of the economy, such as the wholesale trade and ship owning, were legally limited to nobles.

        3. The number of noble families was fixed and no upward mobility into the class was possible. This resulted in the gradual shrinkage of the noble class over the years as families died out and were not replaced, creating a major social and political problem by the late 16th century.

    D. The Venetian government was also unique.

        1. The head of government, called the *doge*, was elected from the noble elite by the Senate, a hereditary body of 60 nobles. Together, the doge and the Senate ruled the city, depending heavily on a secret police that investigated anonymous accusations of disloyalty.

        2. The Grand Council was an assembly of representatives of all noble families, but it was not a functioning organ of government.

        3. Venice was a rigid society and stable government in the hands of a minority.

E. For much of the early Renaissance, Venice was content to ally with other cities, most notably Florence, in order to maintain the balance of power in north Italy.

   1. After 1450, however, certain factors forced Venice to begin a policy of expansion on the Italian mainland. Chief among these factors was the need to secure a mainland food supply, because Venice itself could not grow much food.

   2. Wars against Milan and Florence followed, and some territory was gained, but weaknesses in the economic and military structure of Venice limited and ultimately reversed most of these gains.

   3. Venice was, by 1500, entering economic decline. Her eastern trade had been severely hurt by a combination of factors, including Turkish conquests in the eastern Mediterranean and the competition of both the Dutch and Portuguese in the spice trade.

   4. Venice underwent a slow decline over the course of the 16th century.

III. The Kingdom of Naples was a major power in the south of Italy and another state that was different from the typical Italian city-state.

   A. Naples was the only state in Renaissance Italy that resembled the typical medieval state: ruled by a king, mainly rural with only one large town, nobles and poor peasants making up most of the population.

   B. Naples tended to ally with the papacy to create the southern axis of power in Italy.

   C. Naples also controlled Sicily and was sometimes called the Kingdom of the Two Sicilies.

   D. Naples was conquered by the Normans in 1054 and ruled by the French dynasty of Anjou until 1434, when it was conquered by Alfonso of Aragon. In 1498, Alfonso's line died out and Naples was claimed by Charles VIII of France, leading to the French invasion that was a turning point in the history of Renaissance Italy. The French conquered and ruled Naples for a while, but in 1503, Ferdinand of Aragon re-conquered Naples for Spain, and from him, that area passed into the empire of Charles V.

E. With its feudal structure and string of foreign rulers, Naples was atypical in Renaissance Italy.

IV. The Papal States was the secular domain of the pope in central Italy.

A. The Papal States was made up of a string of small states running in a band through central Italy from Rome in the west to the old Byzantine capital of Ravenna in the east.

B. In the early Middle Ages, the area had been controlled by Byzantine forces under Emperor Justinian and was called the *Exarchate*, for its ruler, the *Exarch*. Later, it was taken from the Byzantines by the Lombards, from whom it was taken by the Franks, who later gave it to the pope as the Donation of Pepin.

C. The pope made the Papal States into his own secular state, from which he collected tax money and levied troops. The pope believed that only by controlling a secular state would he have the power to remain independent of the secular powers surrounding him.

D. When the pope moved to Avignon in 1308, the Papal States declared their independence and the papacy lost their revenue. Not long after, the pope began a slow campaign to re-conquer the Papal States. Enough progress was made for the pope to return to Rome in 1378, but the last portions of the Papal States were not re-conquered until well into the Renaissance.

E. Many of the popes were great patrons of Renaissance art and learning and they turned Rome into a center of Renaissance culture. The Medici popes Clement VII and Leo X were especially significant in this regard.

Essential Reading:

Anthony Molho, *The Italian City Republics*.

Supplementary Reading:

Frederick Lane, *Venice*.

Questions to Consider:

1. How did rivalry between the Italian towns help to stimulate the Renaissance?

2. Was dictatorship or oligarchy the more effective system for ruling Italian towns?

Lecture Nine—Transcript
The Italian State System

In our last lecture we were looking at the political history of Florence as being part of the context for the growth of the Renaissance and humanism. I'm going to say a few last things about Florence here at the beginning of this lecture. Then we'll take a look at a few of the other major Italian powers during the Renaissance period and look at their political situations and economic situations and how they also helped to foster Renaissance culture, because one of the things we have to realize is that the Renaissance and humanism didn't just flourish in Florence, even though that's considered to be kind of the capital of the Renaissance. However, it flourished in many other towns and cities all throughout Italy and eventually all throughout the rest of Europe. So we'll see a little bit today about how that worked out, and it also gives us some interesting questions to ask, which I will try to pose at the end of the lecture, about the growth of the Renaissance and humanism.

I want to start out saying just a few last things about the republic which took power in Florence after the fall of Savonarola, at the beginning of the 16th century. You will recall from the last lecture that chancellor Piero Soderini and his close aide Niccolo Machiavelli were instrumental in setting up and ruling this republic. It was a much broader and more participatory form of government or form of the Florentine governmental system than had been around in quite a long time. The government was more democratic, if you will—but maybe "participatory" is a better word—than it had been under the Medici or really even under the Albizzi. So you have to go back almost to the Ciompi period to find a period of as much and as broad a participation in government. This, in fact, produced a controversy in Florence, because the republic ruled, in many cases, or governed, with the interests, not just of the patricians at heart, but the interests of the whole population, including the lower classes, at heart. This irritated many of the patricians in Florence and gave rise to interesting political debates, which we might want to consider now and just briefly again later.

The famous Florentine historian Francesco Guicciardini became the spokesman for the patrician party, if you will, in Florence during the Republican period. He argued that the republic as it was set up by Soderini was really not the best form of government for Florence, because it didn't contain enough experienced people, and according to Guicciardini, it was the patricians who had this political experience, and they who should really be in charge of the government and running things, because they knew the history of Florence, they knew the traditions of Florence, and they could better govern the city.

On the other hand, Machiavelli and Soderini argued that, no; in fact, a republic was the best possible form of government, just like the one they had set up, despite the fact that there weren't as many patricians in it. The reason for that was that the Florentine Republic was modeled upon the Roman Republic, and the Roman Republic had, of course, led to the great glory of Rome and the birth of the Empire. Obviously this Roman Republic had been a very successful form of government. By imitating this form of government, the Florentine Republic could also be very successful. So that was pretty much their argument.

This brings up another issue, and that is, is there any ideal form of government? Was the Roman Republic the best government? If the Florentine government imitated it, was it the best government? The people in the republic of Soderini and Machiavelli pretty much argued, "Yes. There is a perfect government, and that is a republic, because it's based on the Roman Republic." Guicciardini, on the other hand, argued that, "No, there really is no one perfect or ideal form of government. Governments have to adjust and be flexible, and it's whichever one works best in the particular circumstances that you have and the particular conditions that you have, that is the one you should adopt and will help the city be more prosperous. So there really is no ideal form of government."

This also leads us into a question which we'll take further a little bit later on, and that is, to what extent did political forms, governmental forms, influence the birth and growth of Renaissance culture and humanism? In Florence you could easily make the argument that the broad participatory government in Florence in its republican form throughout the years, and even during the Medici to a great extent, promoted the growth of civic humanism and the need for civic education and therefore the birth and growth of the Renaissance. That's a very effective argument.

The problem with that is that there were many other centers of Renaissance culture which were not broad, participatory governments—which were really anything but that—and we see Renaissance culture flourishing there just as well. So what is the role of politics in the birth and growth of the Renaissance? Or, perhaps, is economics a more important factor? We've seen in Florence that the woolen-cloth industry was extremely important in providing the money for the growth of the Renaissance. Is a successful and prosperous economy the one thing that most importantly promotes the growth of the Renaissance and humanism?

I think that Cosimo and Lorenzo de Medici probably thought that peace and prosperity were the most important things behind the growth of the Renaissance, and in these other cities we're going to be looking at in just a second, you will see that their economic prosperity made them centers of Renaissance culture.

So we will turn next, after this brief look at Florence—we will turn next to the city of Milan. We'll look at the structure and history of Milan during the 15th century, essentially—late 14th and 15th century. Milan was a big city. It's one of the three most important cities in all of northern Italy, along with Florence and Venice. Like Florence, it was an industrial city, but it wasn't an industrial city based on the woolen-cloth industry. This made it a little bit different, because in most cities across Europe at this time the major industrial sector was woolen cloth, because that produces clothes, and people need clothes, and, after food, which the agricultural sector produces, clothes are the things that are in most demand.

But instead, Milan's industrial base was constructed on the manufacture of tools used in the woolen-cloth industry. So it was a tool-making industry, and because of this it obviously had many contacts with Florence, because it would sell its tools to Florence and to the woolen-cloth industry there. So there were important economic ties between these two even though there were also great political rivalries.

So the tool-making industry is one source of Milanese prosperity. Another source of prosperity for Milan was the fact that Milan is located right in northern Europe [sic Italy], at the foot of the Alps. Being located at the foot of the Alps means it pretty much controls the passes through the Alps, and the passes through the Alps are the trade routes. There is a lot of trade going on between Italy, Germany,

France in this period—even England, as we've seen. So if you control the trade routes, you have power. The Milanese did that, and they charged high tolls for people to move through the passes and carry on trade. So they got rich as toll collectors, as well.

In terms of the Milanese government, we've already seen that the prominent ruling family during the Renaissance was the Visconti family. They ruled essentially as dictators. They were appointed by the emperor as dukes, because Milan was legally, theoretically part of the Empire, but in fact Milan was completely independent, and the Visconti family ruled as completely independent rulers, or dictators. They weren't beholden to the emperor at all, and they didn't maintain any kind of a façade of a republic. They made it very clear: "We are dukes. We rule this place. This is not a republic. This is not a participatory government." It's very different from Florence.

We've seen that the first great Visconti was Gian Galeazzo Visconti. He's the one who conquers a lot of northern Italy, and virtually builds an empire in northern Italy in the late 14th century, until he becomes involved in the siege of Florence from 1380 to 1402. Of course it is during that siege that he (Gian Galeazzo) dies, and the siege is broken. That's the moment that civic humanism is born in Florence, as Salutati and Bruni realize that they have to change their educational system to make the city more viable. So Florence survived that crisis. Milan lost. Milan's power then began to shrink.

After Gian Galeazzo, the ruler of Milan was Filippo Maria Visconti. He was not nearly as capable a ruler or military leader as Gian Galeazzo, even though he did defeat Florence in a war in 1425. Between 1402 and 1447—he ruled for a fairly long time—he pretty much lost all of Milan's conquests in north Italy, and the hope of a north Italian empire just went with these.

Filippo Maria himself died without a male heir, and at this point Cosimo de Medici in Florence seized his opportunity. He sends his personal general Francesco Sforza with his personal mercenary army to conquer Milan, which happens between 1447 and 1450, and Sforza is installed by the Medici and, by this conquest, as the new ruler of Milan.

You might expect a kind of mercenary general who conquers a place by force and just kind of takes over wouldn't be a great ruler of the city, because he really wouldn't have the interests of the city at heart, but that wasn't the case with Sforza. Sforza actually became a very effective ruler of Milan and a very important figure in Italian politics, and a very important patron of Renaissance art and learning. We know that, right after he was installed, he signed a peace treaty with Florence which guaranteed peace and prosperity between these two cities. We also know, from the last lecture, that he was part of the Peace of Lodi in 1451, which was a northern military alliance designed to maintain the Italian balance of power. So there again, he's thinking—probably with a lot of advice from the Medici in Florence—he's thinking about the larger diplomatic situation in Italy. He's thinking about how to make his city more prosperous.

He also does not ignore the economic side of things, because he realizes that, while the economy of Milan is prosperous, it can always be improved and that things can always happen, so he takes measures to increase, to improve the Milanese economy. For example, he introduces the cultivation of rice in the Po Valley, and that was a really new thing for Italy. He also brings in mulberry trees and introduces silk worms, and starts a silk industry. That's very interesting, because what it shows is that Milan does not want to get into the business of being a competitor in the woolen-cloth business with Florence and other cities, because they couldn't ever really catch them in that area, but the silk industry is another thing. There were silk merchants in Florence, as well, but silk is a very high-value thing, purchased only by wealthy people. It's a luxury industry. It's not a high-volume industry. Therefore it didn't occupy huge sectors of the economy in Florence or other places. So he sees silk as a way to make the Florentine [sic Milanese] economy more rounded and more prosperous.

As I mentioned before, Sforza also was a terrific patron of Renaissance art and learning. He brought Leonardo da Vinci to Milan; he had "The Last Supper" painted there; all sorts of important contributions as a patron of the arts.

He was followed as ruler by Ludovico Sforza, his son, also known as il Moro or "The Moor," because he was very dark-complected, apparently. Ludovico ruled from 1476 to 1500. He continued to foster Renaissance culture in Milan, and Milan does, in fact, become a major center of the Renaissance. Unfortunately, it's Ludovico who is in charge of Milan in 1498, when Charles VIII of France invades Italy, and Milan is the first city in Charles's path. Charles's French army, as we mentioned before, was a much more effective military organization than anything in Italy at the time. Milan was easily conquered in the beginning of this invasion, just like Florence and the Medici would later be conquered. So, at that point, the Sforzas fall from power, driven out by the French invasion.

The French, then, rule Milan up to 1535, when it is conquered by Emperor Charles V of Hapsburg, the Holy Roman Emperor. That's where I want to leave Milan right now.

We'll turn next to the other major northern power, Venice. Venice was a very unusual city, built entirely on islands off the northeast coast of Italy, founded by Roman citizens fleeing to escape the barbarian invasions. In fact, it's quite far off the coast. Today if you go to Venice, you've got to drive across a very long bridge to get there. So it was very well protected by the sea. Largely because of its protected situation, and because of its merchant fleet, Venice was one of the major commercial cities of the Middle Ages—probably the most important commercial city in Italy during the Middle Ages. Along with the cities of Genoa and Pisa, it led a revival of Mediterranean trade between Italy and the Middle East after about the year 1000. This, of course, means all sorts of trade, but especially the spice trade. Venice got richer and richer by its participation in the spice trade. Spices would come overland, mostly from India, into the Middle East, and they would be purchased in the Middle East by Venetian merchants, the main competition being Byzantine merchants, up until the fall of Byzantium in 1453. Venice traded Florentine wool for these spices. So the Florentine woolen industry actually helped Venice become more wealthy, because it gave then an entree into the spice trade.

Venetian society was controlled by rich commercial families, just like Florentine society and every other town in Italy, just about. These rich commercial families controlled the economy and they controlled politics. Unlike in Florence, though, these rich commercial families declared themselves to be nobles. So we do, in fact, have a nobility in Venice; no such thing in Florence any more. Government office, as well as many sectors of the economy, as we shall see, was limited to nobles, but these are not typical medieval nobles. These are not rural, agricultural, feuding nobles. These are rich commercial families who just want to be seen at the top of society and who give themselves the designation of nobles. There were a fixed number of noble families in Venice. There was no upward mobility into the class. So that made for a stable society, in a way, but it also meant that, over the years, the nobility was going to shrink and shrink and shrink as families died off, as families generally do after a few generations, and no new families can move up. This becomes a major problem for Venice as the noble class or noble group shrinks and becomes less able to govern and less able to manage the economy, but, at least in the early Renaissance, this was not a major problem. It really didn't become a major problem until the 17th century in Venice.

In Venice, only nobles could own ships, which meant that only nobles would be the ones profiting from the very wealthy maritime trade, particularly spice trade with the Middle East. Also, only nobles could engage in wholesale trade, which was the most prosperous kind of trade, even though other people could engage in retail trade. So it really is a commercial nobility that was profiting from this.

The government of Venice is headed by an official, actually an elected official, called the doge. The doge is chosen, or I guess you would say elected, from among a small, elite group of noble families. He's the chief executive of the city. The legislative branch of government was called the Senate. That was a hereditary body of between 50 and 60 nobles. It was the Senate who actually elected the dodge; it was not a general election. The Senate would come together and elect the doge. The Senate did not include all the noble families. It included 50 or 60 chosen noble families—I guess the most important ones or those closer to the top.

There was another body, called the Grand Council, which included representatives of all noble families, but this was really just a rubber-stamp body. It didn't meet very often. It didn't really make important decisions, and was largely controlled by the doge and by the Senate.

The doge and the Senate were obviously the two most important governing entities in Venice. They governed by use of a very effective secret police force. There were spies throughout the city, there were policemen throughout the city, and people were watched and the society was regulated. The doge himself lived in a huge palace on St. Mark's Square, right next to the cathedral. The palace has a very interesting thing on the front side of it. The official symbol of Venice was the Lion of St. Mark, because during the Crusades, the story was, Crusaders from Venice had gone and found the bones of St. Mark and brought them back to Venice and put them in the cathedral. So Venice was known as the city of St. Mark, and his symbol was the lion. On the front of the doge's palace there was a little sconce kind of thing in the shape of a lion head, with its mouth open. What that was there for was that anybody—anybody in Venice—who thought there was somebody disloyal to the city or not patriotic or not doing his duty, you could write down an anonymous accusation. "I think so-and-so is not a loyal Venetian." You don't have to sign your name to it. Put it through that lion head, and the officials in the doge's palace are going to read it—put it through the mouth—they are going to read these accusations and they are going to send the secret police out to round people up, which happened.

Right behind the doge's palace there's a bridge over a canal—there are no streets in Venice; it's all just canals—and over the canal right in back of the doge's palace there is this arched bridge, called "the Bridge of Sighs." That's where they would take the essentially political prisoners from the doge's palace across to the prison and back, where people often spent many, many years, locked up for comparatively small offenses.

So Venice was a rigid society. The government was stable, but it was in the hands of a tiny minority. Nevertheless, it was a terrific center of Renaissance culture. It's not the dictatorship Milan was, but it's certainly not the republican participatory kind of government that Florence was. Yet, it's a very important center for humanism, maybe the second most important after Florence, and a very important center for art, especially, and the growth of Renaissance culture.

In the 1400s (15th century), Venice becomes an even more important political force in northern Europe [sic Italy], as it expands on to the mainland. I mentioned in an earlier lecture that one of the problems that Venice had was that, being out there on those islands, every inch of land is built up. There's no open land, so they don't have any place to plant food crops. They had depended for many years on the importation of food from the mainland, from various allied cities like Padua and Bologna and other areas. They would just simply buy the food, but it was clearly not a very good situation for Venetian security. The Venetians were sure that if they were ever besieged, and that supply cut off, they probably couldn't supply their whole population by ship. So, in the 1400s, they set out to create an empire on the mainland in northern Italy. They are kind of the successor of

Milan in this attempt to form an empire in northern Italy. They have pretty much success trying to obtain land to grow food on, which they directly control and they can rely on. Unfortunately, they are blocked in their conquest by an alliance, the important north Italian alliance of Milan and Florence, so Venice is ultimately unsuccessful in conquering any kind of mainland empire.

Its efforts to do so pretty much end around 1500. That's because the economy starts to have serious troubles in Venice around 1500. One of the reasons is that the Turks have conquered a good part of the Middle East, and this has disrupted the spice trade and other elements of Venice's Mediterranean trade. So that's a problem.

Another problem that we'll see, developing more in the next lecture, is that the Portuguese, first of all, then later the Dutch, actually find a way to intervene into the spice trade and cut off a good deal of the spice flow from Venice, and take it back to their countries and profit from it. These commercial setbacks really hurt the Venetian economy, because it was so dependent on maritime trade. Like I said before, the fact that the nobility is shrinking and becoming less able to really govern—it's becoming less able to handle the economic system; the government is becoming ever more rigid—but even while all this is happening, Venice is still a very important center for Renaissance culture.

There are only two other Italian powers that I want to talk just briefly about, and we might have a few minutes to consider a couple of questions. In the south, the two major powers (really the only two significant powers) are the kingdom of Naples and the Papal States. We'll talk just briefly about those two.

The kingdom of Naples is a very different place from anything in north Italy. In many ways, it doesn't really fit in with the Italian Renaissance very well, although Naples itself had a Renaissance culture—the city of Naples. The kingdom of Naples is a feudal monarchy. It has a king in charge of it. It has a class of nobles. It's a rural, agricultural state, and in that sense it really resembles a lot of northern European states much more than it resembles the north Italian city-states and even central Italian city-states. So it's a very different place. It also has passed through a number of different hands over the years. In 1054, the Normans, who come from the north of France, conquer Sicily and then, later, Naples. (Naples and Sicily make up the kingdom of Naples.) These Normans are the same ones who, a few years later, from the same place, will conquer England. The Normans rule Sicily and Naples for a number of years. The dynasty is an Angevin dynasty. They don't change very much. They just rule the area.

Then, in 1434, King Alfonso of Aragon invades Naples and conquers it, and he becomes the king. In 1434, Spain is not a unified monarchy, but Aragon is among the two or three most important kingdoms in Spain, and so they have now expanded into Naples, and they become kings of Naples, so it becomes a Spanish monarchy.

In 1498, the line of Aragon, the dynasty of Aragon, in Naples dies out. That's the opportunity that we see King Charles of France taking to claim the throne of Naples. He simply says, "Look. We conquered it back in 1054 (we French, we Normans). There was an Angevin dynasty there. We have as much right to it as anybody else. "Of course the Spanish Aragonese also said, "We have a right to the throne, too." There was a local claimant to the throne, as well. So in order to actually establish power in Naples, Charles had to invade. We have seen that he did invade in 1498. He marches south with his huge army, conquers Milan, conquers Florence. He gets Savonarola coming in, in Florence. He makes it all the way down to Naples, and he actually conquers Naples and establishes himself on the throne of Naples, but he finds that he can't stay there, that he's got to go back to France and tend to his duties as ruler of France, because, as we will see later on, the king of France is not yet powerful enough to be gone from the country for such a long time and not have trouble develop. So, not long after he conquers Naples he makes his way back north through Italy again, this time in a much more peaceful way, not having to conquer everybody for a second time.

After he leaves, the French claim just collapses. In 1503, the Aragonese come back. In this case it's Ferdinand of Aragon who conquers Naples, and once again Spain controls Naples. So Naples goes back and forth. It later on passes into the inheritance of the Holy Roman Emperor Charles V.

The only other power we need to mention right now, the only other major power in the south, is the Papal States, a very unusual power, because, first of all, it's not one state; it's really a series of small states. They stretch in a line from Rome in the south, kind of doing an S-shape up to Ravenna in the north, right through the middle of

Italy. They are all directly controlled by the pope. He is their secular ruler. The pope got these territories in the early Middle Ages. They used to be controlled by the Byzantines. The Byzantines had invaded Italy. The Franks conquered them from the Byzantines. The Franks—King Pepin of the Franks—gave them to the pope as the Donation of Pepin, and the pope then made them into the Papal States.

The pope depended on these Papal States for the revenues to run the Church, as we've already seen, but he also depended on these states for troops and for money to defend Rome and to defend the Church against its foreign enemies, because the Church was, essentially, a secular political player, and needed a power base from which they could draw recruits and draw money and taxes and put an army in the field and maintain the Church's independence. This had become very apparent during the Middle Ages during the clash with the Holy Roman Emperor. So the Papal States was an essential part of the pope's power, and it not only helped him run the Church, it also made him a major political player, a major secular ruler, in south central Italy.

Lecture Ten
The Age of Discovery

Scope:

This lecture will examine the period of European overseas expansion known as the Age of Discovery that took place as the Renaissance flourished in Europe. Some historians have argued that the renewed confidence in man's abilities fostered by the Renaissance gave Europeans the courage and curiosity to sail the world's seas in search of distant lands. However this may be, economic motives were clearly in evidence as first Portuguese, then Spanish explorers set off for far-flung destinations. The Portuguese pioneered a sea route to India to take advantage of the spice trade, and the Spanish discovered, explored, and exploited a whole new world in their search for riches. The Dutch, English, and French would become part of the expansion at a later stage. It was the beginning of European knowledge of other parts of the world—and the beginning of European imperialism.

Outline

I. The Age of Discovery began in a somewhat unlikely place, the tiny nation of Portugal.

   A. Portugal was a nation of poor farmland that had always looked to the sea for its prosperity. Maritime trade was important in Portuguese tradition.

   B. In the 15th century, its ruler, Prince Henry the Navigator, became interested in finding a sea route to India as a means of taking part in the wealthy spice trade.

      1. The trade in Asian spices originated in the spice islands of the East Indies (today Indonesia), moved on to India and then to the Middle East, where Italian merchants took the spices to Europe.

2. Because the Italians controlled the Mediterranean trade routes, the only way for other Europeans to enter the spice trade was to pioneer alternative routes. The chief of these was around the southern tip of Africa and on to India to interdict the trade before it reached the Middle East. The only problem was that no European had ever reached the tip of Africa.

3. Portuguese expeditions inched their way down the African coast until, in 1487, Bartolomeu Dias rounded the Cape of Good Hope and proceeded on to India. Ten years later, in 1497, Vasco da Gama took the first big Portuguese trading fleet along the same route to India. The Portuguese were now participants in the spice trade.

C. Several factors contributed to the Portuguese success in trade and exploration.

1. The Portuguese did not attempt to conquer or colonize the peoples they traded with overseas. They simply established bases and maintained good (and profitable) trading relations.

2. The Portuguese made a number of important innovations in ship technology, beginning with Prince Henry's patronage of map makers and interest in new navigational devices.

3. The Portuguese also were the first to combine on their ships two principal types of sail: the triangular lateen sail used in the light winds of the Mediterranean and the much bigger and heavier square-rigged sail used in the heavy winds of the Atlantic. Thus, Portuguese ships could maneuver under a variety of conditions.

4. To fend off pirates and rivals, the Portuguese were the first to put heavy cannons on their ships. They pioneered ship-to-ship artillery warfare.

II. The Spanish were the next power to enter the expansionist movement.

A. Spain had only become a united country in 1469, with the marriage of Ferdinand of Aragon and Isabella of Castille following the successful re-conquest of Spain from the Moors.

1. In 1492, Genoese sea captain Christopher Columbus convinced the royal pair of his plan to find a shorter and easier route to India and the spice trade by sailing west and circumnavigating the globe. He was given three small ships and set off on his journey.

2. After 33 days at sea, Columbus landed in the Bahamas, thinking he was in Asia. He went on to Cuba and Haiti before returning to Spain to report his discoveries to Ferdinand and Isabella.

3. Other expeditions followed, and by Columbus's death in 1506, it was apparent that he had not reached Asia but instead had discovered a whole new world.

B. Spanish exploration of the New World continued, and in 1513, Vasco de Balboa crossed Central America and discovered the Pacific Ocean. This rekindled Spanish hope for a westward passage to India.

1. During 1520–1522, Ferdinand Magellan set out to pioneer this westward route. His expedition succeeded in sailing around the world but at tremendous cost.

2. First, the distance was great. It took Magellan 98 days just to cross the Pacific. Second, the journey was dangerous. Ships were lost and many sailors died, including Magellan himself.

3. The Magellan expedition taught the Spanish that the western voyage to India was too long and expensive to ever be profitable. They gave up the idea.

C. The Spanish now focused on exploiting the riches of the New World, specifically South and Central America, to which they were still virtually the only claimants.

1. The Spanish, unlike the Portuguese, built their empire on conquest and colonization, not on trade.

2. Small Spanish armies used the benefits of firearms, horse-mounted soldiers, and terror tactics to defeat the native American states. Cortez conquered the Aztecs of Mexico in 1519–1521 with 600 men, 13 muskets, and horses. The Spanish took the Aztec emperor hostage, demanded and were paid a large ransom, then murdered the emperor. Pizarro conquered the Incas of Peru in similar fashion.

3. Spanish viceroys were put in charge of conquered areas and colonists streamed in to search for riches. Missionaries arrived to convert the native population. European diseases, such as syphilis and plague, also made their arrival and began to decimate the natives.

4. Colonists established large agricultural plantations worked by slave labor at first drawn from the local population, later brought from Africa. These plantations grew cash crops, such as sugar cane, to be sold in Europe.

5. Because many native Americans wore much gold jewelry and had many golden implements, the Spanish became convinced that there was a large source of precious metals to be found in the New World, giving rise to the legends about El Dorado, or the Seven Cities of Gold.

6. Spanish soldiers, called *conquistadors*, led numerous expeditions in search of this gold, Coronado even penetrating as far north as what is now Kansas. No golden cities were found.

7. In 1545, however, the Spanish did discover, high in the Andes of Bolivia, the Potosi mine, one of the richest mines of precious metals ever discovered.

8. Potosi had been worked by native Americans for generations. It contained gold, silver, and even jewels. The Spanish forced the native Americans to work the mine as slaves, smelted the ore on the spot, and loaded it aboard Spanish ships bound for the home country. Thus began the famous treasure fleets that left the New World almost yearly for nearly a century, packed with coins,

bullion, and other precious items mined, looted, or stolen in America.

9. As this treasure arrived in Europe, it was to lead to economic, social, and political changes across the continent that the Spanish could never have dreamed of.

III. After 1500, the European economy experienced a period of inflation and expansion as a response to several different stimuli.

A. Despite the fact that the treasure fleets all sailed back to Spain, their riches did not stay long in that country.

1. Spain had been constantly at war for generations, and to fight these wars, the crown had taken loans from mostly foreign bankers.

2. Now the riches from the New World had to be used to repay these bankers, and the gold and silver flowed right through Spain into Germany, Italy, and elsewhere in Europe.

B. For centuries, Europe had suffered from a shortage of precious metals because of the exhaustion of local mines and a trade imbalance with the East. Now, that shortage suddenly ended.

1. The gold and silver supply suddenly increased—by 1650, the silver supply tripled—and the result was booming inflation, the first in European history.

2. After 1460, the European population started to grow again for the first time since the plague, and this increased economic demand. Between 1460 and 1600, the population grew by 50 percent. Cities grew at an even faster rate.

3. Renewed political stability in Europe contributed to an increase in trade. Growing demand also increased trade volume, especially in the Baltic Sea region. Commercial profits rose. All of these factors kicked off a period of economic expansion.

4. Food prices increased. Over the course of the 16th century, the price of wheat increased by a factor of five.

5. The woolen cloth industry boomed as a result of increased demand for clothes. The English and German woolen industries led the way.

6. Banking grew, in part because of investment in trade. The Fugger bank of Augsburg was an example.

C. The constant increase of prices as a result of inflation and growing demand, along with the population growth, brought social change.

1. As the population increased, wage levels fell. This hit the lower classes hard because they were also faced with rising food prices. Peasant poverty increased.

2. High prices for food tended to enrich noble landlords whose estates were relatively self-sufficient. Those who depended on the market economy were also hit by higher prices.

3. The middle class profited from the increase in trade and banking and continued its economic and social rise.

Essential Reading:

Donald Wilcox, *In Search of God and Self*, chapters 9–10.

Supplementary Reading:

Charles Boxer, *The Spanish Seaborne Empire*.

———, *The Portuguese Seaborne Empire*.

Questions to Consider:

1. What would have happened had the Portuguese, rather than the Spanish, funded Columbus?

2. Was trade or colonization of foreign lands more profitable?

Lecture Ten—Transcript
The Age of Discovery

In the last several lectures we've been looking at Italy during the Renaissance period, in particular Florence, but also some other Italian cities. In the next couple of lectures we're going to expand our focus a little bit and look at the rest of Europe. In particular we're going to be looking at European overseas exploration and overseas expansion, which happened at the same time as the Renaissance, right along with the Renaissance, in fact. We're also going to be looking at some of the effects this overseas expansion had on Europe and the economy of Europe, European politics, and the development of European society. That will be the plan for the next couple of lectures.

You could argue that the new confidence that Europeans had coming from the Renaissance, this new desire to develop a whole new world and all, would have encouraged European overseas expansion and exploration. It makes plenty of sense that this new atmosphere would encourage exploration of other areas, but in fact, a lot of the overseas exploration and expansion occurred for purely economic motives. We'll see how that works out in this lecture. When we talk about European overseas exploration, perhaps oddly, we're going to be beginning with a tiny little Iberian state known as Portugal, which we haven't even mentioned in the course so far.

Portugal took the lead in the period of European overseas expansion, and was only later caught up to by Spain and other powers. It's not really that strange that Portugal would be a leader in overseas expansion, because Portugal was not a particularly wealthy agricultural state. It doesn't have the wealth of fertile soil that France does, for example. It tends to have rocky, hilly soils, and it's not very productive agriculturally. So the Portuguese had always looked to the sea and trading by ship (maritime trading) as their source of wealth. So it's not really surprising that they would be the first ones to engage in overseas exploration. In the 15th century, Prince Henry the Navigator of Portugal became particularly interested—he was interested in all kinds of exploration—but he became particularly interested in finding a sea route down around the bottom of Africa and then on to India. The point of this was to intervene in the spice trade. The Italians had the spice trade from Italy through the

Mediterranean to the Middle East pretty much locked up. So it wasn't going to be easy to be involved in that, but there were other possibilities for getting to India, because the spices came to the Middle East largely from India, but also from Indonesia. They came overland into the Middle East and then they were taken by the Italians through the Mediterranean.

But Henry thought it might be possible to find another sea route and go directly to India and sort of cut out the middleman (the Italians), and intervene directly in the spice trade. The problem is, and if you look at maps from this period you can tell, geographical knowledge was still very, very limited. No one knew how long Africa was, and no one knew how long it would take to get around it or even if you could get around it. So Henry started out by patronizing sailors and mapmakers to explore in this area down around Africa. They made many, many expeditions down the coast of Africa. They went first to the Azores and they went to Africa, and they would inch their way down the coast, mapping the coast as best they could, going a little ways every time, until they would finally find the end of it. That discovery came in 1487, when the explorer Bartolomeu Dias rounded the Cape of Good Hope and continued on to India. So he did prove that it was possible to sail around the southern tip of Africa and go all the way to India. He himself just had a small exploratory party, but 10 years later the Portuguese sailor Vasco da Gama, in 1497, took the first big Portuguese trading fleet on the same route around the southern tip of Africa to India. At that point, the Portuguese became very involved in the spice trade, and Portugal became a very prosperous country almost immediately.

In this activity Portugal did not create colonies. They did not attempt to colonize the areas they went to. They didn't attempt to conquer the native peoples that they met. All they wanted to do was trade, and pretty soon they are trading all the way from India to Indonesia, which is another really big source for the spice trade. Of course, Portuguese ships are key in this trading network. A couple of advances that Portuguese shipmakers and sailors made really accounted for a lot of the Portuguese success in this area. One of the innovations the Portuguese made was creating a new kind of rigging for ships. Up to this point, when you talk about the sails that sailing ships have, there are basically two kinds of ships and sails. If you're talking about the Mediterranean, where there's not a lot of wind and the winds are mild, ships were usually smaller and the sails were triangularly shaped. The point of that is that you're not going to catch a lot of wind, because there's not a lot of wind, but the triangular sails can be easily maneuvered around, so you can catch the wind coming from any direction. That makes your ship maneuverable and able to sail in light winds.

On the other hand, if you're in the Atlantic, which was the other main area Europeans sailed in, there you have high winds, and the ships are mainly equipped with these huge square sails, which would catch vast amounts of wind and move the ship across the Atlantic. What the Portuguese did was, they combined both these kinds of sails. They put triangular sails at the front and back of ships and used square ones in the middle, and that way they could do either thing. They could catch small winds or they could catch big winds. They could go faster, farther, in different kinds of circumstances. That was one thing they did.

Another thing they did was pioneer the use of artillery on their ships. Up until this point, even fighting ships (navies) didn't really use much heavy artillery. Most ships had what they called "castles" built up on the back and front of them. The way ships would fight each other is that they would put soldiers in these "castles," these built-up places, and just like soldiers on the land, they would shoot arrows or fire firearms or attack the enemy in that way. They didn't really use artillery. The Portuguese began using cannon on ships. This proved a lot more effective than putting lots and lots of soldiers on ships—especially effective because it was good defensively. They weren't out, really, to attack anybody. They just needed defense in case someone attacked them. These cannon provided good defense with a much smaller crew. You didn't need a huge group of soldiers to man them. The Portuguese were very successful at doing this and were later imitated by everybody, as you know.

So the Portuguese kick the whole period off and become very prosperous in the spice trade. By 1492, a lot of people are interested in the spice trade, in particular, a Genoese sea captain named Christopher Columbus, who starts to believe that there is yet another sea route to India that could get someone involved in the spice trade; not around the southern tip of Africa, not through the Mediterranean; he thinks it would be possible to sail all the way around the world and back, and get to India that way. This again shows you the severe lack of geographical knowledge. People didn't really even know how big the world was. So Columbus could legitimately believe that maybe sailing around the world might even be shorter than going around Africa, because unless you can find a shorter route, it's not going to be a lot more economical, and you won't be more successful than the Portuguese, for example.

You know the story. Columbus eventually convinces the king and queen of Spain, Ferdinand and Isabella, who just recently united Spain into one country, to finance his try to sail around the world and reach India and get Spain involved in the spice trade. So Columbus sets off with his three ships, is at sea for about 33 days—which to us doesn't sound that long, but his sailors were almost desperate towards the end—and finally he reaches land in the Bahamas. You can almost imagine—he thought he was in Asia. He thought he had reached Asia. You can almost imagine him getting off the boat, looking around and saying, "Hey! Where are all the Japanese?" He didn't find what he thought he would find, but he still thought he was in Asia. He continued on from there to Cuba. He went to Haiti. Then he went back and reported his findings to his patrons.

They were all excited because they thought he might have been to Asia, as well. He made a number of additional voyages. He came back, sailed down the whole coast of Central America, sailed off the coast of Venezuela, sailed to other Caribbean islands, and really mapped and charted out a large part of that area. He never found any Japanese, but he named the natives he did find "Indians" because he thought he had reached India. He was convinced to the end of his life that he had indeed reached Asia.

By the time of Columbus' death in 1506, it was pretty clear to most people that he hadn't gotten to Asia, but that he'd done something even more amazing: he had discovered a whole new world, a completely new world that nobody had ever known about before, that was there to be explored, and who knows what else? Imagine the excitement of this, if, all of a sudden, we discovered another Earth right next to ours, that hadn't been explored at all. Imagine the possibilities that people must have been feeling about this new world that could be explored, and who knows what riches might be there, and so forth. Of course, the Spanish were quick to take advantage of this opportunity. Many more Spanish explorers began sailing over to what became known as the "New World" and later as "America."

But they never gave up the idea of getting to Asia. So far they hadn't given it up. In 1513, a Spanish explorer named Vasco de Balboa crossed the isthmus of Central America and discovered the Pacific Ocean. To him, this suggested, "Maybe if we just sail across this ocean we'll find India, and we'll find Asia, and we'll get into the spice trade." So again, it seemed possible to do that—to circumnavigate and get into the spice trade in Asia.

Of course, the guy who tries to do it is Ferdinand Magellan. His trip around the world, from 1520 to 1522, had an outcome that the Spanish really didn't expect: it convinced them that, yes, you can go around the world and you can go to Asia, but it's too dangerous a trip. It's much too far, it's much too expensive, and it will never, ever, be profitable to engage in the spice trade this way. For example, it took 98 days just to sail across the Pacific, and when they realized that, they just gave up the idea of circumnavigating the globe for the purposes of the spice trade.

Spain now focused on colonizing America—the New World. For that, of course, it sends over its *conquistadors*, and begins a long process of subjugating most of Central and South America. Unlike the Portuguese, the Spanish built their empire not on trade, but on conquest and on colonization and on exploitation of native peoples. So it's a very, very different process from what the Portuguese were involved in. Many famous *conquistadors* were involved in this process, of course. Cortez, for example, conquered the Aztec empire in Mexico between 1519 and 1521. He did so with an army of 600 men, 13 muskets, and a few horses. With that force he brought down the very large empire of the Aztecs.

How did he do it? For one thing, there were the muskets. The Aztecs, of course, had never seen firearms. They had never seen muskets. These muskets were large, bulky things. You had to load them in the muzzle. They had a fuse on them. They were so heavy, you often had to put them on a tripod to fire them, although you could possibly carry them. They were terribly inaccurate. The barrels, of course, were not rifled. When the gun went off, the shot would spray everywhere, and you had to be very close to somebody to actually hit them. So they weren't terribly effective militarily, but when you fired these muskets with black powder, they gave off this huge flame and all this smoke, and it was a scary, scary thing that really panicked the Indians who faced these muskets, not because they were really lethal that much, but because they were just frightening.

The other thing is the horses. There were no horses in the New World; therefore, the Aztecs had never seen horses. They thought they were monsters, and the Spanish themselves—large people, larger in stature than the Aztecs, with suits of armor and helmets and all these fancy things—so this essentially panicked the Aztec forces. You had these giant people riding on monsters, charging them, firing these flames at them. It just caused the Aztec armies to break and run, and made the Spanish conquest pretty easy.

There are other aspects to the Spanish conquest, such as the fact that they kidnapped the Aztec emperor and held him for ransom. They got paid the ransom and then killed him anyway. It's a pretty sad story, but the Spanish effectively conquered Mexico that way, and they conquered the rest of Central America. Pizarro conquers the Incas in Peru in much the same manner. By about 1550, all of Central and South America is in Spanish hands. Spain sends officials it calls viceroys who come over. A viceroy is somebody who rules in the name of the king. The viceroys are set up in special districts and they rule directly on the authority of the king in Spain. The rule the area directly. There is no autonomy left to the people living there.

Also, the Spanish begin to set up huge agricultural plantations. They begin to grow cash crops, which they then send back to Europe for sale, and they make lots of money off these cash crops, like tobacco and sugar cane and other kinds of cash crops. Because the amount of land in Europe was limited, it seemed unlimited in America. You could have these huge plantations. Of course, one of the problems is that you've got to have labor to work these plantations, and that is later on going to lead to the import of slaves into the area, which begins to happen a little bit later after the Spanish conquest.

Something else interested the Spanish. Ever since Columbus's day, they had noticed when they came over that a lot of the natives they met seemed to have an awful lot of gold things—gold jewelry, gold implements—and they would ask them where they got them, and they would never really get a straight answer. The Spanish developed this theory that somewhere in the New World there must be an immense amount of gold that these Indians were getting all their gold stuff from.

That led to the theory about El Dorado, the City of Gold, somewhere, waiting to be discovered and basically melted down by the Spanish and taken back to Europe. So they start to search all over for El Dorado or whatever other kind of gold they can find. They go everywhere. The *conquistador* Coronado comes up into North America and goes as far north as Kansas looking for El Dorado. Of course, they never find it, but they do find something else.

Down in Bolivia, in the mountains, the Spanish stumble upon what is, in fact, the wealthiest silver and gold mine anybody had ever seen. It was called the mine of Potosi. It was worked by the local Indian population. It turned out precious metals. It even turned out jewels. It was probably better than finding El Dorado, because you don't have to melt this down. All you've got to do is get it up out of the mine. Of course, there are not nearly enough Spanish to do this mining, so they conquer all the local Indians and turn the local Indians into slaves, virtually. They send them down to the mines. They bring the precious metals up. They have smelting furnaces right there on site. They smelt the precious metals. They make them into either bars or coins or other objects, and they put them on ships and they send them back to Spain—whole fleets, entire fleets full of gold and silver and other precious things, going back to Spain every single year. These are the famous "treasure fleets." A lot of these Spanish who are involved in this trade become wealthy beyond their wildest dreams, and Spain itself, in some ways, becomes quite wealthy from it.

These discoveries and explorations had a profound impact on wider European society and the development of the European economy and the European political system. We'll just finish up this lecture by talking about some of the social/economic impacts of it, and then we'll take a look at the political impacts of it in the next lecture.

So, huge amounts—fleets loaded with gold and silver—coming back into Spain. Now, you'd think that that would make Spain the world's wealthiest nation. In fact, it does turn Spain into a major power, militarily and economically, but one of the problems is that almost as soon as the money came back into Spain, it really flowed out of Spain. The reason for this was that Spain had been constantly fighting wars: the wars of unification, the wars in other areas in Europe. They had taken out many, many loans to fight these wars from foreign bankers, and as soon as the gold and silver flows into

Spain, they pretty much owe it to the bankers they have taken loans from. So the money goes out of Spain, like a revolving door, into the coffers of mainly German and Italian bankers who had supplied the previous wars that Spain had fought.

So Spain does not get the opportunity to invest these riches in its economic infrastructure. Some wealthy, upper-class people in Spain become even wealthier by keeping some of the money, but it doesn't really fortify the Spanish economy. However, it does give Spain enough wealth to build a powerful military apparatus. Spain pretty soon has the biggest, most effective infantry in Europe. It has one of the biggest fleets and best-equipped fleets. So militarily they do prosper from it.

As the silver and gold and other precious items spread all over Europe, it really revolutionizes or changes in a profound way the European economy. There had long been in Europe a shortage of precious metals. The gold and silver mines were just simply mined out, and there weren't really very many other sources of specie coming into Europe. Another problem was, when Europeans traded with Asia, in many cases the Asians would only accept gold and silver as payment. They didn't want European goods. So there was a precious metal drain out of Europe to Asia. Now, the first thing that happens is the balance of trade is restored. Precious metal is coming in to Europe from the New World, stays in Europe for a little time, and then a lot of it flows back out to Asia in the Asian trade.

Also, the European money supply grows. By 1650, for example, the supply of silver has just about tripled, and any time you introduce a large amount of new money into the money supply, which is essentially what's happening, you have inflation. That's what happens here in this case. The influx of precious metals into Europe kicks off a booming period of price inflation all through Europe.

An interesting thing happens from this price inflation. I mean, a lot of things happen from it, but one of the interesting things is, it was misunderstood, because the European economy really had not experienced inflation in hundreds of years—maybe never. They really didn't understand what inflation was. So when, all of a sudden, prices started to go up and profits appeared to be going up, they thought, "Well, the economy is expanding. We're doing great." As a result of that, many businessmen expanded their businesses and expanded their trade, and began trading on a bigger scale, and the inflation actually led to a period of real economic growth, which wouldn't happen in the modern world, where inflation is considered a plague. However, it really set off a period of true economic expansion that had all sorts of consequences.

Another reason that we see inflation and prices going up in Europe during this period is that after about the year 1460, the European population starts to increase again. That, of course, is the first time the European population has increased since the plague. Historians are not clear exactly why, in 1460, the population began to go up again, but it did. As a result of that there was an increased demand for food, to begin with, for clothes and other items, even for manufactured goods, and this drove up prices but also encouraged business expansion.

Another aspect that helps the European economy, that we will come back to later, is that Europe at this point is engaged in a period of relative political stability. This political stability, peace, and prosperity, for the most part, as we've seen in Renaissance Italy, does lead to economic prosperity and cultural flourishing, and all this also had an effect on the wider European social scene.

Let me say a few things about how increasing population affected Europe in the years after 1460, and then we'll bring this lecture to an end.

It's very hard to have specific figures about population growth in the early modern period, because records were just simply not that accurate. There are good tax records remaining from certain cities, like Florence, for example (the *Catasto*), and certain countries like England kept very good treasury records and from that you can trace taxes; you can trace households. You can make an estimate of the number of people in the household, and you can get an idea about the population. So from these kind of rough ways, we estimate that between 1460 and 1600, European population grew by about 50%, which is a dramatic population growth.

Cities grow even faster. The general population is growing, but at the same time, populations of cities are growing and people are moving into cities. So urbanization and the increasing size of cities goes at a faster rate than even the general population growth. To give you an example, London, in the century between 1500 and 1600, goes from a city of 50,000 people to a city of about 200,000 people, which makes it one of the top couple of cities in all of Europe.

Prices continue to go up. Increased demand for food and other things drives prices up. When you look at the overall economic situation, food prices tend to drive other prices. So when food prices go up, it brings other prices along with them. During the course of that century, the 16th century, which is a century of economic expansion, the cost of wheat, for example, increases about five times. That's important, because wheat is a staple of everybody's diet. Most peasants live off of different kinds of grains, usually not totally wheat, but barley, oats, rye, other kinds of grains, but the upper classes are more reliant on wheat, because they make white bread from the wheat. When wheat prices go up, it just elevates grain prices in general, food prices in general, and all prices in general.

Along with this, the growing demand of a growing population causes trade volume to increase all around Europe. The two main trading areas nearby Europe are the Mediterranean, which the Italians still pretty much dominate, and then the Baltic area, which the Dutch and the Swedes dominate pretty much. These are two very different trading areas. In the Mediterranean, the top trade is the spice trade still, even though the Portuguese have cut into it. In the Baltic, on the other hand, the trading is more in bulk goods: wheat coming from the Ukraine; timber, tar, and pitch used in ship making; lumber used in ship making, coming from Scandinavia. All these things are brought back, largely on Dutch ships, to Amsterdam and other Dutch cities, where they are stored up and sold to the rest of Europe, and the Dutch are making a lot of money in this trade.

Industry begins to expand all across Europe. The demand for clothes is going up, so the demand for woolen cloth is going up. Here, especially, the English and German woolen cloth industries really expand. The Italians are a little bit lagging behind in this expansion as far as woolen cloth goes.

Banking expands. No longer are the Italians the main bankers. There are a lot of other bankers now, a lot of bankers in Germany, for example. The well-known Jacob Fugger the Rich establishes the Fugger Bank, which later on has a key role in the Reformation. A lot of important money is being made in banking in this period.

Social change begins to happen. As the population goes up, wages go down. As wages go down, peasants can't afford to buy food, and they are miserable. However, as the population goes up, prices go up, and the owners of agricultural plantations, the nobles, they get higher prices and they get higher profits. They are making a lot of money, and they are happy. So there's a gap between rich and poor. That's another important social aspect of change in this period.

Lecture Eleven
Inflation and New Monarchy

Scope:

This lecture will survey developments in European economic and political life prompted by the great influx into Europe of New World treasure, largely on Spanish ships. A great period of economic inflation transformed the European economy. Price rises corresponded with the beginnings of population growth to stimulate a period of economic expansion. These economic factors also played a role in the changing nature of European monarchy as countries rebuilt their governments on a new basis after the near-collapse of the 14th century. Instead of partnering with nobles for power, kings now chose to work with the middle class, which encouraged the rise of this class at the nobility's expense. After 1500, Europe entered a long period of economic and political expansion.

Outline

I. By the 16th century, the crisis of the 14th century was but a distant memory for most Europeans.

    A. The Renaissance and Humanism beginning in Italy had brought a new confidence and optimism to many people.

    B. Population growth after 1460 ended the depopulation crisis of the 14th century and its related problems.

    C. Economic expansion caused by demographic growth ended the depression of the plague's worst years.

II. The Age of New Monarchy: European governments began to reconstruct themselves after the collapse of the 14th century and the earliest beginnings of the modern state were in evidence.

    A. Medieval monarchy had been built on a partnership between the king and his nobles, many of whom were as rich and powerful as the king himself.

        1. This partnership broke down in the 14th century because of the increased cost of warfare, which caused tensions between king and nobles, and civil wars and economic depression, which weakened nobles.

2. By the 15th century, kings were rebuilding their power based on new foundations.

B. New Monarchy began to grow after 1450 in a de facto way but, because of conditions, on very different foundations from medieval monarchy.

   1. Nobles were beginning to be replaced as the king's governing partners by the middle class. Rich middle-class merchants and bankers began to purchase government office, as well as nobility, and they started to form a new professional administrative class.

   2. Although kings made an effort to exclude nobles from positions of great power, at this early date, this could only be partially accomplished. Nevertheless, their lessening role in government, as well as the inflation of nobility caused by kings' sale of titles, contributed to the decline of the nobility while the middle class profited from its increasing commercial wealth and role in government.

   3. Kings began to build powerful new bureaucracies and armies, mostly with middle-class money.

C. But the higher prices brought by inflation and economic expansion affected kings as well, especially when it came to building bureaucracies and armies. These effects only accelerated the growth of New Monarchy.

   1. It simply cost kings a lot more to run government. On the military side, costs were increasing quickly because of the evolution of firearms and the need to pay mercenaries, but even the costs of day-to-day administration of the government were increasing.

   2. Kings were forced to collect more in taxes to cover these costs.

   3. To accomplish this, even bigger bureaucracies were needed, which in turn, cost even more money. More offices were sold to raise needed money.

   4. The practice of sale of office raised money for the royal treasury but led to ineffective operation of the bureaucracy. We will examine this further in later lectures.

5. The modern military bureaucratic state was beginning to emerge.

D. New Monarchy in France began with Louis XI.

    1. In the early 15th century, France could barely be governed by its king, and the government still lay in ruins from the Hundred Years War.

    2. Many nobles were strong and relatively independent of the king, and the royal government was small.

    3. The taxes the king could levy directly were few. Most taxes had to be voted by local assemblies called *Estates*. The army consumed fully one-half of royal revenues.

    4. Louis XI (1461–1483) began to reverse some of these trends and started France down the path to New Monarchy. His biggest contribution was reasserting the power of the monarchy by confronting and defeating in battle the most powerful and independent of French nobles, Charles the Bold of Burgundy. Although a vassal of the king, Charles was in the process of turning Burgundy into an independent state. After Charles's death, Burgundy was brought safely back under royal control.

    5. The increasing power of the French monarchy was demonstrated by the 1498 invasion of Italy by Charles VIII, who claimed the crown of Naples.

E. The greatest of all the French New Monarchs was Francis I (r. 1515–1547).

    1. He continued the practice of sale of office to raise revenue and increased the size of the bureaucracy.

    2. He emphasized the hiring of middle-class officials in the bureaucracy instead of nobles whenever possible. He began the creation of a new professional governing class.

    3. In 1516, he obtained from the pope control over all church appointments in France and began to use church wealth and power to benefit the state.

F. The New Monarchy in Spain developed along different lines.

1. Medieval Spain had been a collection of small feudal states. In 1469, Spain was unified into one kingdom by the marriage of Ferdinand of Aragon and Isabella of Castille.

2. Because Spain lacked a significant middle class, hiring middle-class bureaucrats for the government was not possible. Instead, the monarchs took advantage of Spain's large and partly impoverished nobility to hire minor nobles who could be counted on to be loyal. Unfortunately, they could not supply the crown with much money.

3. The crown controlled appointments to the Spanish church and used this mechanism to increase royal power.

4. The crown consolidated state power by enforcing religious uniformity: In 1492, Jews were expelled from the kingdom, and in 1502, Moors were expelled.

G. New Monarchy in England began with Henry VII.

1. The first New Monarch of England, Henry VII (1457–1509), came to the throne following the disastrous civil war known as the War of the Roses. He established the Tudor dynasty.

2. Henry had large family land holdings and funded his government with his own money to avoid having to deal with Parliament. This allowed him greater freedom of action.

3. He established the Court of Star Chamber, a royal court in which a royal judge could try Henry's enemies while avoiding English common law and its guarantee of trial by jury.

4. His successor, Henry VIII (1491–1547), consolidated royal power and established control over the English church as a result of divorcing his queen. We will learn much more on this in a later lecture.

H. The Holy Roman Empire (Germany) was governed differently.

1. The Holy Roman Empire was the only major European power that did not go down the path of New Monarchy.

2. It was still a dynastic state of many different political entities and almost no central government, held together only by its ruler, Charles V, who was elected in 1519. Charles was Flemish, born in Gent. When elected emperor in 1519, he was already king of Spain, as the grandson of Ferdinand and Isabella. From his grandmother, he had inherited Burgundy and The Netherlands.

3. Charles V thus presided over a worldwide empire, including the Holy Roman Empire; Spain; Spanish possessions in Italy, the New World, and the Pacific; and The Netherlands. He could not possibly rule such a vast territory effectively. In the Holy Roman Empire, real power devolved upon local nobles known as the princes. Each one of their tiny principalities functioned almost as a sovereign state. Thus, Germany was following a trend of political decentralization, the opposite of the rest of Europe. This will help to explain why the Reformation started in Germany.

Essential Reading:

George Huppert, *After the Black Death*, chapters 1–2.

Questions to Consider:

1. Would the modern state have begun to evolve without the 14th-century crisis?

2. What was the most important single difference between medieval monarchy and New Monarchy?

Lecture Eleven—Transcript
Inflation and New Monarchy

By the 16th century, Europe had pretty much recovered from the 14th-century crisis. The Renaissance and humanism, which started out in Italy, had ended the pessimism and despair that the 14th century had brought. Population growth, beginning around 1460 and continuing on for the better part of a hundred years, was ending the depopulation brought on by the plague years. Economic expansion caused by, number one, population growth and, number two, the influx of American treasure, had ended the economic depression, which stretched from about 1350 to 1450. We also are going to see in this period, and in this lecture, that there is significant political restructuring and rebuilding going on. That has to do with the birth of what we call New Monarchy. New Monarchy in the 15th, 16th century, is a rebuilding of royal governments (monarchy) that had collapsed in the 14th-century crisis.

You might recall from one of the first lectures in the course that medieval monarchy—which was really very different from what we're going to see evolving in the Renaissance and Reformation period—had been based on a partnership and cooperation between the king and the important nobles of the kingdom, because these important nobles were very wealthy and very powerful, and the king really couldn't rule without their help and consent. This cooperation, this partnership which caused medieval monarchy to work, had collapsed in the 14th century largely due to the pressures of warfare and other economic conditions. As we've seen before, long, expensive wars, like the Hundred Years War between England and France, had driven a wedge between the king and nobles. The king is now having to hire mercenary soldiers; he's having to buy firearms; he's not able to rely on the nobles anymore as his knights and armor and fighting wars for him, essentially for free. So he's got a lot of economic problems, and the king kept on going back to the nobles asking for more and more money to fight wars, more and more contributions, and they did make their contributions, but after a while they just got fed up with it and they said, "We're not going to pay any more money." The king insisted they pay more money. They refused. Essentially the king and nobles became more adversaries than partners by the end of the 14th century.

That was a real problem. When the structure of monarchy breaks down like that, kings just became unable to really govern their kingdoms. Another factor was that nobles themselves were declining in power. They were fighting civil wars with each other in the 14th century, killing each other off, spending lots of money doing that. The economic depression came in and hit their landed wealth and drove prices and profits down. So nobles are declining in power and the monarchy can't rely on them anymore.

And even kings—kings are losing tremendous amounts of power by the end of the 14th century, because warfare has exhausted their treasuries and their partners in government have turned away from them, and they just don't really have many options left. So medieval monarchy really collapsed in the 14th century.

By about 1450, we start to see monarchy being rebuilt, but on very different foundations than before, and it's going to become a very different animal than it was before. In the first case, I will just go through some of the differences here, and then we'll look at some specific examples of new monarchs and what they did.

One thing that happens is that kings attempt to replace nobles in government with middle-class officials. Now, at this early stage (we're talking about 15th, 16th century), there's only so much of that you can do. There are going to be nobles in the government because there are some powerful nobles here and there, and you can't get rid of all of them, but the kings are attempting, whenever they can, to take nobles out of office and put loyal, middle-class bureaucrats who just follow orders in office, to make the government more responsive to what the king wants. That's one aspect.

The second aspect that's happening is that wealthy, middle-class merchants, bankers, industrialists, etc., are actually purchasing government office, and they are purchasing nobility—both of these from the king. This has a significant impact on government, as we will see in a few minutes. These middle-class people who purchase office and nobility are going to turn into a new professional administrative class, which is going to be the main staff for this new monarchy, this new kind of government. So the king is going to attempt to rule without nobles as much as possible, and with the aid of middle-class bureaucrats and their money, because don't forget that nobles can't be taxed, but middle-class people can be taxed. They are commoners. So the king becomes extremely reliant on taxing the middle class. That's another aspect of the way the monarchy is rebuilt.

Finally, kings need to build large new bureaucracies and large new armies to enforce their power—bureaucracies largely to collect taxes and armies both to fight foreign opponents and to fight domestic opposition. Both of these are differences. Big bureaucracies and armies are differences from the Middle Ages. Medieval monarchy really did not involve big bureaucracy. For most medieval kings, the entire central government was their court and their household officials—the chamberlain, the chancellor, the constable, the steward, the marshal, people like that—a very small circle of people who ran the central government. Even tax collecting was contracted out to independent agents. So there really weren't large bureaucracies at all in the medieval monarchy. So this is going to be a big change.

Also, medieval armies were small—until the 14th century, at least, they were small—and they were fairly cheap when you could just call on your nobles to fight for you. So these big, new professional armies is going to be another big change that we're going to see in monarchy. This is really the beginning of the evolution of what you might call the modern military bureaucratic state, although it's a long process. It's going to start, say, around 1450, continue on through the 17th century, into the 18th century, but this is the beginning point.

There are very definite social consequences to these kinds of changes. Nobles are declining in power. Now, true, they start out as the top group in society. They have a lot of power so they have a long way to decline, but they really are declining. They have a lesser role in government than they used to. Because middle-class people are buying nobility, there's a phenomenon known as the inflation of nobility, which means the more nobles there are, the less each noble title is worth and the less prestige each noble has. That's also hurting noble power.

On the other hand, the power of the middle classes is going up. They have more role in government, although it's still in an early stage, it's still just kind of getting started. They have more political power in the new monarchy, and they have great wealth, which they make in the economic expansion in trade, in industry and in banking and areas like that. So we're starting to see a trend that really will continue through the 18th century—in fact, through the end of this course—the decline of the nobility and the rise of the middle class, and it is really connected to changes in the state as well as in society.

What exactly set off this change in monarchy? What started the growth of New Monarchy? You might look back and say, "Well, monarchy in the Middle Ages, in the 14th century it collapsed, so they had to rebuild it, they had to do something." However, there wasn't that immediate recognition that something could be done or what should be done. It really was more economic conditions which forced things to happen and actually molded this new image, this new shape of monarchy. We are talking here about the economic expansion that is the result of geographical expansion into the Americas. We're talking about the inflation, the price climbs, all through the 16th century. Expansion and especially inflation means that it just simply costs kings a lot more money to run the government than it ever had cost them before, and they simply have to find a way to get this money. Other things that are costing them even more money: firearms are advancing, getting more complex, more expensive; artillery, hand-held firearms—all this you have to purchase for your military—the use of mercenaries. All that is causing the cost of government (doing business as a ruler) to increase.

So really, the only thing kings can do in this situation is they have to increase taxes, and to increase taxes they have to get someone to go out and collect these taxes, so they have to get a big bureaucracy to collect the taxes that they need to feed their expenses, especially their military machine. We see them relying more and more on the sale of office and the sale of nobility. Both of these things are not really new. In France, at least, the sale of office goes back into the 13th century to Philip Augustus, and in other countries almost that far, but in the Middle Ages it was a small thing. It wasn't really a major thing. Now the sale of office starts to become a major source of royal revenue, and kings become dependent on it, and they've got to go on selling offices, and the more they sell, they have to create more to keep selling more, because they sell them all out, and this creates a problem. There are other problems the sale of office creates, as we will see later on in the course.

Sale of nobility is also a case in point. Kings do it for financial gain now. In the Middle Ages it hadn't really been a source of big revenues. Now it's becoming a source of big revenues, and also causing increased tension between king and nobles who don't want to have their titles devalued. Big new armies to enforce royal rule; big new bureaucracies; this is all something very new and something, in a way, very modern. This marks it as a different system from the Middle Ages.

Let's take a look now at some specific examples of New Monarchies and how they developed. We'll start off in France, and then we'll continue on with Spain, England, and some other examples.

In France in the 15th century, before the real beginning of New Monarchy, the kings were hampered by a number of things. They were hampered by the fact that nobles were still fairly strong—so strong that especially local nobles could create opposition—and they were hampered by the fact that the king still had, at this early stage, a pretty small central government, so he didn't really have the power to reach out and control all areas of the country.

Another problem the French king had was that a large part of his tax revenues had to be voted by local assemblies known as estates. These estates usually were provincial estates (provincial assemblies). They were representative assemblies where the three different estates, the nobles, the clergy, and the commoners, would all send their deputies to meet and hear the king's plea for money. Then they would have the ability to vote yes or no on whether they would grant new taxes in their province for the king. There were a few taxes that the French king could just levy directly, like the *taille* and a few others, but they didn't make up nearly enough revenue for the royal government to prosper. So having to have these local votes on taxes was a real problem, and the king often got turned down. Stack that up against the fact that even at this early stage, the royal army ate up fully one-half of the king's total revenue. So that means that these early kings of France in the 15th century have a real revenue problem.

Louis XI, who becomes king in 1461 and rules until 1483, takes over the French monarchy (the French throne) at a low point, at the very end of the Hundred Years War, which France had sort of won, but it bankrupted the country. The country was ungovernable. It was torn up by war. Really, it was just a disaster, and Louis had to figure out some way to rebuild the monarchy and the country from this terrible low point it was at.

To make matters worse, one of the French nobles, the duke of Burgundy, who ruled Burgundy, a substantial province in the south, had become so powerful that he was essentially an independent ruler. He was a rival of the king of France for power in France, so much so that he even expanded his power into the Netherlands and the Low Countries and was building, in fact, his own state. You could say, in a way, that in this early period Burgundy was not a part of France, because the duke was so powerful and such a thorn in the side of the king. Probably the most important thing Louis XI does is he goes to war against Burgundy, he wears them down, and he defeats the duke of Burgundy, Charles the Bold, in 1477, and brings Burgundy back into allegiance to the king of France, which is really a big step, because if they had lost Burgundy, if they had become an independent nation, then the king would have been seriously weakened.

The next king, Charles VIII, who rules from 1483 to 1498, is the one who invades Italy. He has this claim on the kingdom of Naples. He invades; conquers Milan; conquers Florence; marches down to Naples and claims the throne there, but then has to come all the way back to France because the country is not really governable when he is not there. All these military efforts in Italy seriously weaken the French monarchy. It costs a lot of money. It distracted the king from things at home. That was really a setback in the growth of the French monarchy.

The turning point for France was the rule of Francis I, who ruled from 1515 to 1547. He is the first truly New Monarch that we find in France, and a major European figure—a major figure in European politics. He sets France on the path towards a stronger new monarchy. One of the things he does is he greatly increases both sale of office and sale of nobility.

Sale of office, especially, is a deceptive thing. It brings you two things. It brings you instant money in your treasury, because these offices are expensive. They are sold to middle-class people with money, and it brings you an instant bureaucrat, because the guy has just bought the office. The trouble with it is, when that person buys an office, that office becomes his personal property. It no longer belongs to the king or the state, and the person who buys that office can essentially do with it what he wants to.

The king hopes, of course, that he will get the official, he will get the money, and the official will do his job—collect taxes, keep records, whatever the job might be—and the person might well do that. However, the person also might not do that, and if he doesn't, what you've just done is you've chopped off a part of your own government and sold it like a piece of cake. That's not a very good direction to be going in. A lot of officials didn't do the job they were supposed to do, or they would keep a lot of revenue for themselves and only pass a bit along to the king. So it's a real double-edged sword, the sale of office, because the kings of France become dependent on it for revenue, and so it's both a good and bad thing.

Francis also makes an attempt to put more middle-class officials in government office, and to kind of nudge out the nobles wherever he can, although he can't nudge them all out, or even a majority of them, but he's on the way to creating, as much as he can, a new administrative class for the country: a loyal, middle-class, administrative group.

Another big thing Francis I does is, in 1516 he makes a deal with the pope. This goes back to the pope's battle with the Conciliar movement. You will remember after the Great Schism was healed, the Church council really did take control of the Church for a while, and the pope had to make deals with kings to get their backing against the Church councils. This was a kind of a late stage in these deals being made by the pope with the king. This deal gave Francis control over almost all important Church appointments in France, so he could appoint the people he wanted to the Church. That meant that he could control the Church's wealth and the Church's power and use it for the purposes of the state, which is a big advantage when you're trying to build up the power of the state. So Francis I, by the time he dies in 1547, has re-established the French monarchy on a pretty strong foundation.

We'll move next to Spain, and talk a little bit about Spain. Spain is an unusual case, because for most of the Middle Ages it was controlled by the Moors and was not a unified kingdom. There was a long war of re-conquest to make it into a Christian, unified kingdom. In 1469, this process comes to a kind of climax when Spain is united into one kingdom by the marriage of Ferdinand of Aragon and Isabel of Castile. That's a very important turning point in the creation of the Spanish state.

Now the king and queen of Spain have the problem of building up the power of the monarchy as it's being built up in other countries, especially right to the north in France, because Spain and France are rivals, and if France is increasing the power of the king, the Spanish have to do the same thing to keep up. Unfortunately, the king and queen of Spain cannot remove all the nobles out of government office and replace them with middle-class people, because Spain doesn't have much of a middle class. However, Spain does have a very large class of nobles, and many of the nobles towards the bottom of that class are pretty poor and pretty dependent on royal favor. So what happens in Spain is that more powerful nobles are edged out, and weaker, smaller nobles are brought in who will be more responsive to the king, because they are more dependent on the king for their welfare, their fortunes, and for their whole livelihood. So that's a first step, and it's similar to what is happening in France.

Also, the king and queen of Spain make a deal with the pope, and they get control over Church appointments in Spain. So they get the same power of the Church behind them that we see behind the king of France.

What happens in Spain which is a little bit different from other countries is that the king and queen of Spain consolidate their power by enforcing a very strict religious uniformity. You have to be Catholic in Spain, or else you are going to be in trouble. This becomes a political tool, because the king says, "I am the protector of the Church, and therefore if you do anything against the Church you do something against me." So heresy also becomes treason. The king and queen set out to enforce religious uniformity. In 1483 they establish the Spanish Inquisition, which is a court of traveling judges who go around the country hearing cases of people accused of heresy or people accused of treason, which is really the same thing in Spain now. People are locked up; people are executed for being heretics/disloyal to the monarchy. So the king and queen use the power of religion to support their own political power.

In 1492, the last Moors are driven out of Grenada, so that part of Spain becomes Christian. The same year, all the Jews are expelled from Spain by the monarchy and their wealth is confiscated. In 1502, all the Arabs are expelled. So pretty soon you've got a very solid Catholic country, and that means a very solid country loyal to the king, because these are almost the same thing in Spain.

On to England. In England, the first New Monarch is Henry VII, who comes to the throne in 1485 and goes to 1509. He comes in, again at a low point like we saw in France, at the end of the War of the Roses, which was a war between two noble families for control of the English throne. Both of these noble families, Lancaster and York, essentially lose out in this war and Henry, who is a member of the Tudor family, establishes a brand-new dynasty and sets on the road to restore royal power. One of the ways he does this is by doing what the English call "living off his own," meaning he paid a large part of the government expenses from the revenues of his own private estates and private lands. So he's using his own personal money to pay for the operation of government, which didn't really happen in France and didn't really happen in Spain. The reason it happened in England is because the alternative—if you want tax money, you have to go to the Parliament, the House of Commons, get their consent to new taxation. This has been the tradition in England since the Middle Ages. It's a very strong tradition. No king can overcome it. Once you go crawling on your knees to Parliament for tax money, they will ask you to make concessions. They will take away parts of your power and you will be weaker. You will be dependent. So not having to do that is a big plus. Henry was happy not to do that. He was happy to use his own money to pay for the operation of the government.

Henry also established something called the Court of Star Chamber, which becomes a major institution in English government all the way up until the 17th century. The Court of Star Chamber is essentially a royal court, where Henry can take nobles, largely, who oppose him, put them on trial for treason, and get them convicted. Why did he have to establish a new court for that? Well, other courts in England operate by English common law, and that means that everybody accused of a crime gets a trial by jury of their peers. So if you've got a noble you are accusing of treason, and you take him to a common law court, he's going to get a trial with a jury of nobles, and you can imagine what's going to happen there. They are not going to convict him. They are going to let him off because they don't want to see the king's power increased, and Henry knew this. He knew he's never going to make progress if he has to depend on common law courts. So he decides to set up a whole separate court system, the royal court system, of which the Court of Star Chamber was the first one.

It doesn't replace common law. It's just a parallel court system. The difference is the royal courts don't operate on English common law. They operate on the Justinian Code, the law of the Roman Empire, recently revived by the humanists and studied intensively. Justinian Code or Roman law says that when somebody gets a trial, it's in a court with a judge appointed by the king. So Roman law gives tremendously more power to the king, the monarch, the emperor in the case of Rome, than would otherwise be the case. That is exactly why Henry sets up this parallel court system and starts trying his opponents with Roman law. People don't like it; people in the common law courts don't like it; Parliament doesn't like it, but there is nothing they can do about it. Henry is exercising his power.

He is followed by Henry VIII, who rules from 1509 to 1547, who continues to consolidate royal power with the help of several important prime ministers, the first of whom is Thomas Wolsey and the latter of whom is Thomas Cromwell.

You probably know that the main issue in Henry's rule was he needed a divorce from his wife Catharine because she was childless. He had no male heir. He was afraid his dynasty, the Tudor dynasty, would come to an end after two kings. So he wants to get a divorce and he wants to marry his mistress and get a male heir, he hopes. You can't just get a divorce in the Catholic Church, so he sent a messenger down to the pope to ask the pope for special permission to get a divorce so he could remarry, and the whole process. Unfortunately, he found the pope, we might say, indisposed.

The pope had just been involved in a war as an ally of the king of France, in an alliance called the League of Cognac, in which they were fighting in Italy against the Holy Roman Emperor Charles V, who had expanded his power into southern Italy. He was threatening the pope. The French didn't like this imperial influence in Italy, and so the pope and France fight this war of the League of Cognac against Charles V, the Holy Roman Emperor, but Charles V wins. He captures Rome and he puts the pope in jail.

When Henry VIII's officials come down and say, "Could you please give our king a divorce?" Charles V tells the pope, "You know, he's asking for a divorce from Catharine of Aragon, and she happens to be my niece. We have a nice alliance with England right now because of this marriage, and I don't want to see it spoiled, so if you grant this divorce, you're going to rot in jail." So the pope says, "No. No divorce."

At that point Henry fires his prime minister, Wolsey, hires a new prime minister, Cromwell, and decides to break with the Catholic Church and establish the Church of England, of which he himself is the head. We'll talk a lot more about this later in the course; there's a lot of Parliamentary legislation that goes into making this break, but they essentially do break away from the Catholic Church and establish a new church. Then what happens essentially is that Henry grants himself a divorce, but as a by-product of this he's got control of the Church: Church appointments, Church monies, Church lands. He takes Church land. He sells it off to the highest bidder and puts the money in his treasury. So he has greatly increased royal power.

The only place in Europe we don't see a New Monarchy developing is in Germany, where Charles V is Holy Roman Emperor. The problem there is that Charles V doesn't just rule Germany. He has inherited the rule of a massive worldwide empire. He's king of Spain, also, because he's a grandson of Ferdinand and Isabella. He is duke of Burgundy, because his grandmother was Mary of Burgundy. He gets elected emperor because his father was the previous emperor. So he controls this empire that includes Spain, Germany, the Low Countries, the Philippines, Spanish America, Spanish Pacific possessions—a vast empire that he can't possibly govern—and there is no way he can establish a new, centralized monarchy to control these vastly separated lands with all different problems. The lack of a New Monarchy in Germany is going to be a major factor in the rise of the Reformation there.

Lecture Twelve
Renaissance Art

Scope:

In this lecture, the new style of art that emerged during the Renaissance will be examined. The Renaissance was one of the greatest periods in art history, and this lecture will offer one interpretation of the evolution of the Renaissance style. Patronage patterns will be examined and changes in these patterns will help to explain the changing style of art. We will look at the great artists of the early Renaissance and note the contributions of each toward the emerging Renaissance style. The lecture will also look at how the giant figures of the High Renaissance—da Vinci, Michelangelo, and Raphael—mastered the techniques developed by early Renaissance artists to create some of the greatest masterpieces of all time. Finally, we will explore the place of art within overall Renaissance culture.

Outline

I. Changing patterns of patronage taking place during the Renaissance had a profound impact on the emerging style of Renaissance art.

    A. In the Middle Ages, the main patron for art was the church.

        1. The church had the money to buy art and it exercised control over the artists producing it.

        2. Not only subjects of artworks were determined by the church but often how the subjects would be painted and sculpted.

    B. During the Renaissance, the increasing wealth of lay society led to a demand for art from that sector. Art was seen as a stable investment in unpredictable economic times.

        1. Lay patrons did not control artists as the church did; thus, working for lay patrons gave individual artists more opportunity to express their own artistic originality.

        2. Greater artistic individualism was a key in the development of many of the new techniques involved in Renaissance style.

C. Religious feelings also helped mold the new style of art.

    1. As will be seen in more detail in later lectures, the 14th-century crisis had encouraged among the population an upsurge in personal piety. This personal piety tended toward a more emotional expression of religious faith and a more active involvement in religion.

    2. Both wealthy families and guilds built more churches, chapels, and altars and needed art to decorate them. The new Renaissance style of art was influenced by this emerging emotional piety.

D. The Renaissance style of art can be thought of as a kind of visual rhetoric designed to move the will and heart of the viewer to religious piety.

    1. It did this by using the elements of art—color, line, and shape—to manipulate the eye of the viewer and cause it to focus on the point of greatest religious emotion in the painting or sculpture.

    2. This would get the viewer emotionally involved in the subject of the artwork and move his or her will to piety.

II. The great artists of the early Renaissance pioneered different techniques that would help to achieve this new style of emotionally charged art.

A. Giotto (c. 1266–1336) was the first pioneer of this new style.

    1. When he painted Madonnas, he did not paint them as saintly figures, as had been done in the Middle Ages, but rather, he portrayed them as real women with all the human emotions of motherhood expressed on their faces. Viewers could easily understand and identify with these emotions.

    2. Giotto painted a series of paintings of the life of St. Francis that also stressed emotional expression.

    3. His series of paintings on the life of Christ portrayed the human side of Christ with his emotional sufferings.

    4. Giotto's masterpiece, the *Lamentation*, portrayed the love and anguish of Mary and the disciples at the death of Christ. It is located in the Arena Chapel in Padua.

B. Brunelleschi (1337–1446) transferred Giotto's techniques to architecture.

    1. When he designed churches, he used architectural line to manipulate the eye of the viewer inside the church and cause the viewer to focus his or her eye on the point of greatest emotion in the church: the altar, where the central miracle of the church—the mass—took place.

    2. He revived Classical Roman architecture and built the most famous structure in Renaissance Florence: the cathedral dome.

    3. No dome had been constructed in Europe since antiquity; for this reason, Brunelleschi went to Rome, where he meticulously studied the construction of the dome on the Pantheon before returning to Florence to build what has been called Brunelleschi's Dome.

    4. In other buildings, he revived the rounded Roman arch and Classical lines.

C. Masaccio (1401–1428) continued the stylistic innovations of Giotto and Brunelleschi.

    1. He studied the way Brunelleschi used lines of perspective in architecture, then pioneered the use of three-dimensional depth perspective in painting.

    2. At first, he created the illusion of depth by painting figures inside architectural frameworks to exactly copy Brunelleschi's lines. Later, he developed and used grids to create three-dimensional space.

    3. The use of the three-dimensional technique was not only to give the illusion of realism but also to lead the viewer's eye around the painting to focus on the point of most emotion.

D. Fra Filippo Lippi (1406–1469) and Piero della Francesca (c.1412-1492) were two other important early Renaissance painters.

    1. Lippi painted Madonnas of great emotion.

    2. Francesca specialized in depth perspective and even wrote a book on the technique.

E. Lorenzo Ghiberti (1378–1455) founded the Renaissance style of sculpture.

1. He won a contest to construct the doors of the Baptistry in Florence. His giant bronze creation he called *The Gates of Paradise.*

2. In multiple panels depicting biblical scenes, he used line to simulate rhythmic movement, producing a stark realism in imitation of nature.

F. Donatello (1386–1466) was an outstanding early Renaissance sculptor.

1. He trained with Ghiberti and traveled with Brunelleschi to Rome, where he studied Roman sculpture.

2. Returning to Florence, he revived Classical Roman sculpture with all its realism and admiration for the human body. His bronze *David* was the first Renaissance nude.

G. The greatest universal genius of the early Renaissance was Leon Battista Alberti (1404–1472).

1. Painter, architect, scholar, and theoretician of art, he was born to a Florentine family rich from the wool trade.

2. By the age of 20, he had written a Latin play in Classical style, become a brilliant organist, invented a machine to raise sunken ships, and studied art and architecture in Rome.

3. As an architect, he built in the Classical style.

4. As a Humanist, he wrote a book on architecture modeled on Vitruvius.

5. He wrote *On Painting* in 1435, the first scientific treatise on painting. He also wrote the first book about home economics, *On the Family,* in 1443.

III. The artists of the High Renaissance perfected the techniques pioneered in the earlier period. This period represented the zenith of Renaissance art and was dominated by great geniuses.

A. The great Leonardo da Vinci (1452–1519) was a painter, architect, engineer, and sculptor.

1. Only 15 of his paintings survive, all among the greatest masterpieces of all time.

2. His greatest talent was in portraying human psychology and emotion in his subjects.

3. His *Last Supper* in Milan shows the reactions of the disciples at the moment Christ reveals he will be betrayed.

4. As a scientist, da Vinci had great botanical knowledge, which he transferred to his paintings.

5. As an inventor, he envisioned the airplane, helicopter, tank, and submarine.

6. He worked for Lorenzo de' Medici in Florence and Ludovico Sforza in Milan.

7. His masterpiece, today called the *Mona Lisa*, was bought by the king of France for the greatest sum of money ever paid for a painting to that time.

B. Raphael of Urbino (1483–1520) specialized in painting Madonnas of great serenity and humanity. He made special use of perspective and geographic form.

C. Michelangelo Buonarroti (1475–1564) was a genius at painting, architecture, and sculpture.

1. He portrayed his subjects in moments of psychological transition, when their faces most clearly revealed the inner self.

2. His great marble statue of David portrays the hero at the moment of his confrontation with Goliath.

3. His greatest masterpiece is the Sistine Chapel ceiling, painted on commission for the pope. It is a masterpiece of Neoplatonic symbolism.

D. The artists of the High Renaissance perfected the Renaissance style of emotion and realism and provided one of the greatest periods of artistic advance in history.

Essential Reading:

Michael Baxandall, *Painting and Experience in Fifteenth-Century Italy*.

Questions to Consider:

1. What similarities do you see between the Renaissance style of art and Humanism?

2. What did art contribute to Renaissance culture?

Lecture Twelve—Transcript
Renaissance Art

One of the greatest contributions of Renaissance culture, of course, was art: painting, architecture, sculpture. So in this lecture we're going to take a brief look at the Renaissance period of art, because it really is one of the greatest periods of art in the whole history of Western art, and introduces a new and distinctive style to art that really makes it unique and characteristic of the Renaissance period. We're going to see changing patronage patterns. We're going to actually see a very important change in artistic styles. We're going to see different motivations for the art. This will all end in the production of some of the greatest artistic masterpieces of all time.

What I would like to argue in the beginning of the lecture here is that most of these important changes that we see in art can be tied to broader cultural, social developments in the Renaissance itself. So it's really of a piece with most of the other things we've been looking at in the Renaissance so far.

We'll begin with patronage patterns, because this really is something that influenced the development of Renaissance art a great deal. In the Middle Ages, the main patron for art had been the Church, and the Church was a good patron for art. It paid for quite a lot of art, but the Church often had a very distinct idea of not only what it wanted painted or created in terms of art, but how it wanted it done—the style it wanted it done in. This tended to create a kind of unified style among all the creators of these artistic pieces that perhaps inhibited individualism. In the Renaissance, however, we start to see different patronage patterns. The Church, of course, is still an important patron, but now, lay people—princes, patricians, as well as merchants even lower down in the middle class—are important patrons of art. They buy a lot of art, and they generally don't tell the artist how to paint things. Often they don't even tell the artist what to paint. Sometimes they do, but normally not, and they almost never get involved in the style of the painting. So this tended to free up artists to express more of their own individual styles, and develop more of their own individual styles without the Church requiring certain things.

Another important thing is that the Renaissance is a period of increasing wealth in lay society. We've already seen that with the plague and the demographic collapse that the population was reduced, but the number of people that were left were really more wealthy, because they had inherited the money of the family members who were deceased. So these people tend to buy a lot of art, because they have a good deal of money to spend. So the demand for art goes up. We've also seen that in the 14th, 15th century, in the period of the economic depression, that art was considered a good investment. It was stable; gains in value all the time; safe, and for that reason it was a very popular investment in the depressed economy, and that also increased the demand for artwork. We're not talking just about paintings, but we're talking about the building of chapels, the creation of sculpture, and all sorts of things that we'll take a look at during the lecture.

So art is a good investment, but art also being freed up to express more of an individual style on the part of the artists. That's certainly one really important factor, but another important factor in the distinctive Renaissance style of art that evolves, I would like to argue, comes from religious changes that we haven't talked a lot about yet in the course, but I want to just touch on briefly here.

During the 14th century, when the Church had been in such a crisis with the Babylonian Captivity and the Schism, the Church had really lost a lot of its ability to be the spiritual leader of the people. At a time when there is the plague and the Hundred Years War and famine and all that, and when people really needed the guidance and spiritual comfort of the Church, it was so involved in its own problems it didn't really have the opportunity to provide the comfort and guidance and leadership that the people needed. For this reason, and in kind of miraculous fashion, common people began to develop their own distinctive religious practices. This was known as the development of popular piety. They developed their own religious practices, which usually involved actively doing something, and were always very emotionally oriented, because this is what people were interested in—active involvement in the religion so they could feel closer to God, and safer, and a very emotional involvement. So popular piety was a religion of great emotion.

Just to give you one example: In the Middle Ages, when people went to Mass, they would just go in the church and stand in the nave (there were no pews), listen to the Mass (it's always in Latin and they don't really understand Latin, so they don't know what's going on), and they would leave; not a very fulfilling religious experience. Part of popular piety was the development of the rosary necklace, where while you're standing there listening to this Mass in Latin, which you don't really understand, you can say prayers to the Virgin and count the prayers on these beads by moving them across on the chain, and feel like you're actually speaking to God and getting closer to heaven that way. So it's an active, involved, emotional kind of religion.

Another example: Stations of the cross were invented during this period. Pilgrimages became very popular. So popular piety was people taking religion into their own hands and creating a religion of great emotion and great activity that they could be involved in. What I would argue is that this popular religion of emotion really influenced, in a big way, the Renaissance style of art, because these same people, a lot of these same people who are involved in popular piety, are buying the art. They want to see their religious feelings and their point of view or perspective reflected in the art.

Another really important fact that feeds into this is the humanist belief in rhetoric. We've already looked at the fact that humanists believed that rhetoric was incredibly important—eloquence was incredibly important—to inspire and motivate the will of people to get people to live a good life and make good decisions and be good citizens. I think this also, this humanistic influence, had an impact on the distinctive Renaissance style of art, because you could almost say that Renaissance art becomes a kind of visual rhetoric. It tries to do some of the same things in pictures and images and forms that humanists were trying to do through rhetoric and eloquence and beautiful Latin and great communications.

What do I mean by that? For example—and this is a very important example—painters, first of all, and then other artists, begin to manipulate elements of painting, like shape or line or color. They do this to get the eye of the viewer to go to a certain place in the painting as soon as the viewer looks at the painting. So what the artist is trying to do is get you, if you're looking at a painting, when you first see it, to focus on a really important point in the painting, and they used shape, line and color to lead your vision to that point.

What kind of point are they trying to lead you to? Usually it tends to be the point of most emotion in the painting. Most of these paintings, even though they are done for lay people, are still on religious topics. So it would be the point of most emotion in a religious scene. The point of this visual rhetoric in painting, and later in other forms of art, is to get the viewer emotionally involved in the religious scene that is being portrayed by focusing your view, for example, on a face with definite emotions on it, or another point of great emotion. It will get you involved. You will experience the religious scene that's there, and perhaps it will inspire you to piety. I think that really goes along with the humanist belief in rhetoric and also popular piety's belief in a kind of emotional religion.

The pioneer of this Renaissance style is a painter who actually lived and worked very early: Giotto, who lived from 1266 to 1336, years usually thought to be before the Renaissance, but Giotto is considered to be the pioneer of this particular Renaissance style of painting. He made a number of important early pioneering contributions. He kicks off what I call the "early Renaissance period" in art, where a lot of the techniques are pioneered and developed and tried by artists, and to a great extent perfected. In the later High Renaissance we find tremendous geniuses coming along, who use these techniques already tried and pioneered, and carry them to an even higher level.

What did Giotto do? One of the things he did was he painted Madonnas, such as *The Madonna Enthroned*. His contribution there is that he painted these Madonnas as real people, with emotions. In the Middle Ages they had always been painted as saints or godlike figures with really no emotion on their faces, but the effort here was to get across the message that Mary was a woman, a real person. She suffered. She had emotions. You can identify with that when you see her emotions. So he wanted to get across the idea that these Madonnas were not godlike, even though in a way they were divine. Here also was a very human figure that people could identify with and feel the same emotions and feel close to and feel involved with. In a certain sense, when you feel that way, you feel protected by the religion, when you feel part of such an important icon of the religion.

Giotto also did a whole series of paintings on the life of Saint Francis, including *The Death of St. Francis*. Again, the effort is to portray St. Francis as a person, with great emotional expression on his part and on the part of other people in the painting. So people again could identify with it and feel a part of the scene, feel like they understood what was going on, and feel closer to the religion that way.

Giotto did, as well, a series of paintings on the life of Christ, such as *The Baptism of Christ*. Again, these focus on emotions. Now, Christ being half God, half man, you can't portray as just being a simple mortal, but he attempted to show that Christ was a person with love and compassion and emotions that other people could identify with and understand and feel a part of. This is a very different style from medieval religious painting. You could call it a secular style, but the object is not secular. It's not just saying, "Well, you know, Mary was really a person," or, "St. Francis was really a person." The point of it is to get the viewer emotionally involved in the religious scene or experience that's being portrayed.

Giotto's masterpiece was called *The Lamentation*. That's in the Arena Chapel in Padua. This shows the love and the anguish of Mary and the disciples after they've taken Christ down from the cross, and he's dead, and they are experiencing his death. In this painting you see people experiencing death in a way that people experience death: with sadness, with a kind of love, but anguish about the whole thing. It really comes through, and this is an important piece of work.

Giotto just kicked off these trends. Many people came along to continue them. In architecture, one of the important early pioneers was Brunelleschi, who lived from 1377 to 1446. He made a really interesting contribution because he looked at Giotto's paintings and he said, "What I want to do is use Giotto's methods, but I want to do it in architecture," and the way he would do it, for example, when he designed a church as an architect, he would use line—the architectural lines of the building, the inside of the building—so that when a person entered the church, their eyes would follow these architectural lines and automatically focus on the altar, the altar being the point of greatest emotion in the church. That's where the sacrifice of the Mass occurs. So that's what you should think about when you go into a church. Christ's sacrifice. The Mass. Brunelleschi is getting people to focus their attention on that when they first go in.

Brunelleschi also, in a more humanistic kind of fashion, revived the Roman classical style of architecture. Perhaps he is most famous for the fact that he built the domed roof on the top of the Florentine cathedral. This was a really important contribution, because the Florentines had built this cathedral, and the central part was an octagon. They hadn't really figured out what kind of roof to put on it. Somebody said, "It should be a dome. A dome would work perfectly on this octagonal shape," but nobody had designed and built a dome since antiquity, and no one knew how to do it. Brunelleschi volunteered to do it. He went to Rome. He studied Roman ruins there. Particularly he studied the Pantheon, which has a Roman dome on it. He measured it, and he basically figured out how to build a dome again. He comes back to Florence. He builds the cathedral dome, and it becomes known as Brunelleschi's dome, the first dome built since antiquity. It makes the dome a kind of characteristic part of Renaissance architecture.

Brunelleschi also pioneered other aspects of Roman [sic Renaissance] architecture, for example, the classical straight lines and the rounded arch, which you see in buildings he designed such as the Pitti Palace.

Continuing on in painting, Masaccio continued the work of both Giotto and Brunelleschi. Masaccio—for example in his picture *The Resurrection of Theophilus' Son*—studied Brunelleschi's use of lines of perspective: how you can use these perspective lines to focus people's view, in the architectural case, on the altar of a church. Masaccio decided he would use these lines of perspective to create three-dimensional depth perspective in painting. So he was really the pioneer of three-dimensional depth perspective in painting. At first he painted his figures inside architectural frameworks, so he could use the actual architectural lines used by Brunelleschi. Later on, he uses a grid and he abandons the architectural frameworks. He creates the illusion of depth, of three-dimensional space, on a flat surface, perhaps partly for the purposes of realism, but also because the depth perspective also guides the viewer's eye to certain points in the painting that the painter wants you to look at first, which is going to be the point of most emotion.

Fra Filippo Lippi, another early Renaissance painter, lived from 1406 to 1469. He painted Madonnas, like his *Madonna and Child*, as real women, with emotions, very much like Giotto had, but even more so. So he continues that tradition.

Piero della Francesca, another early Renaissance painter, who lived from 1416 to 1492, develops three-dimensional depth perspective, such as in his *Death of Adam*. He really concentrates on three-dimensional depth perspective. He even wrote a book on it, about how to do it. Again, it was to manipulate people's eyes and lead them to a certain point in the painting, which usually was a point of great emotion or spirituality for Piero della Francesca. So he further develops that trend.

The father of the Renaissance style of sculpture was Lorenzo Ghiberti. He won a contest in Florence to construct the doors of the Baptistry building, which he named *The Gates of Paradise*. There he used line to simulate a kind of rhythmic motion, and made the sculpted panels of these doors seem to actually move before your eyes, and come alive. That would, again, involve people in the scenes and get people to identify with it. It is also, to some extent, more realistic.

But perhaps the best early Renaissance sculptor was Donatello, who lived from 1386 to 1466. He trained with such famous people as Ghiberti. He went with Brunelleschi to Rome, and when Brunelleschi was up measuring the dome, Donatello was studying Roman sculpture and how to do that. When he came back he revived the classical Roman style of sculpture. His bronze *David* is in a style based on realism and admiration for the human form, characteristic of classical architecture [sic sculpture]. This bronze *David* was the first Renaissance nude that was done, and that was considered a little bit shocking at the time.

But the greatest universal genius of the early Renaissance has to be Leon Battista Alberti, who lived from 1404 to 1472. He was not just an artist. He was a painter. He was an architect. He was a man of letters, a scholar, and even a brilliant theoretician of art. Born in Florence to a family rich from the woolen-cloth trade, he did amazing things at an early age. At the age of 20, he wrote a Latin play in the classical style, became a brilliant organist, invented a machine to raise sunken ships, and went to Rome to study art and architecture. As an architect—and he made contributions in all these areas; consider the Rucellai Palace—he built in the classical style, meaning straight lines, rounded arches, just as the Romans had done it. As a humanist, he wrote a book on architecture which was modeled on the classical Roman architectural treatise of Vitruvius, and it became one of the standard books on architecture in the Renaissance period.

He also wrote another book in 1435 called *On Painting*, which was the first really scientific treatise on painting done in the Renaissance. It analyzed specifically proportion, spectrum, and color use, and attempted to tell people how to use these things. In fact, his theories were much used later on by such famous artists as Piero della Francesca and Raphael. Finally, Alberti wrote a book called *On the Family* in 1443, which was the first book on home economics ever written. So quite a contribution there.

Now we come to the period of the High Renaissance. This period I would basically date from about 1450 to 1550. This is a period in which Renaissance reaches its zenith, and the techniques pioneered earlier are, I guess you could say, mastered; but I would just say further developed and brought to an even higher point by some of the most impressive geniuses of this period—you might say dominating geniuses—one of whom, and one of the most famous of whom, was Leonardo da Vinci, who lived from 1452 to 1519.

Da Vinci, as most people know, was not just a painter, but also an architect, an engineer, and a sculptor, and made other contributions, as well. Interestingly enough, only 15 of his paintings actually survive today, but all of these are among the greatest paintings, the greatest masterpieces, of all time. His greatest skill in painting—actually in a lot of the art he did—was in portraying human psychology and emotion in his subjects. Here again, you can see the tie-in to popular piety. He's often portraying religious topics, but he wants to portray them in a way that people can identify with; people can understand the emotion that's involved with the scene. People can say, "Yes, I've felt these things myself. I know what's going on in this scene." They can feel a part of it. Leonardo was really sensitive to drawing people in like that.

One of his most famous works, of course, is *The Last Supper*, which he painted in Milan on the refectory wall. This portrays the moment at which Christ tells his apostles at the Last Supper that he is going to be betrayed. What it does, if you look around that table, and look at the faces of the people at the table, each one has a slightly different emotional reaction to this shocking news: disbelief, sadness, different kinds of reactions that ordinary people would have if someone had told them a thing like this. "How can you know?" "Why would somebody do a terrible thing like this?" And it really draws you into the scene. It's almost as if you were sitting there at the table with them, and you heard it, and you watched them all react. Kind of a moment frozen in time, but in other ways a very dynamic scene, where actually you look at the different faces and there are many different thoughts and emotions being felt and expressed and experienced. It's a whole panoply of human reaction to this kind of extremely important event in Christian history.

It should be pointed out that all of these artists don't just paint religious scenes because someone says, "I want you to paint me a painting of Christ or Adam," or whatever else. They are very Christian and pious people themselves, and they have the intent to try to motivate people to piety, to draw people into the religion. They want to make people feel safe with God. They want to make people feel a part of the religion. So the artists themselves are as involved in these scenes they are painting as they want the people to be, the viewers to be. That's why they used these different means to manipulate the viewer's vision, to manipulate the viewer's reaction to the paintings, to manipulate the viewer's emotions, even. To draw them in and get them involved.

Of course, da Vinci made many other contributions. As a scientist, and he was a great scientist, he had tremendous botanical knowledge, for example. When he paints paintings, when he includes plants, trees, flowers, in paintings, they are real plants, trees, and flowers. You can identify them, because he observed nature and he painted nature just as it really was. He didn't just paint generic bushes and trees. He painted the real thing, because he had the botanical knowledge to do that.

As an inventor, and he was also a great inventor, he left behind notebooks with sketches of inventions that would be realized in the distant future: things like helicopters, airplanes, tanks, submarines. It's kind of interesting that he never really attempted to build almost any of these inventions. He built a few, but not very many. It's even more interesting because he was employed by Sforza in Milan as a military engineer, and presumably he made a number of these sketches as suggestions of things that could be used, like a tank, a conical kind of thing that people would get in. It was armored. They would ride in it. They would fire from it. So it was kind of curious to notice that none of these inventions were ever built and utilized, where, I'm sure, Sforza was paying him good money to have them thought about and designed out and so forth.

Da Vinci worked for a number of very important Renaissance people. He worked for Ludovico Sforza in Milan both as painter and engineer. He worked for Lorenzo the Magnificent in Florence. He had tremendous influence in Renaissance art and culture.

His masterpiece, which everybody is aware of, I'm sure, is the *Mona Lisa*, which is, of course, famous for the fact that her face portrays a very definite kind of emotion that people have ever since speculated about. What exactly is she thinking and saying with this particular facial expression? He painted this picture in Florence. It was appreciated at the time. It was purchased by the king of France, Francis I, for the greatest price ever paid for a painting, taken to Paris, and put in the royal palace. Of course it now hangs in the Louvre, which used to be the royal palace.

Raphael of Urbino, another late Renaissance genius, painted Madonnas, like the *Madonna of the Goldfinch*, with great serenity and great emotion in their faces. He also used perspective and geographic form to great advantage in getting people to focus on their points of emotion that he wanted to concentrate on.

And finally there was Michelangelo Buonarroti, 1475 to 1564, another one of those universal geniuses that most humanists would have loved to think they created, because it was all part of their educational vision to create these many-sided people. He was a genius in painting and architecture and sculpture and many other areas.

It's hard to sum up exactly what the most important aspects of his artistic works were, but at least one of them was his knack of portraying his subjects at the moment of a kind of psychological transition, where they just thought of something and the thought was really represented on their face, with their facial expression. You can almost tell what they are thinking by the expression on their face. Probably his most famous sculpture is the marble *David*, which is in Florence. That, we think, was meant to represent David just as he's decided to throw the rock at Goliath, and while he's thinking of what possibly could happen.

Of course, the masterpiece was the ceiling of the Sistine Chapel, Michelangelo's greatest contribution, considered often a masterpiece of neo-Platonic symbolism. Recently cleaned and restored, it is certainly one of the most important pieces of Renaissance art by any of these geniuses.

Maps

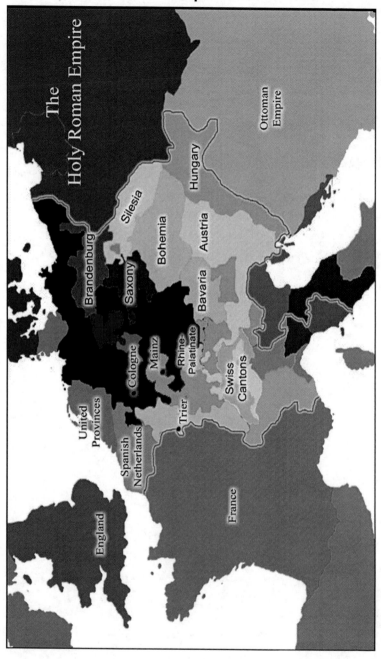

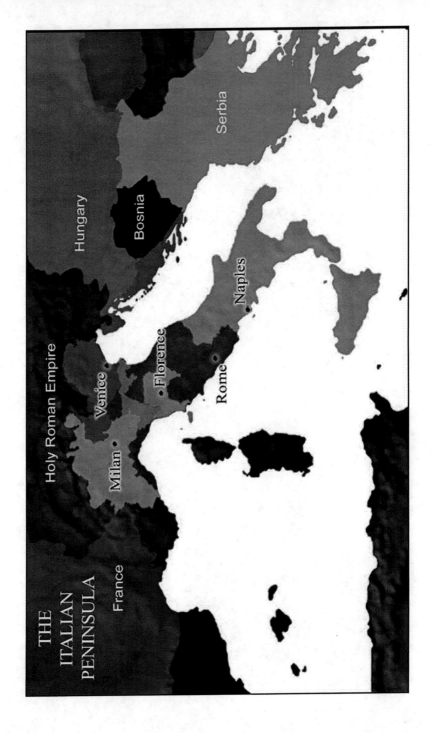

THE ITALIAN PENINSULA

France

Holy Roman Empire

Hungary

Serbia

Bosnia

Venice

Milan

Florence

Naples

Rome

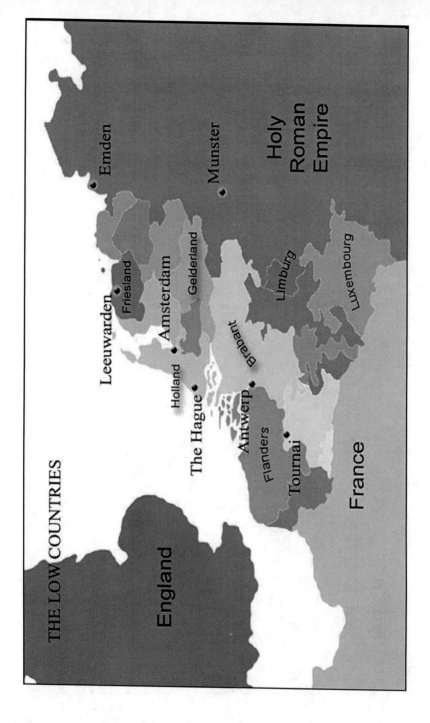

THE LOW COUNTRIES

England

Emden

Munster

Holy Roman Empire

Leeuwarden

Friesland

Amsterdam

Gelderland

Limburg

Luxembourg

Holland

Brabant

The Hague

Antwerp

Flanders

Tournai

France

Timeline

1304	Birth of Francesco Petrarch
1315–1378	The Babylonian Captivity of the papacy
1328	The Hundred Years War begins
1348	The bubonic plague strikes Europe
1378–1415	Great Schism
1382	The English Peasant Revolt
1402	Birth of Civic Humanism in Florence
1415	Council of Constance ends the Great Schism
1434	Cosimo de' Medici becomes ruler of Florence
1453	Constantinople falls to the Turks
1454	Italian states sign Peace of Lodi
1464	Lorenzo the Magnificent becomes ruler of Florence
1487	Bartolomeu Dias pioneers the sea route to India
1492	Columbus discovers America
1497	Vasco da Gama takes first Portuguese fleet to India
1498	French king Charles VIII invades Italy; the Medici fall from power
1509	Henry VIII becomes king of England
1512	The Medici return to power in Florence

1517 ....Martin Luther protests indulgence sales in Germany

1519 ....Charles V elected Holy Roman Emperor

1521 ....Luther faces the Diet of Worms

1523 ....Zwingli wins debate in Zurich; city converts

1525 ....The Peasant War in Germany

1525 ....Charles V defeats Francis I at the Battle of Pavia

1527 ....Charles V defeats the League of Cognac; troops sack Rome

1531 ....Zwingli killed in the Battle of Kappel

1534 ....English Parliament establishes the Church of England

1534 ....Paul III becomes pope; kicks off Counter-Reformation

1535 ....Anabaptist kingdom of Munster defeated by Catholics

1536 ....John Calvin arrives in Geneva

1540 ....Loyola founds Jesuits

1545–1563 ....Council of Trent powers the Counter-Reformation

1546 ....Luther dies; Schmalkaldic War begins religious wars

1555 ....Religious Peace of Augsburg ends the Schmalkaldic War

1556 ....Philip II becomes king of Spain

1558 ....Elizabeth I becomes queen of England

1562 ....French wars of religion begin

1570	Sea Beggars begin Dutch Revolt against Spain
1572	St. Bartholomew's Day massacre of French Huguenots
1576	Spanish Fury in Antwerp
1579	Dutch provinces sign the Union of Utrecht
1584	William of Orange assassinated
1588	Defeat of the Spanish Armada
1589	Henry IV wins religious war, ascends French throne
1603	Elizabeth I dies, ending Tudor dynasty in England
1609	The Bank of Amsterdam is founded
1610	King Henry IV of France assassinated
1618	Thirty Years War begins in Germany
1625	Denmark intervenes in the Thirty Years War
1628	Richelieu defeats Huguenots at La Rochelle
1629	Parliament presents King Charles I with Petition of Right
1630	King Gustavus Adolphus of Sweden invades Germany
1637	Rene Descartes publishes his *Discourse on Method*
1640	English Civil War begins
1640	Frederick William, "the Great Elector," becomes ruler of Prussia

Glossary

Absolutism. Form of monarchy in which all power is located in the monarch, who is said to embody the state. Royal power is not limited by representative assemblies or social groups, such as the nobility. The monarch commands a powerful bureaucracy and army, with which he extends his authority to all groups of people and all corners of the country. Absolutism developed during the 17th century in France, Germany, and elsewhere. Its most well known representative was King Louis XIV of France (r. 1643–1715).

Age of Discovery. The period from 1492 to the mid-16th century, in which European sailors traveled the world's seas and pioneered new trade routes and navigational techniques while exploring the Americas, Asia, Africa, and the Pacific. The Age of Discovery can be said to begin with Portuguese voyages around the tip of Africa to India, and it continued with Columbus and the European settlement of the New World. The era was drawing to a close with Magellan's circumnavigation of the globe in 1520–1522. The age saw the Spanish amass a huge worldwide empire, while the English, French, Dutch, and Portuguese acquired substantial overseas possessions and interests.

Agrarian subsistence cycle. Name given to the inefficient European agricultural system before the 18th century. Unfertile soil and lack of manure to fertilize it dictated that part of the fields be left fallow each year to regain nutrients. This caused from 30 percent to 50 percent of the land to be out of use each year. The remaining land produced only enough food to maintain the population at the subsistence level, and no food was raised for livestock, keeping the animals small and undernourished and producing little manure.

Anabaptists. A radical religious group during the Reformation era. Anabaptists rejected infant baptism as unbiblical; they also rejected the ceremonies, institutions, and clergy of the mainline churches. Many were pacifists who did not recognize state authority, and some practiced communism and polygamy. Because of their unorthodox beliefs, the Anabaptists were persecuted by both the Catholic and Protestant churches and by states. Many were executed by authorities. Those who survived went into hiding.

Apostolic Church. The Christian church as it existed during the days of Christ and the apostles. Many Humanists envisioned this church as pristine and uncorrupted by medieval additions; thus, they based their church reform plans on returning the church to its apostolic purity. During the Protestant Reformation, the Anabaptists and other radical groups also called for reconstructing the church in the image of this apostolic community.

Armada. The great Spanish fleet dispatched by King Philip II to invade England and intervene in the religious wars in France and The Netherlands. It was met in the English Channel by a smaller English fleet commanded by Francis Drake and Martin Frobisher, scattered by English fireships, battered by storms, and ultimately defeated. The Armada returned to Spain with fewer than half its ships.

Augsburg Interim. The peace agreement that followed the defeat of Protestant forces at the Battle of Muhlburg, which ended the first phase of the Schmalkaldic War in Germany. Because the Interim outlawed Lutheranism, the Protestants resumed the war in 1550, this time with France on their side. By 1555, the war had ground to a stalemate and the two sides agreed to the Religious Peace of Augsburg.

Babylonian Captivity (1305–1378). The period in which the Catholic Church moved its headquarters out of Rome to the city of Avignon in southern France. During this time, the papacy fell under the influence of the French crown and the church lost much prestige. Without the revenues of the Papal States to finance the church, the pope had to raise church taxes on ordinary believers, which prompted a wave of popular anti-clericalism. Finally, the papacy returned to Rome to stem the tide of bad feelings toward the church.

Brethren of the Common Life. A lay religious group that flourished in The Netherlands during the 15th and 16th centuries. Devout Catholics, the Brethren wanted to live together in compounds and lead a strictly religious life without actually becoming regular clergy. They also established schools where students were taught practical piety, as well as Humanist ideas. Two important centers of Brethren activity were the cities of Deventer and Zwolle. Among their students was Erasmus of Rotterdam.

Bubonic plague. Epidemic disease that struck Europe in 1348, killing one-half to one-third of the population. This population catastrophe touched off an economic depression that lasted 100 years and contributed to a century of political instability. The plague recurred at regular intervals after 1348, not disappearing from the scene until after 1730. The plague was bacterial in nature and was carried by fleas hosted by rats. It has also been called the *Black Death* for the dark swellings it caused.

Church Ordinance of 1541. John Calvin's plan for organizing the Reformed Church in Geneva. Four types of church officials were established: pastors, doctors (theologians), elders, and deacons. The governing body of the church was the Consistory Council, on which sat elders and pastors. It was the elders' job to supervise the private moral lives of church members. Calvin himself was appointed as the only doctor.

Ciompi Revolt (1378). Revolt by the lower guilds of woolen cloth workers in Florence against the city government's attempt to freeze worker wages below market levels to relieve the labor crisis produced by the death toll of the bubonic plague. Similar revolts occurred among workers and peasants across Europe in response to wage freezes. The lower guilds succeeded in seizing control of the city government and holding it until 1382.

Colloquy of Marburg. Religious conference between Martin Luther and Ulrich Zwingli held in 1529. The meeting was arranged by Lutheran Prince Philip of Hesse, and its goal was for the two Protestant leaders to work out their theological differences as a prelude to a military alliance between German and Swiss Protestant states. The conference failed when Luther and Zwingli could not agree on the issue of the real presence of Christ in the mass.

Consubstantiation. Luther's theory about the real presence of Christ in the mass. He did not believe that the priest was able to effect a change from bread and wine to the body and blood of Christ (*transubstantiation*), but he did believe that the real body and blood of Christ were present in the mass, in the inner essence of the bread and wine, not in the outward appearances.

Council of Constance (1414–1418). One of the biggest church councils of the Middle Ages, it healed the Great Schism by electing Martin V as the sole legitimate pope, restoring to the church prestige lost during the Babylonian Captivity and Great Schism. The council also convicted Jan Hus, a Bohemian follower of John Wycliffe, of heresy and burned him at the stake. The council took for itself some of the pope's powers to govern the church, powers that later popes would recover.

Council of Trent (1545–1563). Church council called by Pope Paul III that played a key role in the Catholic Counter-Reformation. Rather than seek compromise with the Protestants, the council upheld the validity of the very church practices and beliefs that the Protestants rejected. The council maintained that good works were needed along with faith for salvation, that church tradition and papal decrees were sources of religious truth along with the Bible, that all seven sacraments were channels of divine grace, and that transubstantiation took place in the mass. The council clearly differentiated the Catholic position from that of the Protestants.

Counter-Reformation. The massive effort made by the Catholic Church after 1530 to counter the Protestant Reformation and re-convert the European masses to the Catholic faith. The effort began with the papacy of Paul III (1534–1549) and continued with the founding of the Jesuit order by Ignatius Loyola in 1540 and the decrees of the Council of Trent (1545–1563). Key components of the Counter-Reformation were the Inquisition, which tried Protestants as heretics, and the Index of Forbidden Books, which condemned Protestant books. The Counter-Reformation re-converted large areas of Europe to the Catholic Church and sent Catholic missionaries abroad.

Court of Star Chamber. A special royal court established by the first Tudor monarch of England, Henry VII (r. 1485–1509), to try political opponents of royal power. The court operated on Roman law, not English common law, and thus, did not provide for trial by jury. The king appointed the court's judge.

Defenestration of Prague. Episode in 1618 in which representatives of Holy Roman Emperor Ferdinand II were thrown from a tower in Prague Castle after notifying the Bohemian States assembled within that the emperor was withdrawing privileges earlier granted to Bohemian Protestants. This symbolic rejection of Ferdinand's sovereignty was followed by a formal deposition of him as king of Bohemia by the States. These events sparked the beginning of the Thirty Years War (1618–1648), when imperial forces invaded Bohemia.

Diet of Worms (1521). German national assembly where Luther confronted Emperor Charles V and representatives of the pope over his rejection of Catholic Church doctrine. Given a chance to recant his beliefs, Luther refused and, in consequence, was branded an outlaw. After the Diet, Luther was protected from prosecution by the ruler of Saxony, Frederick the Wise. Luther's stand at Worms greatly increased his popularity among the German people.

Dutch Revolt. The prolonged war of independence fought by the Dutch against their Spanish rulers between 1570 and 1648. Provoked by Spanish taxation and persecution of Dutch Protestants, the revolt was led by William of Orange. Spanish King Philip II sent the ruthless Duke of Alva to crush the revolt, but his military tactics were unsuccessful. A truce was declared in 1609, giving the Dutch de facto independence, which was formally recognized in the Treaty of Westphalia in 1648.

Dutch War. War fought by France under Louis XIV against the Dutch Republic between 1672 and 1678. The war was prompted by the role of the Dutch in building the coalition that had defeated France in the earlier War of Devolution (1667–1668). Louis bribed Dutch allies into neutrality as French armies poured into the republic, occupying much of the country and bringing down the government of Grand Pensionary Jan de Witt. The French advance was halted and the situation ultimately salvaged when the Dutch opened the dikes and flooded the countryside.

Edict of Nantes. Issued in 1598 by Henry IV after the former Calvinist had assumed the French throne and converted to Catholicism. The edict guaranteed religious toleration to French Huguenots and allowed them to fortify their towns as a defensive measure. The right to fortify was withdrawn by Cardinal Richelieu after the siege of La Rochelle in 1628, and Louis XIV later revoked the entire edict.

Evangelical Rationalists. A group of believers during the Reformation era who based their beliefs on a rational interpretation of Scripture. They accepted nothing as true that was not in the Bible; thus, they rejected many key theological doctrines of the mainline churches, including the Trinity and the divinity of Christ, the sacraments, resurrection of the body, and predestination. Leaders of the group included Laelius (1525–1562) and Faustus Socinus (1539–1604).

Fronde. Revolt of French nobles against the crown that occurred in 1648, during the minority of King Louis XIV. The Fronde was the last revolt against French absolutism before the French Revolution of 1789. The revolt started among nobles of the robe, administrative and judicial officials who bought nobility with their offices, but spread to involve traditional nobles of the sword, as well. Cardinal Mazarin, the king's first minister, was instrumental in the defeat of the Fronde.

Gentry. Wealthy upper-middle class industrialists and landowners who became the ruling class of England after the civil war of 1640–1649. Before the civil war, this class was already displacing the nobility in England's social and political structure because of their wealth and their control of the House of Commons. During the war, the gentry made up the backbone of parliamentary opposition to King Charles I. Religiously, many members of the gentry favored Puritan positions and expressed religious opposition to the Church of England in Parliament and, ultimately, in the civil war.

Great Schism (1378–1415). The period following the end of the Babylonian Captivity, when disputed papal elections resulted in at first two and later three popes competing for control over the church. One pope was based in Rome, another in Avignon in France, and a third (after 1409) in Pisa. All Europe was divided by this crisis as each country, city, university, and even individual had to decide which pope to follow. The Schism was finally healed by the Council of Constance (1414–1418), which established Martin V as sole pope.

Holy Roman Empire. The name given to the German monarchy since the days of Charlemagne (800). Originally Charlemagne envisioned it as a revival of the Western Roman Empire, but over the course of the Middle Ages, the power of the emperor weakened as the power of local nobles increased. There was a brief revival of imperial power under Charles V (r. 1519–1556), but after the Treaty of Westphalia (1648), the emperor's power became largely a fiction and the empire, a collection of small sovereign states ruled by local nobles.

Humanism. The revolutionary educational plan introduced during the Italian Renaissance. It featured a return to the study of the ancient classics and a revival of interest in the liberal arts. The goal of Humanism was to produce well-rounded individuals and good citizens. There was also an emphasis on practical morality. Among the founders of Humanism were Francesco Petrarch, a Florentine living in exile in Avignon, and Caluccio Salutati, a chancellor of Florence.

Hundred Years War (1337–1453). War fought between England and France over English King Edward III's claim to inherit the French crown. This long war featured several truces and temporary lulls in fighting. The major battles were Crecy (1346), Poitiers (1356), and Agincourt (1415), all English victories, but in the end, the war saw English armies driven from France by Joan of Arc. The war featured the first use of the English longbow and gunpowder and the decline of the mounted knight as a military weapon.

Iconoclasm. The destruction of religious artwork and images in Catholic Churches during the Reformation period. Some Protestants believed that religious artwork violated the biblical injunction against worshiping graven images, and outbreaks of iconoclasm followed the introduction of Protestantism in Germany, Switzerland, and The Netherlands. Such outbreaks were sometimes spontaneous and other times orchestrated by Protestant agitators. Protestant leaders such as Luther and Zwingli did not sanction iconoclasm.

Indulgence Crisis of 1517. The incident that precipitated Luther's break with the Catholic Church. The church sold documents called *indulgences* to believers, claiming that these documents relieved the recipient of the burden of doing certain good works. Luther objected to the pope's selling of these documents, saying that such relief should be available free of charge to all members of the church. When the pope learned of Luther's objections, he made claims of papal infallibility not made before, and Luther's rejection of these claims led to his excommunication in 1520.

Inquisition. Also called the Holy Office, Catholic Church court that prosecuted heresy cases. Founded in Rome in the 13th century, the Inquisition was active against the Albigensian and Waldensian heresies. A separate Inquisition was founded in Spain by the crown in the 15th century to move against Moslems, Jews, and other nonbelievers. After 1485, both Inquisitions prosecuted witchcraft cases in Spain and Germany. During the Reformation and Counter-

Reformation, the Inquisition focused on Protestants, especially in The Netherlands.

Intendants. A new kind of French royal official created by Cardinal Richelieu. These officials were not venal but appointed by the king; thus, they were more responsive to royal wishes than venal officials. Intendants became the king's chief representatives in local areas. They enforced royal decrees, recruited soldiers, and worked with private contractors known as *tax farmers* to collect royal taxes. Because of their loyalty to the king, intendants were hated by the populace, and several revolts occurred against their power.

Jesuits. Catholic religious order founded by Ignatius Loyola and approved by Pope Paul III in 1540. The Jesuits were the foot soldiers of the Counter-Reformation, specializing in re-converting the masses to the church by means of preaching, teaching, hearing confessions, and doing missionary work. They were highly educated and trained, and they founded many schools throughout Europe. Jesuit confessors were influential on leading Catholic rulers. Their efforts at re-conversion met with considerable success.

Junkers. The name given to Prussian nobles residing on large rural estates in East Prussia. They cooperated with the rulers of Prussia in creating royal absolutism, and in return, they were given officerships in the military and unfettered control over peasants on their estates.

Liberal arts. The seven subjects taught to free Roman citizens in antiquity. The liberal arts were revived by Renaissance Humanists as an appropriate education for well-rounded individuals. The liberal arts consisted of grammar, rhetoric, and logic (the *Trivium*), as well as mathematics, astronomy, geometry, and music (the *Quadrivium*). To these subjects, the Humanists added history, poetry, and literature.

Magisterial Reformation. Name given to Luther's tactics after the 1525 peasant revolt of spreading Lutheranism not by preaching to the masses, whom he concluded had misunderstood his message, but by preaching to and converting the princes of Germany, who would, in turn, decree the conversion of the people they ruled.

Mercantilism. An economic theory that was at the foundation of most European states' economic policies prior to the 18th century. Mercantilism held that there was a limited amount of wealth in the world and states became powerful by obtaining as much of this wealth as possible through a kind of economic warfare. States strove for a favorable trade balance that would create a flow of bullion into the country. State regulations and subsidies were mechanisms to promote industry and trade and achieve this favorable trade balance. Leading practitioners of mercantilism included French finance ministers Sully and Colbert in the 17th century.

Millenarianism. The belief of some radical religious groups and figures during the Reformation era and afterwards that Christ would return to earth before the end of the world to set up a thousand-year kingdom of the holy, in which true believers would live in a kind of paradise, while sinners would be punished. Some millenarians, such as Melchior Hoffman, took it upon themselves to get the world ready for this holy kingdom.

New Monarchy. The name given to European monarchies that rebuilt their power in the 15th century after the disasters of the previous century. Such New Monarchs as Francis I of France and Henry VIII of England used partnerships with the middle classes, as well as expanded bureaucracies and tax structures, to reestablish royal power.

Nobles of the robe. French nobles who bought nobility along with a government office. They were called *nobles of the robe* for the long robes worn by the jurists of the Paris Parlement, the supreme court of France, the offices of which were purchased and conferred nobility. Other such offices were on provincial parlements and even local government. Nobles of the robe adopted many of the habits and ways of thought of traditional nobles, called *nobles of the sword*. They had the same privileges as traditional nobles and guarded them just as fiercely. Nobles of the robe started the Fronde revolt against the king in 1648. In the 18th century, nobles of the robe pressured the king to reduce the sale of ennobling offices because of the inflation of nobility that resulted.

Open-field system. The name given to the organization of European agricultural fields before the 18th century. Fields were divided into multiple strips, each farmed by a different peasant family. Because of the close proximity of the strips, the farmers had to agree to common farming techniques, times, and crops. This communal method of farming prevented innovation, because most farmers were unwilling to take risks.

Pacification of Gent. Treaty signed in 1577 that brought the southern provinces of The Netherlands into the rebellion against Spain alongside the northern provinces. The treaty was precipitated by the Spanish Fury of 1576, in which Spanish troops rioted and plundered the southern city of Antwerp because they had not been paid. After the treaty, Spanish power was, for a time, confined to the area of Luxembourg.

Papal States. A band of small states running through central Italy from Rome in the south to Ravenna in the north. The pope was secular ruler over these states and they provided him with tax money and troops that were crucial for the papacy to remain independent of more powerful secular rulers, such as the Holy Roman Emperor. The Papal States were possessions of the Byzantine Empire in the early Middle Ages, but when the Byzantines left Italy, the states passed into Frankish possession and from there to the pope. The pope lost control of the states during the Babylonian Captivity (1315–1378), necessitating a lengthy war of re-conquest.

Pavia, Battle of. Decisive victory by the forces of Charles V over those of French King Francis I in the first Hapsburg/Valois War in 1525. As a result of the battle, the French king was captured and all of Italy lay open to imperial domination. After his release, Francis signed a military alliance with the papacy called the League of Cognac and the two allies launched a new war against Charles to prevent his conquest of Italy.

Peace of Lodi (1454). Military alliance uniting Florence, Venice, and Milan and establishing a balance of power in Italy, countering the southern alliance of the papacy and Naples. The alliance was engineered by Florentine ruler Cosimo de' Medici as part of his policy of maintaining peace among the Italian powers, a peace he believed would benefit Florentine economic and cultural development.

Peasant Revolt of 1525. Massive revolt of German peasants against landlord and princely taxation. The peasant leaders claimed that the revolt was inspired by Luther's ideas on Christian freedom, a claim Luther vehemently rejected. Luther called for the peasants to obey their lawful rulers, but this did not stop the revolt. Luther then called on the German princes to put down the rebellion.

Philology. The study of the changes in style and form the Latin language underwent over time. Renaissance Humanists used this science to revive Classical Latin style, to date manuscripts and books, to identify stylistic periods in the language, and even to prove the Donation of Constantine a forgery. Perhaps the greatest Humanist philologist was Lorenzo Valla (1407–1457).

Politique Party. A group of officials at the French royal court during the wars of religion in France. The party was led by Queen Marie de' Medici and favored separating religious from political considerations and ruling the country by making all decisions only because of "reason of state," leaving religious issues aside. It was an attempt to preserve royal power in a country increasingly divided religiously.

Popular piety. The name given to certain religious practices that originated with ordinary believers during the Catholic Church's period of crisis with the Babylonian Captivity and Great Schism. Feeling ignored by church leadership, the people developed practices focusing on the use of their senses and emotions and making them feel closer to God. Among the practices, validated by church authorities only much later, were the rosary and the stations of the cross.

Pragmatic Sanction. An agreement between King Charles VI of Austria and major European rulers that recognized the claim of Charles's daughter Maria Theresa to become ruler of Austria upon her father's death. Charles had no male heir and a female had never before held the Austrian throne.

Predestination. John Calvin's belief that God selected which people would go to heaven and which ones would go to hell before he created the world. This selection would be in effect for the entire history of the world. Those chosen for heaven Calvin called the *Elect*. God's choice was absolute and arbitrary. It was not influenced by anything people did, and no one could know the reasons for God's choices or even who was among the Elect.

Priesthood of All Believers. Luther's idea that ordinary Christian believers could read and correctly interpret Scripture. The Catholic Church taught that only the clergy could do so because Christ gave the church the holy spirit and, thus, the power to do so at the Ascension.

Puritans. An English Protestant religious group who called for change in the Church of England during the 16th and 17th centuries. Despite the fact that the church had broken its ties to the pope during the reign of Henry VIII, much of the church's doctrine and practice remained close to Catholicism. Puritans called for the introduction of more Protestant elements into the church. Moderate Puritans, called *Presbyterians*, desired the introduction of Calvinism into the church, whereas more radical *Puritans*, called Independents, wanted complete religious freedom for local congregations. Puritans were influential in the House of Commons during the 17th century and played a key role in the English civil war (1640–1649). One of their leaders was Oliver Cromwell, who ruled England from 1649 to 1658

Radical Spiritualists. A group of Christian believers during the Reformation period who rejected all external elements of religion, including ceremonies, institutions, and clergy. The essence of religion for the Spiritualists was direct divine revelation in the individual soul, which brought grace and salvation. This revelation they called the "inner light." Leaders of the Spiritualists included Kaspar von Schwenkfeld (1489–1561) and Sebastian Franck (1499–1542).

Religious Peace of Augsburg (1555). Treaty ending the Schmalkaldic War between Lutheran and Catholic princes of Germany. The treaty's main principle, expressed by the Latin phrase *cuius region eius religio*, stated that each German prince could choose the religion for the people of his state. There was no provision promoting religious toleration, and Calvinism was not recognized in the treaty. The treaty left Germany religiously divided.

Sale of office. A practice that dates to at least the 13th century in France, in which the king sold offices in the royal government to the highest bidder. The office, once sold, became the personal property of the purchaser. Sale of office raised revenue and increased the size of the bureaucracy: By the time of Richelieu (fl. 1610–1642), fully one-third of royal revenues came from the practice. But these venal offices were alienated from royal control, which decreased the king's control over his government. As more offices were sold, their value decreased and the bureaucracy became a mass of overlapping and redundant offices.

Salvation by faith alone. The revolutionary theological concept of Martin Luther that formed the theological foundation of the Protestant Reformation. From his reading of St. Augustine and Paul's Epistle to the Romans, Luther concluded that good works were irrelevant to individual salvation, which came only to those who had faith in Christ's promise of salvation. The Catholic Church maintained that both faith and works were needed for salvation.

Schmalkaldic War. The first religious war in Germany between Lutheran and Catholic princes. Fought between 1546 and 1555, the war pitted Lutheran princes Philip of Hesse and Frederick of Saxony against the Catholic emperor Charles V. Catholic forces were victorious in the first phase of the war, ending in 1548, but the war resumed when France allied with the Lutheran side, and the ultimate result was indecisive. The war left Germany religiously divided.

Scientific Revolution. The 17th-century intellectual movement that overturned the traditional scientific system based on Aristotle's ideas and put in place a new and radically different science based on the ideas of Copernicus, Kepler, Galileo, and Newton. The old geocentric picture of the cosmos was replaced by the Copernican heliocentric picture, and Aristotelian motion theory was replaced by Galileo's theory of inertia, as well as Newton's laws of motion and gravitation. Modern science emerged.

Sea Beggars. A group of maritime raiders who fired the first shot in the Dutch Revolt against Spain in 1570. The Sea Beggars originally raided shipping in the English Channel, but after being deprived of their base in London because of attacks on English ships, they raised the banner of William of Orange and captured the Dutch port of Brill in Zeeland. A military force from Brill then won the surrender of several towns in inland Holland, making that province the first base of the Dutch Revolt.

Second serfdom. The re-imposition of serfdom by landlords on peasants in the wake of labor shortages created by the bubonic plague. This took place in Germany and parts of Eastern Europe. Serfdom had vanished in most of Europe in the 14th century as a result of the greater social and political power the peasantry possessed during the labor shortage. Only in Germany was serfdom reinstituted in the 15th century, and it continued on into the Reformation period, giving more power to landlords and creating tension between nobles and peasants that led to the Peasant Revolt of 1525. In the 17th century, the greater power of noble landlords resulting from the second serfdom affected the evolution of royal absolutism in Germany.

Signoria. The name given to the city council of Florence during the Italian Renaissance. It was an executive and administrative body and consisted of many different types of officials responsible for police activities, taxation, the regulation of commerce, and other tasks. Its officials were elected for short terms (six months to two years) by a complex indirect electoral process called the Scrutiny.

Spanish Fury. Riot by Spanish troops in Antwerp in 1576 that devastated the city. Caused by the Spanish crown's failure to pay the troops over a period of months, the looting of Antwerp turned the southern provinces of The Netherlands against their Spanish rulers. These provinces joined the northern provinces in revolt by signing the Pacification of Gent in 1577.

Thirty Years War. The last great religious war, fought in Germany between 1618 and 1648. German Protestant princes were joined by Danish, Swedish, and French forces to fight the Catholic alliance of the emperor, German Catholic princes, Spain, and the papacy. The war ended in a virtual stalemate after early Catholic victories. The Peace of Westphalia concluded the war in 1648, leaving the emperor almost powerless, German princes fully sovereign, and parts of Germany in foreign hands. Germany was devastated by the war.

Transubstantiation. The miracle of the mass in which the bread and wine is transformed into the actual body and blood of Christ when the presiding priest speaks the words *hoc est corpus meum*, or "this is my body." The Catholic Church taught that with this miracle, the sacrifice of Christ was repeated in every mass. Following Luther, most Protestants rejected transubstantiation. While Luther denied the transformation but maintained the real presence, Zwingli saw the mass as simply symbolic.

Treaty of Westphalia (1648). Peace treaty ending the Thirty Years War. It decentralized power in the Holy Roman Empire by making the princes of German states fully sovereign. Parts of German territory were also given to France, Denmark, and Sweden, and the independence of the Dutch Republic was recognized.

Trilingual colleges. Colleges founded by Humanist scholars in the Renaissance period with the purpose of teaching students the three so-called "sacred languages," Hebrew, Greek, and Latin. The goal was to enable people to read the Bible in its two original languages or in Latin translation. The mission of these colleges grew out of the Humanist conviction that ordinary believers could read and understand the Bible and follow its moral examples, an idea spread by Erasmus, among other Humanists. Erasmus himself founded one such college at the University of Louvain, while King Francis I of France founded one in Paris.

Union of Arms. Plan of the Count-Duke of Olivares, first minister of King Philip IV (r.1621–1625) of Spain, to spread royal taxation more equally over the Spanish provinces to increase collection and save the crown from bankruptcy. At the time, Spain was trying to finance its renewed struggle against the Dutch Revolt. The plan failed when provinces that had previously paid few taxes rebelled against the crown.

Union of Utrecht. Military alliance against Spain signed by the seven northern provinces of The Netherlands in 1578. The treaty was in response to the Union of Arras in 1577, in which the southern provinces of the country returned their allegiance to Spain. In 1581, the northern provinces formally declared their independence from Spain as the United Provinces, but warfare continued until 1609, when a truce delivered de facto independence to the new Dutch state.

War commissars. The name given to military officers appointed to Prussian government office by Elector Frederick William (r. 1640–1688). These loyal officials helped the elector to mold Prussian absolutism.

War of Austrian Succession (1740–1748). War fought by Queen Maria Theresa of Austria for the right to occupy the throne as outlined in the Pragmatic Sanction. She faced a coalition led by King Frederick the Great of Prussia, whose invasion of Austrian-controlled Silesia started the war. At the war's conclusion, Maria Theresa remained on the throne, but Prussia kept Silesia.

War of Spanish Succession (1701–1713). War fought by King Louis XIV of France against a coalition of European states for the right to install his grandson as king of Spain. The war concluded with the Treaty of Utrecht in 1713. It was Louis' last war. While his grandson was allowed to become king of France, the treaty stipulated that France and Spain could never be united into one kingdom under the Bourbons.

Biographical Notes

Adolphus, Gustavus (1611–1632). King of Sweden and major figure in the Thirty Years War (1618–1648). As a Lutheran, Gustavus was troubled by Catholic victories in the war between 1618 and 1630, and with the encouragement of an anti-imperial coalition of England, The Netherlands, and France, he brought Sweden into the war on the Protestant side in 1630. A military genius, Gustavus defeated Tilly's imperial army at the Battle of Leipzig and routed Catholic forces in north Germany. After invading the Catholic heartland of south Germany, he met the imperial army of Albrecht von Wallenstein at the Battle of Lutzen in 1632. While the Swedish army won the battle, Gustavus was killed. The Swedish advance halted and the war fell into a stalemate.

Agricola, Rudolf (1444–1485). The father of German Humanism. Born near Groningen in The Netherlands, he was educated at the universities of Erfurt, Cologne, and Louvain. He studied in Italy during the years 1469–1479 and, at this time, fell under the influence of Humanism. Becoming a disciple of Petrarch's ideas, Agricola returned to Germany and accepted a teaching position at the University of Heidelberg. From there, he spread Petrarch's ideas. His greatest student was Conrad Celtis (1459–1508), who became a classical Latin poet and lecturer on Tacitus's *Germania*.

Calvin, John (1509–1564). Founder of the Reformed Church, a major branch of the Protestant Reformation. Calvin was born in France and studied at the universities of Paris, Orleans, and Bourges, earning a law degree. He was also influenced by Humanism. After he developed Protestant sympathies in 1533, he was forced to flee France, going to Basel in Switzerland, where he wrote his theological masterpiece, *The Institutes of the Christian Religion*, which advocated predestination. In 1536, Calvin went to Geneva to help reform the city, and he spent the rest of his life there. In Geneva, he built a theocratic state, which he believed was the model Christian society. He also sent Calvinist missionaries into France.

Charles I (r. 1625–1649). The second of the Stuart dynasty to take the English throne, his conflict with Parliament led to the outbreak of the English civil war (1640–1647). Charles disliked cooperating with Parliament in his government of the nation and, at one point, ruled on his own for 11 years without calling a Parliament. He rejected a list of parliamentary demands known as the Petition of Right in 1629, tried to arrest members of the House of Commons, and led the crown into a military conflict with Parliament over the right to rule the country in 1640. Parliamentary forces under Oliver Cromwell defeated the king's forces in the civil war, and King Charles was tried by Parliament for treason. He was convicted and executed in 1649.

Charles V (r. 1519–1556). Hapsburg Holy Roman Emperor under whose reign the Protestant Reformation was born in Germany. He was also ruler of The Netherlands and king of Spain and, thus, ruled over all of Spain's possessions in Italy and the New World. His was the greatest worldwide empire of the age. He fought a series of wars with King Francis I of France for control of Italy, and he fought off several attempted Turkish invasions of Europe. He also was involved in the religious wars in Germany, but he was unsuccessful in stopping the tide of Lutheranism, despite condemning Luther at the Diet of Worms in 1521 and several times declaring Lutheranism illegal in the empire. In 1556, he retired to a monastery and divided his inheritance between his brother Ferdinand and his son Philip.

Columbus, Christopher (1451–1506). Italian navigator who, sailing for Spain, discovered the Americas in 1492. The Genoa-born Columbus was seeking a westward passage to India and the valuable spice trade when he made first landfall in the Bahamas. Believing he was in Asia, Columbus visited many other locations in the Caribbean during his initial trip and several later ones. He went to Hispanola and Cuba and traveled along the coast of Central America and the north coast of South America. His discoveries laid the foundation for the Spanish empire in the New World.

da Gama, Vasco (c. 1469–1524). Portuguese navigator who led the first Portuguese trading fleet around the tip of Africa to India in 1497 to engage in the spice trade. He followed in the footsteps of another great Portuguese sailor, Bartolomeu Dias, who 10 years earlier, had pioneered the route around the cape to India after years of Portuguese expeditions had inched their way down the west coast of Africa. The Portuguese explored many navigational techniques and instruments during these voyages.

da Vinci, Leonardo (1452–1519). Perhaps the greatest universal genius of the Italian Renaissance. Painter, inventor, architect, sculptor, and engineer, among his masterpieces are the so-called *Mona Lisa*, the fresco painting of the *Last Supper* on the wall of a monastic refectory in Milan, and the great marble statue *David* that stands today in Florence's Ufizzi gallery. As a military engineer and inventor, he worked for Lorenzo the Magnificent in Florence and Ludovico Sforza in Milan. In his sketches, he foresaw such modern machines as the tank and the helicopter.

De' Medici, Cosimo (r. 1434–1464). Called *Pater Patria*, or "father of the country," he was the first of the Medici family to rule Florence during the Italian Renaissance. Rich from the banking business, he took power from the Albizzi family in 1434 during a period of civil unrest in Florence, using his mercenary army headed by Francesco Sforza. He ruled the city as a dictator from behind the scenes but maintained the appearances of republican government. He was a great patron of art and learning, and the Renaissance flowered in Florence under his rule. In 1447, he installed his general Sforza as ruler of Milan, and in 1454, Florence joined Milan and Venice in a military alliance known as the Peace of Lodi, designed to preserve the balance of power in Italy and maintain the peace.

De' Medici, Lorenzo (r. 1464-1494). Known as Lorenzo the Magnificent, he was de facto ruler of Florence at the height of the Italian Renaissance. He was a great patron of the arts and Humanism, and Renaissance culture flourished in Florence under his leadership. He pursued a foreign policy of peace as best suited to his city's prosperity, and under his guidance, a modern diplomatic system featuring resident ambassadors grew up among the cities of Italy. He ruled Florence from behind the scenes by controlling the city's complicated electoral process and getting his supporters elected to office. His death in 1494 ended the glory of the Renaissance in Florence and precipitated a governmental crisis.

Descartes, René(1596–1650). French philosopher and inventor of the philosophy of Rationalism during the Early Enlightenment. In his *Meditations on First Philosophy*, published in Leiden in 1637, Descartes used his method of doubt to reject as false every proposition that he could mistrust. By doing so, he arrived at his first indubitable and, therefore, certain truth: *Cogito ergo sum*. Then, by adopting reason as his new criterion of truth, he built his philosophy by accepting into it only those propositions agreeable to reason. Descartes established human reason as the core of Enlightenment epistemology and became one of the most influential thinkers in the Western tradition.

d'Etaples, Jaques Lefèvre (c. 1450–1530). One of the greatest of French Humanists. He called for a reform of the church by returning to the model of the apostolic church, which he considered pristine. He made a Humanist translation of the Greek church father John of Damascus and wrote an influential commentary on Paul's Epistle to the Romans. In this latter work, he anticipated some of Luther's ideas.

Elizabeth I (r. 1558–1603). The Virgin Queen of England. The last of the Tudor dynasty that came to the throne following the War of the Roses, Elizabeth was extremely popular among her subjects. She ruled in close cooperation with Parliament and considered herself subject to the laws of England, just as were her people. She issued the Thirty-Nine Articles as a charter for the Church of England, and she promoted members of the gentry class to positions of wealth and power in her government. Her failure to produce an heir led to the accession of the Stuart dynasty, which ultimately led to the English civil war (1640–1647).

Erasmus of Rotterdam (1466–1536). This Dutch scholar, called the Prince of Humanists, was the greatest of the northern or Christian Humanists. The illegitimate child of a monk and a nun, he was educated by the Brethren of the Common Life. From them he adopted his "philosophy of Christ," which called on believers to read the Bible and imitate the life of Christ. He favored a morally based religion founded on reading the Bible and the great church fathers. Erasmus made translations and new editions of the work of many of the Greek and Latin church fathers, as well as of pagan Classical writings. His edition of the works of St. Jerome was especially famous, as was his Greek and Latin New Testament edition and translation. He greatly influenced such figures as Ulrich Zwingli and Thomas More.

Francis I (r. 1515–1547). King of France during the age of New Monarchy, he fought a series of dynastic wars against Holy Roman Emperor Charles V. He built up the power of the French crown by allying his government with the wealthy upper middle class of the country. He was a great patron of the arts and learning, establishing a royal library that would later become the French national library, patronizing Humanist scholars, and establishing a trilingual college at the University of Paris. He purchased Leonardo da Vinci's painting popularly known as the *Mona Lisa* for the greatest price ever paid for a painting at that time.

Franck, Sebastian (1499–1542). A leading radical spiritualist during the Reformation era. He rejected all external aspects of religion, including institutions, ceremonies, clergy, and sacraments, even rejecting the Bible as a source of religious truth. For Franck, true religion could be based only on the "inner light," direct divine revelation or the indwelling of the holy spirit in the individual soul of the believer. He began his career as a Catholic priest before becoming a follower, first of the Humanist Erasmus, then of Martin Luther. He became a spiritualist in 1528. He was a wandering preacher in southern Germany in the 1530s and 1540s.

Henry IV (r. 1589–1610). Also known as Henry of Bourbon, Huguenot leader during the French wars of religion during the late 16th century who took the throne as king of France at the conclusion of that conflict. In order to better rule largely Catholic France, Henry converted to that faith shortly after becoming king. In 1598, he issued the Edict of Nantes, extending toleration to the Huguenots. He began the process of rebuilding royal power after the religious wars by revamping the king's council and hiring the Duke of Sully as finance minister. He was assassinated in 1610.

Henry VIII (r. 1509–1547). Tudor king of England during the age of New Monarchy. His divorce from Catherine of Aragon in an attempt to secure a male heir to the throne led to the English Reformation, which established the Church of England with the king as its head. He also dissolved English monasteries and sold off their lands, keeping the proceeds of the sale for the crown. His reign saw an increase in the power of the English monarchy, and he secured the Tudor succession by having a male heir with a later wife.

Hoffman, Melchior (1495–1543). Anabaptist religious leader during the Reformation era. Like other Anabaptists, Hoffman rejected infant baptism because it did not appear in the Bible. He also rejected most of the religious doctrines and practices not only of the Catholic Church but of mainline Protestant congregations as well. He was a millenarian who believed that Christ would return to earth before the end of the world and establish a thousand-year kingdom or paradise on earth in which holy people would prosper and sinners would be punished. He began his career in Zurich but traveled north to The Netherlands, where his missionaries established numerous Anabaptist congregations in the early 1530s. He was later jailed in Strasbourg for preaching that Christ would return to earth in that city.

Joan of Arc (1412–1431). The savior of France during the last stages of the Hundred Years War. A simple peasant girl, she convinced the embattled king of France, whose forces were surrounded at Orleans, that God had sent her on a mission to save France and its king from the English. She was given arms, military advisors, and command of the French army and she proceeded to break the siege of Orleans and drive the English army back to the channel. After being captured by English allies, she was turned over to the English and burned at the stake as a witch.

Joseph II (r. 1765–1790). King of Austria after the death of his mother, Maria Theresa, he took radical measures to increase the power of the Austrian crown. He took control of the Catholic Church in Austria, dissolved the monasteries, and sold off their lands. He freed the serfs and let them purchase the land they worked, and he established a tax on noble land. A revolt by the Austrian nobility precipitated by the tax greatly weakened the power of the crown and led to the end of many of Joseph's reforms. He is sometimes called an "enlightened despot" for his reforms, but his rule weakened Austrian absolutism.

Locke, John (1632–1704). One of the most important and influential philosophers of the Early Enlightenment. Disagreeing with Descartes' position on innate ideas, Locke held, in his *Essay Concerning Human Understanding*, that people were born with minds blank of ideas. Ideas were then obtained through sense experience, which implanted them on the brain. Reason combined these simple ideas into complex ideas and, from this, flowed all knowledge. The philosophical position that all knowledge comes from experience is called *Empiricism*. Locke stressed the importance of the environment in forming people's knowledge and character. His ideas were tremendously influential on such major later Enlightenment figures as Voltaire.

Louis XIV (r. 1643–1715). The greatest absolute monarch of France, he called himself the Sun King. Coming to power after the defeat of the noble revolt known as the Fronde, he built the splendid royal palace of Versailles, the biggest building ever erected in Europe at the time. He reined in the nobility and built an efficient bureaucracy that extended his control to all corners of the country. He hired Jean Baptiste Colbert as his finance minister and the Marquis de Louvois as war minister. The latter created for Louis the most powerful army in Europe. Louis' power in France was such that he was able to censor the press and revoke the Edict of Nantes. He spent 18 of his last 27 years on the throne at war with various European coalitions in an effort to expand France's boarders. The wars were largely unsuccessful and left the French treasury near bankruptcy.

Loyola, Ignatius (1491–1556). Creator of the Jesuit order, one of the Catholic Church's primary weapons against the Protestants during the Catholic Counter-Reformation. Loyola was originally a Spanish soldier, then a pilgrim, until a religious vision led him to write his masterpiece, *The Spiritual Exercises*, and set him on the mission to fight Protestantism and re-convert the European masses to Catholicism. With three companions, he traveled from Spain to Paris, then to Rome, where he served the pope by ministering to the poor and earned the pope's respect and confidence. After several requests, Pope Paul III authorized Loyola to establish a new order called the Jesuits in 1540. The Jesuits specialized in preaching, teaching, hearing confessions, and performing missionary work. They went on to re-convert large parts of Europe to the Catholic Church.

Luther, Martin (1483–1546). The father of the Protestant Reformation. Born a peasant in Eisleben, Germany, he challenged the Catholic Church's sale of indulgences in 1517, became involved in a dispute over papal power, and was excommunicated in 1520. In several works written in that year, he rejected much of Catholic theology, including transubstantiation, the power of the priesthood, the infallibility of the pope, and the role of the pope as head of the church. For Luther, the Bible was the sole source of religious truth, and holy writ could be interpreted by ordinary people. Faith in Christ's promise of salvation, not good works, was the only route to heaven in Luther's view. Luther attracted a mass following in

Germany after his appearance at the Diet of Worms in 1521; his adherents formed the first Protestant church.

Magellan, Ferdinand (c. 1480–1521). Portuguese navigator who commanded a Spanish expedition during 1520–1522 that was the first one to circumnavigate the earth. Magellan himself died in combat with natives in the Philippines and, thus, did not return to Spain, and many of his ships and crews were lost on the voyage. The purpose of the expedition was to find the long-rumored western passage to India, but the voyage proved so long and expensive that the Spanish concluded they could not profitably engage in the spice trade using that route. It took Magellan's ships 98 days just to cross the Pacific Ocean.

Mary I (1516–1558). Tudor queen of England, daughter of Henry VIII and Catherine of Aragon, she tried to bring England back to the Catholic faith. After assuming the throne on the death of Edward VI (1547–1553), she caused the repeal of all parliamentary acts separating the English church from papal control and invited a papal legate back into the country. She began appointing Catholics to government office and followed an active policy of persecuting Protestants. Called "Bloody Mary," she had many Protestants executed and caused many more to flee to the continent.

Müntzer, Thomas (d. 1525). Radical Spiritualist and leader of the German peasant revolt of 1525. He believed that God spoke directly to individuals by divine revelation called the "inner light." He was also a millenarian who believed Christ would return to earth before the world's end and set up a kingdom of the holy people. Also a social revolutionary, he encouraged the poor in society to revolt against the wealthy and powerful. He was killed leading a peasant army against the princes in 1525.

Paul III (1534–1549). Pope who was instrumental in launching the Catholic Counter-Reformation. He reaffirmed papal control of the church in the face of Protestant opposition, set up the Roman Inquisition to combat the Protestants, reformed abuses in the Catholic Church, and revamped the College of Cardinals. He also called the Council of Trent in 1545, which put the church on the path of Counter-Reformation, and he authorized the creation of the Jesuits by Ignatius Loyola. The Jesuits went on to re-convert large parts of Europe to the Catholic faith.

Petrarch, Francesco (1304–1374). One of the founders of Renaissance Humanism. A Florentine- born scholar who lived with his family in exile in Avignon, Petrarch criticized medieval university education as too abstract and impractical. He called instead for an education based on practical morality, drawing its lessons from the classics of antiquity. Instead of a specialized vocational education, he favored a broad education based on the liberal arts that would create well-rounded individuals. An accomplished poet, he also wrote prose works, such as his essay "The Ascent of Mount Ventoux," describing the human struggle for the spiritual life.

Philip II (r. 1556–1598). Son of Emperor Charles V, he inherited the Spanish crown and overseas empire from his father. He also ruled The Netherlands and fought against the Dutch struggle for independence after 1570. He was a champion of the Catholic Counter-Reformation and led an international crusade to eliminate Protestantism, sending the Inquisition and the Duke of Alva to The Netherlands and the great armada against England. Ruling Spain from his Madrid palace, El Escorial, Philip mismanaged the Spanish bureaucracy and economy and overspent on military plans, causing his government to declare bankruptcy three times. He left Spain in decline from its position as a world power.

Richelieu, Cardinal (1585–1642). He was the first minister of French King Louis XIII (1610–1643) and an architect of French absolutism. Richelieu built up the royal bureaucracy and treasury through sale of office and created a new group of appointed and non-venal royal administrators called *intendants*. He subdued the rebellious Huguenots and took away their right to fortify their cities. He reorganized government finances and increased royal tax income, and he controlled the French nobility through appointments to powerless offices. Richelieu set the stage for the absolutism of Louis XIV.

Salutati, Caluccio (1331–1406). Chancellor of Florence during the early Renaissance and one of the founders of Civic Humanism. After Florence's near defeat by Milan during the war of 1380–1402, Salutati and other Florentine leaders reformed the educational system of the city based on the ancient Roman seven liberal arts and the classics of antiquity, which they hoped would produce well-rounded individuals and responsible citizens. Philosophically, Salutati was a follower of St. Augustine and a devout Christian who believed that Christian meaning could be found in the ancient pagan classics.

Sattler, Michael (fl. 1527). Anabaptist religious leader during the Reformation era, he wrote the *Schleitheim Confession*, the only known Anabaptist confession of faith. Like other Anabaptists, he rejected infant baptism as unbiblical and he rejected most of the doctrines, ceremonies, and institutions of the mainline churches of the day. He favored a purely inward, spiritual, and individual faith. He began his career in Zurich but fled persecution there, going first to Strasbourg and later to the Black Forest region. He was arrested by authorities in Rothenburg and burned at the stake.

Sforza, Francesco (1401–1466). Originally commander of Cosimo de' Medici's mercenary army, he helped Cosimo seize power in Florence in 1434. He was, in turn, installed in power in Milan through the actions of Cosimo in 1447. As dictator of Milan, Sforza proved a generous patron of the arts and learning, turning the city into a center of Renaissance culture. He employed Leonardo da Vinci as artist and military engineer. He aligned Milan with Florence in the alliance known as the Peace of Lodi in 1454. He improved the economy of Milan by introducing to the city the cultivation of rice and silk worms.

Socinus, Laelius (1525–1562). He was the founder of Evangelical Rationalism, a radical anti-trinitarian branch of the Protestant Reformation. Born in Siena in Italy, he studied law at the University of Bologna. After learning Greek and Hebrew, he studied theology on his own and developed radical ideas. Rejecting Catholicism, he was forced by the Inquisition to flee Italy. He then traveled to Wittenberg and other major Protestant centers. Ultimately, he rejected orthodox Protestant beliefs about the Trinity, predestination, the resurrection of the body, and the sacraments. Basing his beliefs only on the Bible and human reason, Socinus denied the divinity of Christ. His nephew Fautus Socinus (1539–1604) later carried anti-trinitarian ideas to Poland.

Theresa, Maria (1717–1780). Queen of Austria, she ascended the throne on the death of King Charles VI as a result of the agreement known as the Pragmatic Sanction. She defeated a Prussian challenge to her rule in the war of Austrian Succession (1740–1748) and, after the war, reformed the Austrian military and bureaucracy to increase the power of the state. She also took the bold step of taxing the Austrian clergy and is credited with helping to establish Austrian absolutism.

Valla, Lorenzo (1407–1457). Great Humanist philologist of the Italian Renaissance. Born in Rome, he was educated as a classical Latin stylist and rhetorician. He became an expert in the formal and stylistic changes in the Latin language over time and wrote the Humanist textbook on the subject, *The Elegances of the Latin Language*, in 1444. He worked as a secretary for Pope Nicholas V. While working in the Vatican library, he studied the Donation of Constantine and wrote a work showing, based on its Latin style, that it was a forgery. He also criticized the St. Jerome's Vulgate Bible as a poor translation from Greek into Latin.

William, Frederick (r. 1640–1688). Known as "the Great Elector," he was the father of Prussian absolutism. Ruler of Prussia in the last years of the Thirty Years War, he built up the Prussian military and won several notable battlefield victories. After the war, he kept his army intact and used it to enforce his absolute rule over his country. He even appointed military officers to the state bureaucracy, calling them "war commissars."

William I, Frederick (r. 1713–1740). Known as "the Sergeant King," his rule represented the zenith of Prussian absolutism. By cutting expenses at court, he built up the army until it was the fourth largest in Europe and constructed an efficient new bureaucracy called the General Directory. He instituted a military draft and opened an officer's training school. He also established compulsory elementary education. He was credited with making Prussia a major European power.

William of Orange (1533–1584). Also known as William the Silent, leader of the Dutch Revolt and architect of the Dutch Republic. A reluctant revolutionary, William was a member of the Dutch Council of State under Spanish rule and urged moderate policies on King Philip II. The excesses of the Inquisition and the policies of the Duke of Alva turned William against Spanish rule, and he became the leader of rebel military forces, as well as a key figure in the building of the new Dutch state. His leadership inspired the Dutch during the dark early days of the revolt, and despite his assassination by a

Spanish agent in 1584, the young republic continued on the path to victory.

Wycliffe, John (c. 1330–1384). English theologian and church reformer of the 14th century, he attacked the corruption of monks, bishops, and popes. He especially targeted clerical marriage, simony, and pluralism. He held that the Bible alone, not church authorities, declared the will of God. He denied the special power of the priesthood in transubstantiation, as Luther later would. He and his followers, called Lollards, were declared heretics by the church.

Zwingli, Ulrich (1484–1531). Father of the Reformation in Switzerland. Originally a Catholic priest, he fell under the influence of the Humanist Erasmus and was particularly influenced by his reading of Erasmus's translation of the New Testament. He came to believe that many Catholic teachings were not supported by the Bible, and this insight set him on the path to launching his religious reform movement. Zwingli's reformation, begun in Zurich, was parallel to but largely separate from Luther's movement in Germany. Zwingli shared some of Luther's ideas but rejected Luther's belief in the real presence in the mass, calling the ceremony wholly symbolic. Switzerland became religiously divided and Zwingli was killed in battle against Catholic forces in 1531.

Bibliography

Essential Reading:

Baxandall, Michael. *Painting and Experience in Fifteenth-Century Italy.* Oxford: Oxford University Press, 1972.

Brucker, Gene. *Renaissance Florence.* Berkeley: University of California Press, 1983.

De Vries, Jan. *The Economy of Europe in an Age of Crisis, 1600–1750.* Cambridge: Cambridge University Press, 1976.

Diefendorf, Barbara. *Beneath the Cross: Catholics and Huguenots in Sixteenth-Century Paris.* New York: Oxford University Press, 1991.

Elliott, J. H. *Richelieu and Olivares.* Cambridge: Cambridge University Press, 1984.

Elton, G. R. *Reformation Europe, 1517–1559.* New York: Harper and Row, 1963.

Geyl, Pieter. *The Revolt of The Netherlands, 1555–1609.* London: Ernest Benn, 1958.

Goubert, Pierre. *Louis XIV and Twenty Million Frenchmen.* New York: Vintage Books, 1972.

Hazard, Paul. *The Crisis of the European Consciousness, 1680–1715.* Cleveland: Meridian Books, 1964.

Hill, Christopher. *The World Turned Upside Down: Radical Ideas During the English Revolution.* New York: Penguin Books, 1985.

Huppert, George. *After the Black Death.* Bloomington: Indiana University Press, 1986.

Israel, Jonathan. *The Dutch Republic: Its Rise, Greatness and Fall, 1477–1806.* New York: Oxford University Press, 2001.

Macartney, C. A., ed. *The Hapsburg and Hohenzollern Dynasties in the Seventeenth and Eighteenth Centuries.* New York: Harper and Row, 1970.

Ozment, Steven. *The Reformation in the Cities.* New Haven: Yale University Press, 1975.

Parker, Geoffrey. *Europe in Crisis, 1598–1648.* Ithaca: Cornell University Press, 1980.

———. *Philip II.* Boston: Little, Brown, and Co., 1978.

———, and Lesley Smith, eds. *The General Crisis of the Seventeenth Century.* London: Routledge, 1978.

Scribner, R. W. *The German Reformation.* Atlantic Highlands, N.J.: Humanities Press, 1986.

Spitz, Lewis. *The Protestant Reformation, 1517–1559.* New York: Harper and Rowe, 1985.

Treasure, Geoffrey. *Richelieu and Mazarin.* London: Routledge, 1998.

Wedgwood, C. V. *Richelieu and the French Monarchy.* New York: Collier Books, 1962.

———. *The Thirty Years War.* New York: Doubleday, 1961.

Westfall, Richard S. *The Construction of Modern Science: Mechanisms and Mechanics.* Cambridge: Cambridge University Press, 1978.

Wiesner, Merry. *Women and Gender in Early Modern Europe.* Cambridge: Cambridge University Press, 1993.

Wilcox, Donald. *In Search of God and Self.* Prospect Heights, Ill., Waveland Press, 1985.

Supplementary Reading:

Baron, Hans. *The Crisis of the Early Italian Renaissance.* Princeton: Princeton University Press, 1955.

Blickle, Peter. *The Revolution of 1525.* Baltimore: Johns Hopkins University Press, 1977.

Bouwsma, William. *John Calvin.* New York: Oxford University Press, 1988.

Boxer, Charles. *The Dutch Seaborne Empire.* New York: Alfred A. Knopf, 1965.

———. *The Portuguese Seaborne Empire.* New York: Alfred A. Knopf, 1969.

Brady, Thomas. *The Politics of the Reformation in Germany.* Atlantic Highlands, N.J.: Humanities Press, 1997.

Brucker, Gene. *Two Memoirs of Renaissance Florence.* Prospect Heights, Ill.: Waveland Press, 1991.

Friesen, Abraham. *Thomas Muentzer: A Destroyer of the Godless.* Berkeley: University of California Press, 1990.

Grafton, Anthony, and Lisa Jardine. *From Humanism to the Humanities.* Cambridge, Mass.: Harvard University Press, 1986.

't Hart, Marjolein. *The Making of a Bourgeois State: War, Politics and Finance during the Dutch Revolt.* Manchester: Manchester University Press, 1993.

Hsia, R. Po-Chia, ed. *The German People and the Reformation.* Ithaca: Cornell University Press, 1988.

Jardine, Lisa. *Erasmus, Man of Letters.* Princeton: Princeton University Press, 1993.

Kamen, Henry. *Philip of Spain.* New Haven: Yale University Press, 1997.

Kittelson, James. *Luther the Reformer.* Minneapolis: Augsburg Press, 1986.

Lopez, Robert. *The Three Ages of the Italian Renaissance.* Charlottesville: University of Virginia Press, 1970.

Martines, Lauro. *Power and Imagination: City-States in Renaissance Italy.* New York: Alfred A. Knopf, 1979.

Mattingly, Garret. *The Defeat of the Spanish Armada.* Boston: Houghton Mifflin, 1984.

———. *Renaissance Diplomacy.* Boston: Houghton Mifflin, 1955.

McLaughlin, R. Emmet. *Caspar Schwenkfeld: Reluctant Radical.* New Haven: Yale University Press, 1986.

Moeller, Bernd. *Imperial Cities and the Reformation.* Durham, N.C.: Labyrinth Press, 1982.

Mullet. Michael. *Radical Religious Movements in Early Modern Europe.* London: George Allen and Unwin, 1980.

Oberman, Heiko. *Luther: Man between God and the Devil.* New Haven: Yale University Press, 1989.

Ozment, Steven. *The Age of Reform* New Haven: Yale University Press, 1980.

Parker, Geoffrey. *The Army of Flanders and the Spanish Road.* Cambridge: Cambridge University Press, 1972.

———. *The Dutch Revolt.* Ithaca: Cornell University Press, 1977.

Perroy, Edouard. *The Hundred Years War.* New York: Oxford University Press, 1951.

Scribner, Robert, and Gerhard Benecke. *The German Peasant War of 1525: New Viewpoints.* London: George Allen and Unwin, 1979.

Strauss, Gerald. *Manifestations of Discontent in Germany on the Eve of the Reformation.* Bloomington: Indiana University Press, 1971.

Struever, Nancy. *The Language of History in the Renaissance.* Princeton: Princeton University Press, 1970.

Tracy, James. *Erasmus.* Berkeley: University of California Press, 1996.

———. *Holland under Hapsburg Rule.* Berkeley, University of California Press, 1990.

Williams, George H. *The Radical Reformation.* Philadelphia: Westminster Press, 1962.